Remembering Katyn

Remembering Katyn

Alexander Etkind
Rory Finnin
Uilleam Blacker
Julie Fedor
Simon Lewis
Maria Mälksoo
Matilda Mroz

polity

First published in 2012 by Polity Press

Polity Press
65 Bridge Street
Cambridge CB2 1UR, UK

Polity Press
350 Main Street
Malden, MA 02148, USA

ISBN-13: 978-0-7456-5576-5
ISBN-13: 978-0-7456-5577-2(pb)

A catalogue record for this book is available from the British Library.

Typeset in 11 on 13 pt Sabon
by Toppan Best-set Premedia Limited

For further information on Polity, visit our website: www.politybooks.com

Contents

List of Contributors

Alexander Etkind is Reader in Russian Literature and Cultural History in the Department of Slavonic Studies at the University of Cambridge.

Rory Finnin is Lecturer in Ukrainian Studies in the Department of Slavonic Studies at the University of Cambridge.

Uilleam Blacker is a Postdoctoral Research Associate in the project 'Memory at War' at the University of Cambridge.

Julie Fedor is a Postdoctoral Research Associate in the project 'Memory at War' at the University of Cambridge.

Simon Lewis is a PhD candidate in the Department of Slavonic Studies at the University of Cambridge.

Maria Mälksoo is a Senior Researcher in the Institute of Government and Politics at the University of Tartu.

Matilda Mroz is Lecturer in Film and Visual Culture at the University of Greenwich.

Acknowledgements

Work on this book was supported by a generous grant from the HERA JRP (Humanities in the European Research Area Joint Research Programme) for the research project, *Memory at War: Cultural Dynamics in Poland, Russia, and Ukraine.* We are grateful to the Department of Slavonic Studies of the University of Cambridge, which has created a unique home for the *Memory at War* project, and to Simon Franklin and Emma Widdis for their support and encouragement. At Polity Press, John Thompson and Jennifer Jahn were enthusiastic about, and patient with, the development of the manuscript. Jill Gather provided crucial help with logistics and bibliographical work. We would also like to thank the helpful and dedicated staff of the 'Katyn' Memorial Complex near Smolensk, and especially Galina Andreenkova. For their invaluable assistance, we are grateful to Clare Ansell, Ąžuolas Bagdonas, Aliaksei Bratachkin, Anna Dzienkiewicz, Filmoteka Narodowa, Toomas Hiio, Olga Kerziouk, Anatol' Mikhnavets, Zmitser Navitski, Ian Tuttle and Eugenia Florek.

List of Abbreviations

AK	*Armia Krajowa* (Home Army)
ECHR	European Court of Human Rights
FSB	*Federal'naia Sluzhba Bezopasnosti* (Federal Security Service)
FSK	*Federal'naia Sluzhba Konttrazvedki* (Federal Counter-Intelligence Service)
IPN	*Instytut Pamięci Narodowej* (Institute of National Remembrance)
KGB	*Komitet Gosudarstvennoi Bezopasnosti* (Committee for State Security)
KOR	*Komitet Obrony Robotników* (Committee for the Defence of Workers)
KPN	*Konfederacja Polski Niepodległej* (Confederation of Independent Poland)
NKGB	*Narodnyi Komissariat Gosudarstvennoi Bezopasnosti* (People's Commissariat for State Security)
NKHBZK	*Niezależny Komitet Historyczny Badania Zbrodni Katyńskiej* (Independent Historical Committee for Research into the Katyn Crime)
NKVD	*Narodnyi Komissariat Vnutrennikh Del* (People's Commissariat for Internal Affairs)
PiS	*Prawo i Sprawiedliwość* (Law and Justice)
PFK	*Polska Fundacja Katyńska* (Polish Katyn Foundation)

PRL	*Polska Rzeczpospolita Ludowa* (People's Republic of Poland)
PWN	*Państwowe Wydawnictwo Naukowe* (National Scientific Publishers)
ROPCiO	*Ruch Obrony Praw Człowieka i Obywatela* (Movement for the Defence of Human and Civic Rights)
ROPWiM	*Rada Ochrony Pamięci Walk i Męczeństwa* (Council for the Preservation of Struggle and Martyrdom Sites)
SB	*Służba Bezpieczeństwa* (Security Service)
SSR	*Sovetskaia Sotsialisticheskaia Respublika* (Soviet Socialist Republic)
TVP	*Telewizja Polska* (Polish Television)
UNKVD	*Upravlenie Narodnogo Komissariata Vnutrennikh Del* (Directorate of the People's Commissariat for Internal Affairs, i.e. regional branch of the NKVD)

List of Figures

A Note on Translation and Transliteration

The translations in this book are ours, unless otherwise stated. Where established English spellings of names and place-names exist, these have been given preference (e.g. 'Beria' rather than 'Beriia', 'Katyn' rather than 'Katyń'). Polish names, however, are consistently rendered according to their Polish spelling (e.g. 'Wałęsa' rather than 'Walesa'), and Ukrainian cities according to their Ukrainian spelling (e.g. 'Kyiv' rather than 'Kiev', 'Kharkiv' rather than 'Khar'kov').

Belarusian, Russian and Ukrainian have been transliterated according to the Library of Congress system. Soft signs are rendered with a quotation mark, hard signs with a double quotation mark. Belarusian and Ukrainian apostrophes have not been given.

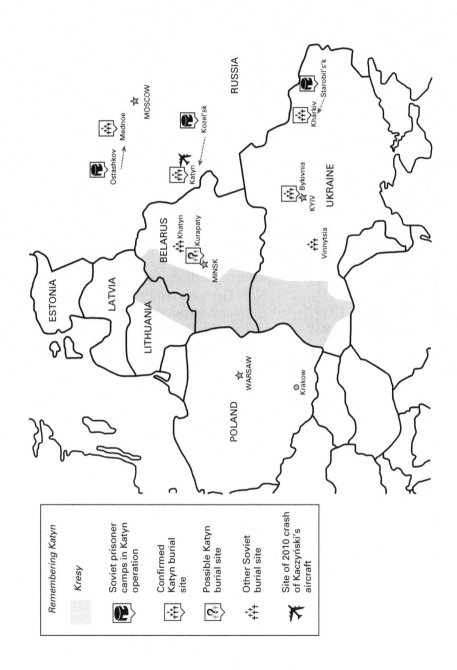

Remembering Katyn

Kresy

Soviet prisoner camps in Katyn operation

Confirmed Katyn burial site

Possible Katyn burial site

Other Soviet burial site

Site of 2010 crash of Kaczyński's aircraft

ESTONIA

LATVIA

LITHUANIA

POLAND

WARSAW

Kraków

BELARUS

MINSK

Khatyn

Kurapaty

Ostashkov

Mednoe

MOSCOW

Kozel'sk

Katyn

RUSSIA

Kharkiv

Starobil's'k

Bykivnia

KYIV

UKRAINE

Vinnytsia

Timeline

23 August 1939	Molotov-Ribbentrop Pact signed by Nazi Germany and the Soviet Union.
1 September 1939	Germany invades Poland.
17 September 1939	Soviet Union invades Poland. 25,700 Polish citizens are arrested and interned on the territory of what is now western Ukraine and western Belarus. They are either incarcerated in local prisons or sent eastward to three special prisoner-of-war camps administered by the NKVD in Kozel'sk and Ostashkov (in western Russia) and Starobil's'k (in eastern Ukraine).
28 September 1939	Soviet-Estonian mutual assistance treaty signed. It enables the establishment of Soviet military bases on Estonian territory.
5 October 1939	Soviet-Latvian mutual assistance treaty signed.
10 October 1939	Soviet-Lithuanian mutual assistance treaty signed.
30 November 1939	USSR invades Finland.
2 March 1940	Soviet party and state leaders take decision to deport up to 60,000 relatives of arrested Polish officers.

5 March 1940	Soviet party leadership approves decision to shoot 'Polish prisoners-of-war (officers and policemen) and arrestees located in prisons of western regions of Ukraine and Belorussia' in accordance with recommendations prepared by NKVD chief Beria.
7 March 1940	Beria orders the heads of the NKVD in Ukraine and Belarus to deport family members of the Polish prisoners to Kazakhstan.
16 March 1940	Registration of camp and prison inmates commences. Ban on correspondence by prisoners comes into force, and security at camps is stepped up.
22 March 1940	Beria orders 'unloading' of NKVD prisons in western regions of Ukraine and Belarus.
April 1940	Official lists of prisoners to be executed are submitted to the camps and prisons. These include 97% of inmates.
Spring–Summer 1940	Deportations of families to Kazakhstan and other remote Soviet locations.
Spring 1940	In accordance with the 5 March order, NKVD staff shoot 21,857 Poles and bury them in numerous killing fields in Russia, Ukraine and, very likely, Belarus.
15 June 1940	Soviet ultimatum and subsequent invasion of Lithuania.
17 June 1940	Soviet occupation of Latvia and Estonia.
21 July 1940	Establishment of Estonian, Latvian and Lithuanian Soviet Socialist Republics (SSRs).
26 October 1940	Beria orders the decoration of 125 NKVD staff involved in the Katyn operation.
14 June 1941	Soviet mass deportations from the Baltic States to Siberia and Kazakhstan (including about 10,000 Estonian, 15,500 Latvian and 40,000 Lithuanian residents).

22 June 1941	Nazi Germany attacks USSR.
24–25 June 1941	Rainiai massacre, in which the NKVD murdered dozens of Lithuanian political prisoners in a forest near Telšiai, Lithuania.
June 1941	Mass deportations of Baltic officers to the 7th Strict Regime Special Camp in Noril'sk beyond the Polar Circle.
July 1941	Nazi occupation of the Baltic States begins. Estonia, Latvia and Lithuania incorporated into the Reichskommissariat Ostland of the Third Reich.
30 July 1941	Agreement signed between Soviet and Polish government in London, whereby Soviet government renounces Polish territory gained under Molotov-Ribbentrop Pact, diplomatic relations are resumed, and creation of Polish army on Soviet territory is approved.
6 August 1941	General Władysław Anders appointed commander of Polish army on USSR territory ('Anders' Army').
12 August 1941	Polish citizens held prisoner in the USSR granted 'amnesty'.
1941–42	Polish officials repeatedly seek information from Soviet government on whereabouts of missing Polish prisoners, but without success.
Autumn 1941	German army occupies Smolensk.
3 December 1941	Stalin receives Anders and Sikorski and tells them missing Polish officers may have fled to Manchuria.
January 1942	Polish construction workers stationed near Katyn discover graves; Germans are informed of the find, but do not announce it until the following year.
March 1942	Soviet censors suppress publication of search announcements placed by Polish families of the missing officers in the Polish embassy newspaper in Moscow.

February–March 1943	German searches and excavations at Katyn are underway, resulting in discovery of eight graves.
13 April 1943	Germany announces discovery of mass graves containing Polish corpses at Katyn.
14 April 1943	Polish Red Cross Technical Commission arrives at Katyn.
15 April 1943	Churchill privately acknowledges to Polish officials that the Soviet regime probably committed the Katyn murders.
16 April 1943	Soviet official propaganda bureau accuses Germany of murdering Poles at Katyn during German occupation of Smolensk.
17 April 1943	Polish government requests International Red Cross investigation of Katyn deaths.
24 April 1943	Churchill informs Stalin that Great Britain will oppose any International Red Cross investigation of Katyn.
26 April 1943	Soviet government breaks off diplomatic relations with Polish Government-in-Exile, which is based in London.
28 April 1943	International Commission formed by Germans commences work at Katyn.
April–June 1943	Eight graves exhumed at Katyn, containing the remains of 4,143 bodies, 2,730 of which are identified.
May 1943	Mass graves of nearly 10,000 victims of NKVD are unearthed by German authorities in Vinnytsia (Ukraine).
June 1943	General Władysław Sikorski dies in plane crash.
September 1943	German *White Book of Official Materials on the Mass Killings at Katyn* published.
22 September 1943	Leading Soviet propagandist recommends to Soviet leadership that it would be timely to create a Katyn investigation

	commission and begin gathering materials to assert German guilt.
25 September 1943	Red Army takes back Smolensk. Soon afterwards, a group of NKVD and NKGB operatives arrive and begin top secret work together with local NKVD staff, falsifying evidence of German responsibility, removing all evidence pointing to Soviet guilt, coaching witnesses, etc.
1943	Memo by Owen O'Malley (British ambassador to Polish Government-in-Exile) asserts Soviet guilt for the Katyn massacres but ends with the words, 'Let us think of these things always and speak of them never.'
1943	Jan Zygmunt Robel begins work on the materials recovered from the Katyn pits.
1944	Publication of Józef Czapski's *Starobil's'k Memoirs*.
1944	Soviet Burdenko Commission conducts investigation at Katyn site. It claims that the Polish officers were shot by the Germans in 1941.
1944/45–1991	Second Soviet occupation of the Baltic States.
1945–1946	Nuremberg Trials.
1945	'Robel's Archive' is lost in a fire during transportation to the West, although some materials, including prisoners' diaries, are either hidden in Poland or spirited to London.
1945	Roman Martini begins his investigation into the Katyn massacres for the new Polish Communist authorities.
30 March 1946	Roman Martini is murdered.
1946	Memorial obelisk erected at Katyn with inscription in Polish and Russian blaming Germans for the crime and dating massacres to autumn 1941.

1947	Ivan Krivozertsev is found hanged in the UK.
1948	Publication of *The Katyn Crime in the Light of Documents*, edited anonymously by Józef Mackiewicz, with a foreword by Władysław Anders.
1949	Publication of Józef Czapski's *On Inhuman Land*.
1949	American Committee for Investigation of the Katyn Massacre established.
1951	Publication, in English, of Józef Mackiewicz's *The Katyn Wood Murders*.
1951	US Congressional Enquiry, known as the Madden Committee, begins.
1955	Publication of Ferdinand Goetel's *Times of War*.
Mid-1950s	Anonymous tributes to the victims of Katyn begin to appear at the Home Army monument at Warsaw's Powązkowski (or Powązki) Cemetery.
22 April 1956	20,000 Poles congregate in central London to commemorate the Katyn massacres, laying flowers at the Tomb of the Unknown Soldier and protesting the visit of Nikita Khrushchev.
3 March 1959	USSR KGB chief Aleksandr Shelepin recommends to Khrushchev that documents regarding the execution of 21,857 Poles in the Katyn operation be destroyed.
1 November 1959	First wooden cross with an inscription dedicated to Katyn placed in the Powązkowski Cemetery. It is removed immediately by the Polish security services.
1964	New edition of the official PWN encyclopedia is published in Poland with no entry for Katyn whatsoever.
1965	Mackiewicz's *The Katyn Crime in the Light of Documents* appears in English.

May 1966	Ukrainian dissident Sviatoslav Karavans'kyi writes to the Union of Soviet Journalists about the unjust incarceration of Katyn 'witness' Andreev in Moscow's Vladimir prison.
7 June 1969	Chairman of the Ukrainian KGB Vitalii Nikitchenko writes to KGB Chief Yuri Andropov and Secretary of the Ukrainian Communist Party Petro Shelest about the public discovery of the Katyn burial site in the Piatykhatky forest on the outskirts of Kharkiv.
End of June 1969	Head of the Kharkiv KGB Petr Feshchenko relays orders from Andropov that the 'special objects' [*spetsob"ekty*] in the Piatykhatky mass grave on the outskirts of Kharkiv be liquidated with a 'corrosive' chemical agent.
30 April 1970	The 'Karavans'kyi Affair' introduces the word 'Katyn' to the prominent *samizdat* journal *Chronicle of Current Events*.
1971	Katyn Memorial Fund set up in London.
1972	USSR pressures British government into preventing erection of Katyn monument in London.
1973	Włodzimierz Odojewski publishes in Paris the novel *Everything Will be Covered by Snow* ..., which features extensive references to Katyn. His emigration two years earlier was partly a result of the impossibility of publishing the novel in Poland.
1975	First Katyn monument unveiled in Stockholm.
5 April 1976	Soviet Politburo resolution 'On Measures to Counteract Western Propaganda on the So-called "Katyn affair"'.
1976	Katyn Memorial unveiled in London. It bears the date 1940 but makes no

	mention of the Soviet perpetrators. Around 8,000 people attend the unveiling. The Stockholm monument is vandalized.
1976	Publication of Stanisław Swianiewicz's *In the Shadow of Katyn*.
1977	Fr Stefan Niedzielak begins his ministry at St Karol Boromeusz parish, where he presides over commemorative activities at Powązkowski Cemetery.
1977	Opposition activist Ryszard Zieliński publishes his underground brochure *Katyn* in Poland under the pseudonyms Jan Abramski and Ryszard Żywiecki (the first and last names on the 'Katyn List').
1978	Opposition activists form the Katyn Institute in Kraków and the Katyn Committee in Warsaw.
1980	Historian and activist Jerzy Łojek publishes one of the most influential Polish underground texts about Katyn, *The History of the Katyn Case*.
21 March 1980	Polish Home Army veteran Walenty Badylak burns himself alive in protest against, among other things, the 'Katyn Lie'.
April 1980	Soviet dissidents issue a public statement 'Look Back in Repentance' on the fortieth anniversary of the Katyn massacres.
3 May 1980	Consecration of the first professionally designed Katyn monument in Poland, by Czesław Majerski, in the Gorce mountains.
1981	Leading activist of the Katyn Institute Adam Macedoński is jailed for seven months.
31 July 1981	A group of activists erects a large stone cross with the inscription 'Katyn,

	Ostaszków, Kozielsk, Starobielsk, 1940' at the Powązkowski Cemetery. It is removed by the security services the following night.
1983	Monument to '500 Soviet Prisoners-of-War' killed by Nazis erected in Katyn at the initiative of the Smolensk City Soviet.
1984	'The Sanctuary of Those Fallen in the East' is consecrated at the church of St Karol Boromeusz.
1984	Włodzimierz Odojewski returns to the topic of Katyn in his collection of stories *Covering the Traces*.
1985	The Polish authorities erect a monument to Katyn at Powązkowski Cemetery blaming the Nazis and bearing the false date of 1941.
1987	Creation of Polish–Soviet Historical Commission with aim of investigating 'blank spots' of history.
1987	First Katyn Family association formed in Warsaw.
1988	Soviet party leadership grants access to Polish memorial to Soviet and Polish citizens.
March 1988	Polish party delegation visits Katyn, replaces old inscription on 1983 memorial 'To the Victims of Hitler's Fascism. 1941' with a new one: 'To the Fallen of Katyn'.
5 May 1988	In the lead-up to Gorbachev's visit to Poland, the Soviet Politburo debates but decides against an official acknowledgement of the existence of the Molotov-Ribbentrop Pact secret protocols.
3 June 1988	Existence of mass graves of NKVD victims revealed at Kurapaty, near Minsk, Belarus.
2 September 1988	Wojciech Jaruzelski makes an unofficial visit to Katyn, during which a wooden

	Catholic cross is erected at the site with the inscription: 'At This Site a Cross Is to Be Erected Immortalizing the Memory of the Death of the Polish Officers'.
26 October 1988	Soviet Council of Ministers resolves to build a memorial complex at Katyn commemorating the deaths of Polish officers and Soviet prisoners-of-war at the site.
30 October 1988	First mass demonstration held at the Kurapaty killing field in Belarus. It becomes an annual event on the *Dziady* feast day.
20 January 1989	Murder of Fr Stefan Niedzielak, 'Katyn's last victim', by unknown assailants.
19 April 1989	Gorbachev is presented with documents from sealed 'File No. 1', including the Politburo resolution of March 1940, just before Jaruzelski's trip to Moscow, but decides to suppress them.
Spring 1989	First Congress of USSR People's Deputies demands that a commission be established to investigate the Molotov-Ribbentrop Pact. Gorbachev continues to deny that original documents confirming the secret protocols have been found.
1989	Findings of the Technical Commission of the Polish Red Cross at Katyn are published for the first time.
1989	Jerzy Łojek's *The History of the Katyn Case* is published legally in Poland, but it is substantially censored.
1989	Katyn is raised at the Round Table negotiations in Poland.
1989	Activists of the Katyn Committee and the Katyn Institute form the Independent Historical Committee for Research into the Katyn Crime (NKHBZK) and the Polish Katyn Foundation (PFK).

Spring–Summer 1989	Soviet historians discover archival documents related to Katyn which confirm hearings by NKVD Special Boards and NKVD orders to transport prisoners out of the three camps (Kozel'sk, Ostashkov and Starobil's'k).
October 1989	Gorbachev allows delegation of Katyn Families to visit Katyn.
28 December 1989	Open access to Katyn territory granted by the Soviet government.
Late 1989	Soviet and Polish sides agree on a new inscription for Katyn memorial, removing reference to German guilt: 'To the Polish Officers Who Perished at Katyn'.
22 February 1990	Leading Soviet official Valentin Falin informs Gorbachev about the recent archival discoveries about Katyn and suggests that continued denial is no longer feasible.
April 1990	Official Soviet media announcement acknowledges Soviet responsibility for Katyn massacres. Gorbachev hands lists of Polish POWs shot to Polish President Jaruzelski in Moscow. Polish TVP broadcasts *Katyn Forest* (Marcel Łoziński, 1990), a project initiated by Andrzej Wajda.
3 June 1990	Soviet authorities publicly announce the discovery of the Katyn burial site in the Piatykhatky forest on the outskirts of Kharkiv.
1990	A plaque is added to the London Katyn monument identifying Stalin and the Soviet secret police as perpetrators.
Late 1990	Soviet and Polish chief military procuracies agree to open investigation at Mednoe, Kharkiv and Katyn.
1991–2004	Russian Chief Military Prosecutor investigates Katyn case.

1991	Excavations are carried out at Katyn as part of Russian investigation.
1991	Some of the materials secretly archived by Jan Zygmunt Robel's team in 1943–5 are discovered in a building in Krakow.
25 October 1991	The Smolensk Regional Soviet Executive Committee declares 100 hectares at Katyn to be a protected zone; mentions the presence of Soviet mass graves for the first time; and calls upon the procuracy and the KGB to conduct studies aimed at establishing sites and numbers of victims.
May 1992	Polish President Lech Wałęsa visits Katyn.
14 October 1992	Russia transfers documents confirming Soviet guilt to Poland.
27 October 1992	Full Russian acknowledgement of existence and authenticity of secret protocols to Molotov-Ribbentrop Pact.
1992	Russian–Polish bilateral agreement to maintain and protect extra-territorial memorial sites.
1992	Katyn Families visit Moscow at the invitation of Boris Yeltsin.
1993	Boris Yeltsin kneels before Katyn cross in Warsaw and asks Poles, 'Forgive us, if you can'.
1993	Polish–Russian negotiations on Katyn memorial begin.
22 February 1994	The Russian–Polish agreement on burial sites and sites of memory of victims of wars and repressions is signed in Krakow.
1994–96	Excavations at Katyn (with stalling and delays on the Russian side).
July 1994	Aliaksandr Lukashenka becomes president of Belarus.
1995	President Lech Wałęsa declares 1995 'The Year of Katyn' in Poland.

1995	Publication of Jerzy Krzyżanowski's *Katyn in Literature.*
31 January 1995	Smolensk procuracy confirms the presence of mass Soviet burial sites at Katyn.
May–June 1995	Foundation stones are laid for a memorial at Katyn; Yeltsin does not attend the ceremony.
1995	Russian excavations at Katyn.
October 1996	Russian government resolves to build memorial complexes at Katyn and Mednoe.
November 1998	Additional explorations carried out at site of Soviet graves at Katyn.
1999	Construction of Katyn memorial complex commences.
Summer–Autumn 2000	Major memorial complexes opened at Piatykhatky (on the outskirts of Kharkiv), Katyn and Mednoe.
June 2001	Lukashenka signs decree to widen ring road around Minsk, threatening to destroy the Kurapaty site. Demonstrations ensue, including a permanent vigil at Kurapaty.
December 2001	Kurapaty is recognized by Belarusian government as a site of mass executions by NKVD. Parliament rejects bid to erect a monument there.
2003	Włodzimierz Odojewski publishes his novel *Silent, Undefeated: A Katyn Story*, originally written at the suggestion of Andrzej Wajda with a view to a future film project.
September 2004	Russian Chief Military Procuracy investigation of Katyn is closed.
November 2004	Polish Institute of National Remembrance launches its own Katyn investigation.
12 April 2007	*Życie Warszawy* announces that Wajda has changed the title of his Katyn film project from *Post-Mortem* to *Katyn*.

17 September 2007	Premiere of Wajda's *Katyn*, attended by President Lech Kaczyński, Prime Minister Jarosław Kaczyński, high-ranking officials of the Catholic Church, members of the Katyn Families, and members of the Russian 'Memorial' Society.
14 November 2007	Polish Sejm declares 13 April the 'Worldwide Day of Memory of Victims of the Katyn Crime'. The date marks the anniversary of the 1943 German announcement.
2008	Latvian author Edvīns Šnore releases the documentary *The Soviet Story*.
2008	Wajda's *Katyn* premieres in Ukraine and Estonia. Andrzej Wajda awarded the Order of Yaroslav the Wise in Ukraine and the Cross of Terra Mariana in Estonia.
2009	Ukrainian government releases letters written by Vitalii Nikitchenko to Yuri Andropov and Petro Shelest in 1969 about the Katyn burial site in the Piatykhatky forest on the outskirts of Kharkiv.
July 2009	Consecration of memorial stone in the Katyn Valley of Death, marking mass graves of Soviet terror victims.
23 August 2009	First Belarusian pilgrimage to Katyn.
13–14 January 2010	Filming begins for *Katyn Epitaphs*. The DVD is released in April 2010.
2 April 2010	Wajda's *Katyn* screened on Russian arts and culture TV channel *Kul'tura*.
7 April 2010	Prime Ministers Tusk and Putin take part in joint commemorative ceremony at Katyn.
10 April 2010	Polish President Lech Kaczyński's plane crashes near Katyn, killing all 96 members of a delegation on its way to commemorate the seventieth anniversary of the massacres.

11 April 2010	Wajda's *Katyn* screened in a primetime slot on Russia's Channel One.
12 April 2010	National day of mourning in Russia for Smolensk plane crash victims.
12–14 April 2010	Three days of national mourning held in Lithuania after the Smolensk plane crash to honour the late Polish president Lech Kaczyński.
17 May 2010	The Grand Chamber of the European Court of Human Rights (ECHR) issues a judgment in the case of *Kononov v. Latvia*, establishing a precedent in applying the standards of the Nuremberg law to victors in the Second World War (i.e. the Soviet Union).
26 November 2010	Russian Duma resolution 'On the Katyn Tragedy and Its Victims' recognizes Katyn as a crime of the Stalinist regime.
December 2010	Medvedev decorates Wajda with the Order of Friendship.
2011	Russian Foreign Minister expresses willingness to consider rehabilitation of Katyn victims.

Introduction

Remembering Katyn

On the clear, crisp afternoon of 7 April 2010, Polish Prime Minister Donald Tusk stood before a phalanx of pines to address his Russian counterpart Vladimir Putin and other dignitaries in a cemetery complex outside the village of Katyn, in western Russia. He began his remarks with a question. 'Why are we here today? Why do we come to this place every year?' He continued: 'Above all, because we remember' (Tusk 2010).

Pamiętamy: we remember. In Eastern Europe, a pivotal object of public memory is Katyn, the mass murder of over 20,000 unarmed Polish prisoners in the spring of 1940 by officers of the NKVD (People's Commissariat for Internal Affairs), the Soviet secret police. 'We will always remember those killed here', declared Tusk, a historian by training. His stirring call to remember the Katyn tragedy was, of course, a call to remember the past, for as Aristotle posited long ago, to remember the future is impossible (Aristotle 1987). Yet three days after Tusk's address, the grounds for Aristotle's claim would feel vacant and forsaken. On 10 April 2010, an aircraft carrying 96 members of Poland's military and political class, including the nation's President Lech Kaczyński, crashed only miles away from Katyn, killing all on board. Time's arrow lurched and fell; the bounds between past, present and future dissolved; only space seemed to matter. 'Katyn is a cursed place, a terrible symbol', said Tusk's predecessor, former Prime Minister Aleksander Kwaśniewski, on the day of the tragedy. 'It sends shivers down my spine' ('Kwaśniewski' 2010).

Yet the 'cursed place' of Katyn and the 'terrible symbol' of Katyn are not congruent. The place is singular; the symbol is, in effect, plural, signifying a multitude of killing fields and burial sites. The majority of those killed in what has become known as 'Katyn' in fact perished in other places well beyond the Katyn Forest in the Soviet Republics of Belarus, Russia and Ukraine. The toponym associated with their murder, moreover, has become a referential touchstone and descriptive shorthand throughout Eastern Europe for other, lesser-known sites of past savagery – Vinnytsia, Bykivnia, Kurapaty – and for sites of more recent savagery – Srebrenica, for instance, at one time proclaimed the 'new Katyn' ('Srebrenica' 1995). Today Katyn circulates with alacrity in public memory and in political discourse in Eastern Europe, fuelling both solidarity and suspicion, fellowship and fear. This book maps its legacy through the interconnected memory cultures of seven countries – Belarus, Poland, Russia, Ukraine and the Baltic States – and explores its meaning as site and symbol, event and idea, fact and crypt.

1.

In the bloody annals of the twentieth century, Katyn stands as one of the first coordinated transnational mass murders of foreign prisoners by a totalitarian state. At the direction of one order from the Kremlin – Politburo Protocol 13/144, drafted by NKVD chief Lavrenty Beria and dated 5 March 1940 – NKVD agents shot 21,857 Poles and buried them in a number of clandestine sites in the Soviet Republics of Russia, Ukraine and, very likely, Belarus (Cienciala et al. 2007, 118–20, 332–3). The victims had been rounded up in the territory known in Polish as the *Kresy*, 'the Borderlands' – encompassing much of today's western Ukraine and western Belarus – during and after the Soviet invasion of Poland in September 1939. They were either incarcerated in local prisons or sent eastward to special camps administered by the NKVD in Kozel'sk and Ostashkov (in western Russia) and Starobil's'k (in eastern Ukraine). In Kozel'sk, Ostashkov and Starobil's'k, they were classified as 'prisoners of war', even though war between Poland and the Soviet Union had never been declared. Months later, they were classified, fatally, as 'enemies', even though they were potential allies. Indeed, as early as 1941, Stalin would begin actively recruiting Polish soldiers and officers to fight alongside the Red Army against Nazi forces. What made these 21,857 prisoners, by contrast, such a threat to the Soviet regime? After all, in the clinical words of Beria's fatal 5 March 1940 memorandum, they were only 'former [military] officers, officials, landowners, [. . .] rank-and-file police, [and] priests' (Cienciala et al. 2007, 119). Among their number were also physicians, pharmacists, veterinarians, lawyers, teachers, rabbis and an eighteen-year-old telephone operator (Cienciala et al. 2007, 125). The victims of Katyn, in other words, were the pride and the promise of the Polish people – young and old, soldier and civilian. In large measure, every memory of Katyn today is a struggle to confront the sheer senselessness of their death sentence, to overcome a persistent and perplexing *why?*

The prisoners' executions were as methodical as they were grisly, involving a formidable state logistical apparatus that, in effect, operationalized displacement. Prisoners were kept on the move. Those held in the *Kresy* were dispatched by train to various NKVD prisons in Kyiv, Kharkiv, Kherson and Minsk, where they were then put to death. Precise details about the location and the identity of these victims remain, to an extent, unclear. What is better known is the fate of the prisoners held in the Kozel'sk, Ostashkov and Starobil's'k camps, who were, in NKVD parlance, 'unloaded' (*razgruzhalis'*) from their cells – sometimes to a lively musical accompaniment, and nearly always under the pretence of imminent release – and sent to Smolensk, Kalinin (today's Tver) and Kharkiv, respectively. At Kalinin and Kharkiv, victims were led into NKVD prisons and asked to confirm their names, one by one, before being shot in the back of the head at the base of the skull. Their bodies were then transported to NKVD burial sites in forests abutting the nearby villages of Mednoe and Piatykhatky and dumped in mass graves, which were, in at least one case, scattered with 'white powder' intended to 'speed up decomposition' (Cienciala et al. 2007, 127). At Smolensk, victims were organized into groups and sent by rail and then by bus to Katyn Forest, where they were largely not afforded the charade of questions from NKVD functionaries. Most were shot immediately upon arrival at the edge of eight pits, in broad daylight and under cover of darkness. By the middle of May 1940, their graves were filled in with dirt and covered over with pine seedlings. Weeks later their executioners were given rewards equivalent to a month's salary for, in the words of one Soviet document, 'successfully completing their assignments' (Cienciala et al. 2007, 272).

Just as the singular term 'Katyn' cannot convey the plural, transnational nature of the massacres, an exclusive focus on the executions themselves cannot convey the extent of the horror of the crime. In the midst of killing these Polish prisoners in cold blood, the NKVD also actively sought out their wives and children and deported them to central Asia, where many perished from malnutrition, mistreatment and disease. In May 1940, four children who survived the arduous journey eastward appealed directly to Stalin for support and assistance, addressing him as their 'great', 'beloved father'. 'We little children are dying of hunger and we humbly ask Father Stalin not to forget about us', they wrote from the village of Rozovka in Kazakhstan. 'We will always be good working people in the Soviet Union, only it's hard for us to live without our fathers' (Cienciala et al. 2007, 198). The 'great father' had these fathers killed in Kalinin and buried at Mednoe.

This heartrending letter captures the particular perversity of the Stalinist disciplinary regime, which so often compelled the victim to honour and supplicate the victimizer. As the Russian writer Aleksandr Tvardovskii would declare sardonically in his poem 'By Right of Memory' ('Po pravu pamiati', 1966–9), 'Be thankful for your fate, whatever it may be,/ And swear one thing: that [Stalin] is great' (Tvardovskii 1991, 111). After the Second World War, with their decimated country firmly within the geopolitical orbit of Soviet power, the Polish people had little choice but to honour the victimizer, to ingest the 'Pill of Murti-Bing' that reconciles one to being ruled by another in Czesław Miłosz's *The Captive Mind* (Milosz 1953, 4–5).[1] In 1951, for instance – the same year that an investigation into the Katyn massacre was being launched in the United States Congress – Communist Poland issued a commemorative stamp adorned with the face of the man responsible for the atrocity. It featured a profile of Stalin as decorated *generalissimo* and celebratory text marking 'Polish–Soviet friendship month'.

---

[1] Originally the brainchild of writer Stanisław Ignacy Witkiewicz, the Pill of Murti-Bing is a drug in the novel *Insatiability* (*Nienasycenie*, 1930) that impedes the realization that the approach of the occupier is an existential danger to one's culture and civilization.

According to the official Soviet narrative, Katyn was a 'monstrous' Nazi atrocity. This lie – known as the 'Katyn Lie', *kłamstwo katyńskie* – was the centrepiece of a relentless Soviet campaign of falsification and disinformation that spanned nearly half a century. Today it constitutes one of the longest and most extensive coverups of a mass murder in history. The Katyn Lie began as a fiercely defensive rejoinder to an announcement, broadcast worldwide from Berlin in April 1943, that mass graves of an estimated '10,000' Polish victims of 'Bolshevik' terror had been found by German authorities near Smolensk (Cienciala et al. 2007, 216, 305–6). The *Wehrmacht* had seized Smolensk in the autumn of 1941 during Operation Barbarossa, and whispered rumours of burial pits in the Katyn Forest soon reached German authorities, who ordered an excavation. Goebbels, who apparently found the whole matter 'gruesome', gleefully remarked in his diary that the discovery would be used 'for anti-Bolshevik propaganda in a grand style' (Lochner 1948, 253).[2] In an effort to shame Moscow and divide the Allies, the Nazis invited the Red Cross and formed an International Commission of forensic scientists to examine the burial site. In the war of perception that attended the Second World War, 'Katyn' became a potent weapon, a chilling refrain.

The Soviet counter-accusation was swift and vociferous. 'In launching this monstrous invention, the German-Fascist scoundrels do not hesitate at the most unscrupulous and base lies in their attempt to cover up crimes which, as has now become evident, were perpetrated by themselves' (Cienciala et al. 2007, 306). Moscow responded by alleging that the bodies found in the Katyn forest were those of Poles who had been taken captive and executed by Nazi forces on Soviet territory in 1941, after the launch of Operation Barbarossa. The date – 1941 instead of 1940 – was everything to the Katyn Lie. Indeed, as we shall see in chapter 1, simply marking the Katyn tragedy as an event from 1940 would constitute a resounding protest against Soviet power in post-war Communist Poland.

Not to be outdone by Goebbels, Soviet authorities set up an investigatory commission of their own upon retaking Smolensk and its environs in 1944, which was preceded by an NKVD operation that

---

[2] Western observers commented that Katyn was 'a gift to Goebbels' (Harvey 1978, 249–51).

doctored evidence and coached local witnesses (Lebedeva 2001, 429–30). The preordained conclusions of the Burdenko Commission gave cover to the Katyn Lie and emboldened Moscow to 'double down' on its claims. In 1944, for instance, the Red Army brazenly considered the formation of a new Polish tank brigade called 'the avengers of Katyn' (Sanford 2005, 206). In 1945 and 1946, they attempted to establish German guilt for Katyn at Nuremberg, only to fail spectacularly in the face of refutations drawn from witness testimony. Talk of Katyn was subsequently abandoned at the international tribunal. The Katyn Lie, however, endured. Only in 1990, when Mikhail Gorbachev handed over cartons of documents attesting to Soviet perpetration of the crime to Polish President Wojciech Jaruzelski, did the truth finally begin to emerge publicly.

The full truth, however, has yet to prevail. In 1992, the President of the Russian Federation Boris Yeltsin offered his Polish counterpart Lech Wałęsa an additional cache of archival documents related to the massacres. Rather than closing the case, these documents confirmed the worst: namely, that there were 11,000 more victims than the 10,000 announced in 1943. Among these documents was the now-infamous protocol of 5 March 1940, bearing the signatures of Stalin and Beria and condemning to death not only the 'former Polish officers [. . .] in the prisoner-of-war camps' but also 'those who have been arrested and are in the prisons of the western oblasts of Ukraine and Belorussia, numbering 11,000' (Wosik 1992, 34–41; Cienciala et al. 2007, 119–20). A letter dated 3 March 1959 from the head of the KGB Aleksandr Shelepin to Nikita Khrushchev was particularly revelatory. It proposed to 'destroy all records of the persons shot' in the Katyn operation, listing the following figures: 'a total of 21,857 persons were shot; of these, 4,421 in the Katyn Forest (Smolensk Oblast), 3,820 in the camp of [Starobil's'k], close to [Kharkiv], 6,311 in the camp of Ostashkov (Kalinin Oblast), and 7,305 persons [. . .] in other camps and prisons of western Ukraine and western Belorussia' (Wosik 1992, 42–7; Cienciala et al. 2007, 332). Whether the prisoner records identified by Shelepin were destroyed or not, these numbers remain, prompting more difficult questions. Where are the other 11,000 victims buried? How did they die? In the words of two Polish historians, in 1992 'the Katyn murder was drastically broadened to include people whom we had previously never connected to the idea of Katyn, about whom we simply did not know' (Strzembosz and Jasiewicz 1992, 161).

2.

The truth of Katyn does not concern some. As we shall see in chapter 6, Katyn deniers in Russia (and elsewhere) cling to the Katyn Lie and its assertion of Nazi guilt, disputing the admissions made by Mikhail Gorbachev, Boris Yeltsin, Vladimir Putin, Dmitrii Medvedev and, most recently, the lower house of the Russian parliament, the Duma. They do so by pitting history against memory, by mixing pseudohistorical research with emotional appeals to Russian national pride and accusations of Polish martyrdom and greed. To understand the place of Katyn in Eastern Europe today is to come to grips with this tense, volatile interplay between history and memory. In recent years, there has been a scramble for memory in the humanities and social sciences, a 'memory boom' (Bell 2003) that has at times thrown the term itself into terminological chaos (Klein 2000). To clarify our usage briefly and abstractly, we refer to a supple distinction made by the historian Jay Winter. 'History', he writes, 'is memory seen through [. . .] documents. Memory is history seen through affect' (Winter 2010a, 12). Defining each by way of the other, Winter underscores that history and memory are inseparable, mutually dependent phenomena. Whereas his formulation hinges on the perceptual, on a 'seeing through', ours hinges on the discursive, on a 'speaking through'. History is memory spoken constatively; it abides to rules of verifiability enforced by a narrow circle of professionals, trained historians and archivists. It is truth-evaluable. Memory, meanwhile, is history spoken performatively; it abides to the poses and practices of a broad circle of priests and pilgrims, politicians and filmmakers, artists and scholars, tourists and their guides. Its relation to historical truth is complex and often unaccountable. The difference between history and memory is both discursive and social; it is also a moving target. As the philosopher J. L. Austin reminds us, there is always a 'danger [in the] distinction between constative and performative utterances breaking down'. History and memory therefore cannot be confined, to borrow once more from Austin, to 'a desert of comparative precision' (Austin 1978,

54, 55). In the case of the Katyn massacres, as we shall see, history and memory overlap and interact with one another constantly, with fact-finding provoking meaning-making and meaning-making perpetuating (and challenging) fact-finding.

If memory is history spoken performatively, the field of memory studies benefits from the employment of the practices of literary and cultural studies, which are attentive to forms and strategies of representation as well as questions of audience and reception. We examine these issues by way of cinematic, literary and memorial texts that commemorate, meditate upon and allude to the Katyn massacres, paying close attention to what might be called the rhetoric of memory. Indeed, rhetoric is the art of persuasion, and memory persuades. Whether painful or heartening, distant or close at hand, memory persuades us of the significance of our past in order to persuade us of the certainty of our present and of the promise of our future. This rhetorical utility makes memory a powerful, and powerfully efficient, political tool. In an instant, it can transform workaday political and economic disputes into pitched battles for collective 'souls'. In the countries of today's Eastern Europe, immersed in an often subterranean conflict over their historical and present-day (in)compatibility, the memory of the Katyn tragedy is frequently put to the service of such alchemy because, in large measure, it productively travels two fundamental rhetorical trajectories: the metonymical and the metaphorical. The first involves a 'concatenation of signs along a string of contiguity'; the second, a 'substitution of one sign for one another within a sphere of similiarity' (Ricoeur 1986, 427). Colliding and colluding with one another across national borders, the Katyn metonym and Katyn metaphor have helped make a tragedy of the past an influential arbiter of the present.

In Poland, Katyn has long been read metonymically, as a part of the country's history meant to stand for the whole. The relation is one of contiguity. In the words of Józef Czapski, 'All of us [. . .] are bound together by an invisible chain, of which one of the final links is Katyn' (Sobolewski 2007). Or in the words of Donald Tusk, 'in a sense, we Poles are one, big Katyn family' (Tusk 2010). In today's Russia, after decades of denial and enforced forgetting, Katyn is at times deployed as a metonym as well. 'All of Russia', declared Sergei Karaganov in 2010, 'is one big Katyn, dotted by the largely unmarked graves of millions of victims of the [Soviet] regime'.[3] The Katyn metonym in the Russian context, however, bears a painful ambivalence. Is 'all of Russia' a site of historical victimhood – or of criminality? If all of Russia is 'one big Katyn', does the Katyn massacre itself lose its specificity and singularity?

Elsewhere in Russia, Katyn resounds metaphorically, as an event meant to evoke another tragedy – the so-called 'anti-Katyn', in which thousands of Soviet POWs perished from hunger and disease in Polish camps during the Soviet–Polish War of 1919–21 (Shved 2006) – by virtue of a putative relation of similarity. The forced metaphorical equivalence between the Polish treatment of Soviet prisoners in 1919–21 and the Soviet treatment of Polish prisoners in 1939–40 has been posited by Vladimir Putin, who in 2010 rationalized the Katyn massacres as Stalin's act of revenge for Soviet losses at Polish hands. In Ukraine, Belarus and the Baltic States, Katyn tends to be employed as a metaphor as well, albeit much differently. Vinnytsia, where the NKVD slaughtered many thousands of Ukrainians in 1937–8, has been called the 'Katyn of Ukraine'; Kaušėnų and Ablinga, where the Nazis killed a total of nearly 2,000 Jews and other civilians during the Second World War, are 'Lithuanian Katyns' (Kamenetsky 1989, 41; ' "Dėkoju jaunimui ir visiems" ' 2010). The expediency of Katyn as a metaphorical vehicle by which to elucidate such tragedies is testament to the fact that, in a region replete with unmarked death pits and ignored atrocities, 'Katyn' is not unknown to the world.[4] Whether it is truly understood remains to be seen.

The metonymicity and metaphoricity of the Katyn massacres are a natural function of their transnational execution, historical resonance and political significance. They cannot but signify something beyond themselves. Yet the circulation of the Katyn metonym and the Katyn metaphor is also at times symptomatic of a failure to remember Katyn *qua* Katyn, on its own terms, in its own way. To borrow a turn of phrase from Roland Barthes: no sooner is Katyn remembered than it must resemble something (1994, 44).

---

[3] Nikolai Burdenko, who led the Soviet investigation of the Katyn graves in 1944, is also believed to have said privately that Russia's soil is full of Katyns (Sanford 2005, 139).

[4] 'Traditionally, metaphor has been represented as a trope of transference in which an unknown or imperfectly known is clarified, defined, described in terms of a known' (Whalley 1974, 490).

Over the course of the chapters ahead, we note these resemblances and follow them wherever they lead, for their itineraries mark an instructive series of differential responses to the Communist legacy in Europe. At the same time, we attend to critical moments in which Katyn's propensity for resemblance gives way to revision and change. Such moments are the consequence of what we call the *memory event*, a revisiting of the past that creates a rupture with its accepted representation.

3.

Memory events are explosive. They are not standard ritual commemorations, anniversaries or holidays – memorial rites, in other words – whose significance and value lie in their repeatability and constancy. Such rites duplicate memories, whereas memory events generate new memories bearing the structural imprint of old ones. In contrast to Pierre Nora's 'sites of memory' (*lieux de mémoire*), which are defined spatially, as material and non-material 'symbolic element[s] of the memorial heritage of any community' (Nora 1996, xvii), memory events are deterritorialized and temporal phenomena, moments of agitation and transformation in the public sphere that generate secondary waves and aftershocks and eventually produce revised memorial rites. Sites of memory 'stop time' by simulating eternity (Nora 1989, 19); memory events 'start time' by endowing the past with new life in the future. Memory events spring from a diverse array of genres – from films, novels, court proceedings, political announcements, textbooks. An instructive example, which is dealt with at length in this book, is the 2007 release of Andrzej Wajda's *Katyn*, a film that emerged out of the realm of private memory to penetrate the public sphere and to change the various ways the tragedy was remembered throughout Eastern Europe. Memory events are typically secondary to the history events that they interpret, but they sometimes attain the status of history events themselves. The 2010 crash of Lech Kaczyński's plane, which was transporting nearly 100 Poles to Katyn to mourn the massacre, is an extreme example of this conflation, by which a memory event became a history event that is today commemorated in its own right.

Memory events may be said to 'reboot' cultural memory. Much like a computer, cultural memory is dependent on an interaction between 'hardware' (e.g. monuments, plaques, street signs) and 'software' (e.g. novels, films, marches) (Etkind 2004, 2009). Monuments are inconspicuous if people are not writing about them, snapping photos of them, laying flowers at their pedestals. Marches have incomplete itineraries without a physical structure designated for commemoration and hewn from stone. Memory events reboot cultural memory by keeping this hardware and software in dialogue while refreshing and updating the code that facilitates their exchange. The memory events in the seven countries surveyed in this book have kept the Katyn massacres a highly fluid, dynamic and contested subject of memory politics in Eastern Europe and beyond. From the Nuremberg Trials in 1946 and the US Congressional enquiry of 1951–2 to Wajda's film and Kaczyński's crash, they have sustained the memory of the massacres while ensuring that their memorial representations change in creative, unpredictable ways.

Tragedies like Katyn impose immense psychological and spiritual burdens on families and communities both bound to the victims and unrelated to them. They also impose considerable burdens on concepts, which by nature seek to define and determine what is for so many indefinable and indeterminable. As a result, the lexicon of catastrophe often eschews concepts for proper names, which work like cultural crypts, simultaneously burying the past and preventing it from dissolution. The Holocaust is one such name, the Gulag another. 'Katyn' functions in a similar way, symbolizing – to borrow from Nicolas Abraham and Maria Torok (1994) – the inability to symbolize. The cultural memory of such tragedies is, to an extent, an implicit struggle to compensate for this inability, to produce public symbols in the present capable of making sense of the past. In Eastern Europe many of the actors shaping this memory today did not experience the horrors of the Gulag or the tumult of the Second World War; in fact, some of them have no experience of the Soviet regime at all. Theirs is the generation of what Marianne Hirsch calls 'postmemory', the memory 'of those who grow up dominated by narratives that preceded their birth, whose own belated stories are evacuated by the stories of the previous generation shaped by traumatic events that can be neither understood nor recreated'

(Hirsch 1997, 22). Remembering things that have not happened to us: this is the work of the imagination. Postmemory in this sense has more to do with poetics than with history, which helps explain why writers like Józef Mackiewicz and Aleksandr Solzhenitsyn have done more to cultivate a memory of Stalinist terror than generations of professional historians.

In the twenty-first century, many scholars of memory (Levy and Sznaider 2006; Rothberg 2010) have issued a call for us to overcome methodological nationalism, which views cultural processes as circumscribed by the nation-state. They posit that one of the most tragic and also most ethnic-bound of losses, the Holocaust, has produced an experience of mourning that has become the subject of global, cosmopolitan memory – 'memory unbound'. We see memories of Katyn and other Stalinist atrocities breaking free of the national as well. Despite a tightly-controlled public sphere, international debates and émigré activities helped to promote and consolidate the memory of Katyn in Communist Poland. More recently, Wajda's film has done much to shape an ad hoc memorial community that extends far beyond Poland; it has moved Ukrainian, Russian, British, American audiences alike and offered them a visceral and graphic vision of the massacres that is difficult to forget. It has helped to inspire East European youth to march together in commemoration of Katyn and to bolster the activities of non-governmental organizations like the 'Memorial' Society, which are increasingly international in scope and reach. Such global, cosmopolitan mourning for the atrocities of the twentieth century is both a cultural reality and a moral responsibility.

Chapter One

Katyn in Poland

In 2008, the Polish rock-punk-ska group Lao Che released 'Are You Human?', a song about the Katyn massacres performed with the stiff, regular cadence of a military march. Its lyrics are a confession of an NKVD agent who recalls leading a Polish victim through the forest to his death. 'If you'd like, I'll tell you/ How I once played God', intones Hubert Dobaczewski, the lead singer of Lao Che. 'How I leaned [my victim] over the pit/ If you'd like, I'll tell you/ How in the back of his head I . . .'. Consigned to ellipsis, the precise moment of the murder haunts the murderer. The echo of the gunshot rings out in his conscience with mockery; the 'wise' eyes of the victim burn in his memory without end. The damned NKVD agent implores the listener, 'Tell me I am human. Tell me, am I human?'

Lao Che have won acclaim in Poland and beyond for their visceral confrontation of the dark events of the twentieth century.[1] With 'Are You Human?' – a song that asserts the humanity of the perpetrators of Katyn by having them question their humanity – the group confronts a particular problem related to the Polish memory of Katyn. The problem is, strictly speaking, that there is no memory. There was no survivor to bear voluntary, direct

---

[1] In 2005, for instance, Lao Che also released an album devoted to the Warsaw Uprising.

witness to the shootings, no one to recollect and *remember* them. 'The survivor's vocation is to remember; he cannot *not* remember' (Agamben 2002, 26). Yet the memory of Stanisław Swianiewicz, a man widely considered a Katyn survivor, ends at Gnezdovo train station outside Katyn forest, where he was pulled aside by Soviet authorities at the last moment. His recollection of seeing his compatriots loaded onto transports at bayonet point, unaware of their fate, is the closest we have to a survivor's memory of Katyn. As Swianiewicz acknowledges at the beginning of his memoir *In the Shadow of Katyn* (1976), 'I am not a Katyn witness . . .' (Swianiewicz 1976, 11).[2] Indeed, no one who entered the space designated for his destruction in Katyn, Kalinin and Kharkiv survived. No one who saw the edge of the pits escaped before the trigger was pulled. And no one who saw any of these 21,857 Poles perish would go on voluntarily to bear witness to their fate. As Lao Che suggest, the cursed memory of Katyn lies with the Soviet perpetrator.

Here we can begin to discern what might be called, for Poland, the singularity of Katyn. *No one* could remember the killings, so *everyone* should remember them. A loss of individual memory, in other words, mobilized the work of 'connective memory', what Jan Assmann calls a 'unifying semantics that "holds [groups] inwardly together" and [stabilizes] a common identity' (Assmann 2006, 11). In this sense, remembering Katyn has been a literal re-membering for Poland, a sustained effort to connect and unite the members of a community around an understanding of a traumatic event of the past beset by lies and deceit. To a degree, remembering Katyn has also been a cosmopolitan undertaking,

---

[2] Another Polish prisoner spared execution during the Katyn operation was Józef Czapski (1896–1993). Son of the Russian governor of Minsk, Czapski graduated from the Faculty of Law of the St Petersburg Imperial University and the Academy of Arts in Krakow. In 1941–2, he was sent by General Anders to search for the Kozel'sk, Ostashkov and Starobil's'k prisoners. In 1942, before learning of the mass graves in Katyn, he met Anna Akhmatova in Tashkent. She documented their meeting in an exalted poem, 'That night we drove each other wild' ('V tu noch my soshli drug ot druga s uma'); he described their promenade in his memoirs. His works *Starobil's'k Memoirs* (1944) and *On Inhuman Land* (1949) would become canonical texts about Katyn. In 1996, a founder of the 'Memorial' Society, Veniamin Iofe, would remember Czapski as a progenitor of the organization.

involving various communities in Europe, North America and beyond whose recognition of the massacre promised assurance, security and vindication for Polish memory and mourning.

For decades, this work of memory and mourning was undertaken both in the Soviet satellite state of the People's Republic of Poland (*Polska Rzeczpospolita Ludowa*, hereafter PRL) and in 'Polonia', the Polish émigré community. Poles at home and Poles abroad interacted with one another – sometimes uneasily, often clandestinely – to achieve the same goal, a discovery and disclosure of the facts of the Katyn massacre. Yet the risks attendant to their activities were very different. For Polish émigrés in the United Kingdom, home of the anti-Communist Polish Government-in-Exile, the work of connective memory involved mounting relentless investigations, educating often disinterested or quiescent publics, and lobbying politicians. For Poles in the PRL, such acts could spell punishment, imprisonment or even death. These many obstacles, from the mundane to the perilous, meant that remembering Katyn also involved, implicitly or explicitly, a meditation on the very limits of memory. Indeed, what we observe in this case is a special type of 'postmemory', which Marianne Hirsch relates to an 'inter- and trans-generational *transmission* of traumatic knowledge and experience' through oral narratives and material artifacts (Hirsch 2008, 106; our emphasis). For Poland, this transmission has been more a *pursuit*. At home or abroad, Poles had to fight to remember Katyn – not only in the face of a state-enforced campaign of forgetting, obfuscation and denial, but also in the face of a stark realization of the literal impossibility of remembering an event for which there was no living and willing witness. Their discourse is symptomatic of what we might call instead *metamemory*: memory about memory, about its loss and disappearance, failures and lacunae. In a verse by poet and literary critic Jacek Trznadel, it is the haunting of a 'Polish Hamlet' by a father executed at Katyn whose ghost cannot speak:

> The ghost of his father in his charnel rags
> with a hole in the back of his head
> wakes him at midnight
> but gives no sign
> his hands are tied behind him
> and from that moment Hamlet constantly hears

that same rap of Nagan pistols in his heart[3]
drowning out the morning song
of Ophelia and the birds   (Trznadel 1995b, 173–4)

Fighting the Katyn Lie

In 1988 Trznadel wrote that in Poland 'there has been no end' to Katyn. Events like the Warsaw Uprising of 1944 had passed into the historical record, but the 'Katyn Lie' lingered and persisted, testifying to the 'falsity of the [Communist] regime, which has tortured the Polish national consciousness' (Trznadel 1994, 128, 12). Indeed, for the anti-Communist opposition, the official narrative of Katyn as a Nazi crime was 'the foundational lie of the Polish People's Republic' (Wasilewski 2010, 87).[4] Exposing the lie would shake the very foundations of Communism in Poland; asserting the truth would provide a 'trench for the spirit', protection and security for a beleaguered resistance (Trznadel 1994, 22).[5]

Asserting the truth in Poland would mean overcoming a policy that went beyond mere censorship: discursive cleansing (Finnin 2011). Discursive cleansing is the process of disciplining speech through coordinated epistemic and physical violence that is both retrospective and prospective in its application. In Communist Poland, it involved silencing and punishing those who dared speak of Katyn; falsifying evidence and fabricating texts related to the massacres; and retroactively effacing references to Katyn in the public sphere, even when such references asserted Nazi responsibility. In tandem with their counterparts in Moscow, authorities in Warsaw were to ensure that Katyn was virtually expunged from public discourse and that its victims were made 'ungrievable' (Butler 2009), that is, cast outside the realm of sanctioned mourning. In principle, Katyn was to remain recognized as a Nazi crime,

[3] 'Nagan' is a reference to the Soviet revolver, named after its Belgian inventor Nagant.
[4] President Lech Kaczyński used the same expression in the speech that he was meant to deliver at Katyn in 2010.
[5] The phrase 'a trench for the spirit' is an allusion to the work of nineteenth-century Polish poet Cyprian Kamil Norwid.

but in practice, after the late 1940s, the event was not to be recognized at all. As Mirosław Golon remarks, 'For most of the period of the PRL, the Katyn crime simply did not exist in its propaganda, or at least was not meant to exist' (Golon 2001, 25).

Following in the footsteps of the Soviet NKVD, which had deported thousands of relatives of Katyn victims and imprisoned circumstantial witnesses, the Polish secret service or *Służba Bezpieczeństwa* (hereafter, SB) threatened, punished and often displaced those who attempted to establish the fate of the loved ones sent to Kozel'sk, Ostashkov and Starobil's'k (Gasztold-Seń 2010, 132). The SB singled out Poles who brought up Katyn in conversation or passed along information about the crime gleaned from Radio Free Europe and other foreign radio services (Gasztold-Seń 2010, 132, 138–9). They also pressured those who had participated in the German exhumations of Katyn in 1943 to recant their testimonies. Writers like Józef Mackiewicz and Ferdynand Goetel, whose reports to the Red Cross and the Polish Government-in-Exile were crucial in establishing an accurate picture of the crime, refused to do so, however. As a result, they were forced to flee to the West, and their names were cleansed from the public sphere.

Even in emigration, Mackiewicz would return, in a sense, to Poland. In 1948 he edited (anonymously) the seminal work *The Katyn Crime in the Light of Documents*, which circulated widely and repeatedly in the Polish underground. In effect, the volume helped establish a 'circuit' of Katyn-related information between Polish émigrés and activists in the PRL. Featuring a foreword by General Władysław Anders, who was invited by the Soviet regime to form a Polish armed force aligned with the Red Army in 1941, *The Katyn Crime in the Light of Documents* is a collection of documents, photographs, testimonies, interviews and other materials, including diary entries of the victims uncovered during the German exhumations in 1943. These latter, fragmentary texts are both records and representatives of the dead, testifying to the aspirations, fears and experiences of the victims but ending abruptly before the moment of execution (Trznadel 1994, 36). In this way, they speak to Katyn by not speaking of Katyn.

The diaries excerpted and collected in *The Katyn Crime in the Light of Documents* were transcribed by Dr Jan Zygmunt Robel and his assistants at the former Polish State Institute of Forensic

Medicine in Krakow, who were responsible for examining the materials discovered during the 1943 exhumation. Robel and his team risked their lives to reproduce each of the twenty-two diaries and to create a secret catalogue of all the documents they handled. Fifteen diaries were passed on to the Polish Government-in-Exile in London; the others were lost. While Communist authorities confiscated some of Robel's catalogued material after the war, a cache of documents, including typed copies of the diaries, remained hidden in the Institute of Forensic Medicine until 1991 (Cienciala et al. 2007, 225).

As these texts made their way to Poland via Mackiewicz's volume, acts of Katyn commemoration proliferated steadily behind cemetery gates and within church walls. Here the secret police encountered persistent resistance from many quarters (Gasztold-Seń 2010, 132–3). At their core, public commemorations of Katyn were a poignant assertion of the right to grieve for the victims, a right denied by Communist authorities whose policy of enforced silence betrayed a *mens rea*, a guilty mind (Finnin 2011, 1104). They typically took place, moreover, within religiously conse-crated space, on or near the holy ground of cemeteries, chapels and churches, where the victims could receive something akin to a symbolic ecclesiastical burial. Indeed, such sites are referred to in Polish as *symboliczne groby*, symbolic graves. These memory events at the crossroads of the worlds of the living and the dead at first sought to honour and remember the victims; they rarely deigned to specify the identity of the perpetrators. Nevertheless, sacralization of Katyn memory posed a threat to the Communist regime. In a country where the Roman Catholic Church repre-sented both a resilient locus of civil society and a repository of national identity, the religious 'situatedness' of commemorative activities bore profound social and political purchase. Indeed, the particular and deep connection between faith, nationhood and memory work makes Poland different from the other countries explored in this book, from protestant, liberal Estonia to an increasingly observant Orthodox Russia.

The most important site of Katyn commemoration in Poland was a space next to a monument to the wartime forces of the Polish underground, the Home Army (*Armia Krajowa*), in War-saw's Powązkowski (or Powązki) Military Cemetery (Łojek 1989, 63). Built in 1946, the monument consists of a black obelisk crowned by a Polish eagle and inscribed with the emblem of the Home Army, the dates 1939–45 and the message *Gloria Victis* ('Glory to the Vanquished'). It immediately became a place of pilgrimage and a focal point for the commemoration of both the Warsaw Uprising and the Katyn massacres, which are intimately connected to one another in the Polish imaginary (Sawicki 2007). In 1959, on All Souls' Day, there also appeared in Powązki a small wooden cross with the following inscription: 'Symbolic grave of the 12,000 Polish officers murdered in Katyn. They were Poles, and they died on foreign soil at the hands of a brutal enemy. They deserve to be remembered and to be honoured' (Sawicki 2007).[6]

The SB immediately removed the cross and undertook an investigation of its provenance. Suspicion fell on former Home Army soldiers until Ludwika Dymecka, the wife of a former prisoner in Kozel'sk who had been caught leaving leaflets and prayer cards on the site, admitted to erecting the cross. Polish authorities later attributed Dymecka's actions to 'mental illness' (Sawicki 2007). In the 1960s and 1970s, others would take up Dymecka's work, marking this 'Katyn place' (*miejsce katyńskie*) in Powązki with more wooden crosses and with flowers, wreaths and ribbons commemorating the tragedy and its victims (Gasztold-Seń 2010, 145–6). The site would eventually become known as the *Dolinka Katyńska* or 'Katyn Hollow'. Time and again, these crosses, messages and mementos were swiftly removed and destroyed by the SB. On such significant religious and historical dates as All Souls' Day, the anniversary of the German announcement of the discovery of the mass grave in Katyn (13 April), or the anniversary of the Soviet invasion of Poland (17 September), the secret police would wait by the gates of the cemetery and detain visitors, who were often forced to throw flowers and decorative items over the fence to avoid arrest (Gasztold-Seń 2010, 145–6).

This sustained assault on Katyn commemoration, which criminalized public displays of grief while perpetuating the Katyn Lie,

---

[6] The writer Melchior Wańkowicz is often credited with initiating the practice of placing lamps around the monument, some appended with the word 'Katyn', upon his return from emigration in 1958 (Juliański 2010; Sawicki 2007; 'Szkic do historii jednej dolinki', in *Biuletyn katyński*, 1992, cited by Siomkajło 2002, 134).

provoked one man to transform his own death into a monument. On the morning of 21 March 1980, a Home Army veteran named Walenty Badylak chained himself to a water pump in Krakow's main square and burned himself alive.[7] On his body was found a metal plate with a note that read 'For Katyn' and lamented what he perceived to be the corruption of Polish youth and the destruction of traditional culture (Wasilewski 2009, 62). As with Dymecka, Communist authorities explained away, with no proof or precedent, Badylak's self-immolation as the act of a mentally ill individual. Over the years to come, Poles would visit the site of his death to recite prayers, sing hymns, light candles, and lay flowers, pictures and letters. Day in and day out, these items would be confiscated by the SB.

On 31 July 1981, amid the rise of the Solidarity movement, a group of thirty-seven people led by sculptor Stefan Melak processed into the Powązki Cemetery and erected a monument to Katyn that would prove more difficult to confiscate (Wasilewski 2009, 66; Siomkajło 2002, 135–7).[8] Melak had participated in Katyn commemorations at the cemetery for years, and in 1979 he, his brother Arkadiusz, the Katyn campaigner Fr Wacław Karlowicz, and others initiated the construction of a massive stone cross weighing nearly four tonnes and standing over four metres high.[9] Its coded inscription invited sensation and controversy: 'Katyn, Ostaszków, Kozielsk, Starobielsk, 1940'. The year 1940 was a searing indictment of Soviet culpability: it predated Operation Barbarossa and contradicted the 1941 chronology upon which the entire official Soviet narrative hinged. The SB immediately confronted Melak and his group and dismantled the monu-

---

[7] In 1968 Ryszard Siwiec set himself ablaze in Warsaw to protest the Soviet invasion of Czechoslovakia (Stolarik 2010, xxv).

[8] The first professionally designed monument to Katyn in Poland was built in the Gorce mountains, south of Krakow, on one of the area's best-known peaks, Turbacz. Designed by Czesław Pajerski and consecrated on 3 May 1980, it features a cross made from birch trees and stone hands bound with barbed wire reaching out from the earth. The monument is situated next to a chapel commemorating Pope John Paul II's visit to the area in 1979. The remote location made the monument an ideal place for unofficial commemorations of Katyn (Roliński and Rybicki 2000, 31).

[9] Stefan Melak was among those killed in the Smolensk plane crash in April 2010.

ment the following night.[10] Four years later, in 1985, Communist authorities took matters into their own hands and erected their own Katyn cross in Powązki, which foregrounded the year 1941 and explicitly held the Nazis to account for the crime. This pre-emptive gesture was futile, however: the inscription was repeatedly vandalized, and in 1987 protestors installed a plaque opposite the monument decrying the 'Soviet murder' at Katyn (Wasilewski 2009, 67). Today this stone cross stands with a corrected inscription alongside Melak's cross, which was recovered in 1989 and reinstalled in 1995 (Siomkajło 2002, 137; Wasilewski 2009, 68).

Not far from the 'Katyn Hollow', in the Old Powązki cemetery (separate from the military one), stands the Church of St Karol Boromeusz, which for many years was guided by Fr Stefan Niedzielak, one of a number of Catholic priests, including former Kozel'sk prisoner Fr Zdzisław Peszkowski, who worked to commemorate Katyn with sensitivity and a call to forgiveness. Fr Niedzielak helped preserve materials recovered from Katyn during the German exhumations and presided over the commemorations in Powązki from 1977, when he began his ministry at St Karol Boromeusz. He frequently invoked the Katyn tragedy in his homilies, appealing for the truth that would finally lay the victims to rest. In 1984, he and Katyn activist Wojciech Ziembiński affixed a large stone cross with the inscription 'To Those Fallen in the East' to one of the church's exterior walls.[11] The memorial forms the centrepiece of what is now known as the 'Sanctuary of the Fallen and Murdered in the East', a collection of plaques and crosses commemorating Poles who died at Soviet hands. For his activities Fr Niedzielak received repeated death threats and endured a series of beatings and attempted kidnappings (Zaorska 2009). He was murdered in January 1989, 'the last victim of Katyn' (Gasztold-Seń 2010, 152).

---

[10] The foundations for another monument were laid in December 1981, but the plan ground to a halt after the onset of martial law and the arrest of Melak.

[11] The memorial now contains the skull of one of the victims of Katyn, which was removed in 1943 by a Yugoslav member of the delegation invited to view the German exhumations. It was used in lectures on the massacres in Zagreb and returned to Poland in 1990 (Siomkajło 2002, 145). A new section was added to the memorial in 2010 to commemorate the victims of the Smolensk air crash.

Émigré Memory

Katyn activism in the late 1970s and early 1980s was the product of both an emerging civil society in Poland and a committed émigré community abroad. For decades after the Second World War, Polish émigré circles had engaged in an energetic campaign to establish the truth of the massacres. In fact, Katyn was ultimately one of the few points upon which the wider Polish émigré community, at times sharply divided, could unite and speak with one voice (Wolsza 2008, 7). News of émigré political activities and copies of their publications circulated in Poland, educating and emboldening new generations of local Katyn activists 'on the ground'.

While they ultimately failed to raise the question of Soviet responsibility for Katyn at the Nuremberg trials, émigré activists in the 1950s succeeded in lobbying the US House of Representatives to form a committee led by Ray Madden and charged with investigating the massacres. The Madden Committee's resounding verdict of Soviet guilt for the crime of Katyn was a central memory event, one made possible by the work of Polish émigrés (Wolsza 2008, 111). The Committee's recommendation that the Katyn case be heard before an international tribunal, however, was never implemented.

The epicentre of émigré activities was London, the base of the Polish Government-in-Exile from 1940 to 1990. Poles in London organized yearly 'mourning academies' (*akademii żałobne*), which were held in prestigious venues (Westminster Cathedral Hall, Brompton Oratory) and featured all possible genres of memorial software – political appeals, masses, marches, poetry readings, plays, films, speeches and lectures (Wolsza 2008, 92–3, 126–30). Katyn commemorations reached a peak in 1956 during the visit of Soviet leaders Nikita Khrushchev and Nikolai Bulganin to Great Britain. On 22 April, 20,000 Poles gathered at Brompton Oratory for a mass dedicated to the Katyn massacres and then marched to the tomb of the Unknown Soldier at Westminster Abbey, underlining the lack of memory hardware relating to Katyn in Britain (Wolsza 2008, 141).[12]

[12] Sixty thousand Poles also presented a petition to the British Foreign Office at this time, demanding, among other things, a complete revelation of the Katyn case (Wolsza 2008, 132–6).

In 1976 Polish émigrés and British supporters addressed this lack and prevailed in erecting a monument to Katyn in London. While the first monument to Katyn appeared in Sweden in 1975, the most controversial and high-profile memorial outside of Poland was without a doubt the one in the British capital.[13] Plans to create the monument had been launched in 1971, when historian Louis FitzGibbon led the development of a Katyn Memorial Fund. Its construction was delayed by official protests from Moscow and Warsaw as well as a reluctant British government, which tried to persuade the Polish community not to contradict the Katyn Lie openly and advocated an inscription bearing the date of 1941 and a location far from the centre of the city. The Poles finally accepted an outlying site at the Gunnersbury Cemetery in west London. The monument, a large black obelisk, bears the word 'Katyn', the date 1940, and the invocation 'The Conscience of the World Calls for a Testimony of Truth' (FitzGibbon 1977). Approximately 8,000 people are believed to have attended its unveiling, including Stanisław Swianiewicz and Józef Czapski (Siomkajło 2002, 65). The British government sent no official representatives to the unveiling and forbade British military personnel to attend in uniform, but this rule was not observed (Cienciala et al. 2007, 244). The monument drew criticism from a number of Poles, including Mackiewicz, for its failure to name and shame the perpetrators of the crime. Jerzy Łojek described the monument as 'cowardly and opportunistic' (Łojek 1989, 62, 5). In 1990, it was augmented with a plaque condemning 'Stalin' and 'the Soviet secret police'.

Mobilization of Polish Civil Society

While Polish émigré communities sought to raise awareness of Katyn in Washington DC, London and other Western capitals, they also worked to protect and preserve the threatened memory of the massacres in Poland itself. Articles from émigré periodicals and seminal works like Mackiewicz's *The Katyn Crime in the*

---

[13] The Swedish monument, which is located in the centre of Stockholm, was doused with acid in 1976 and damaged by vandals again in 2011.

Light of the Documents and Czapski's *Starobil's'k Memoirs* found their way into the Polish underground press, helping to inform and spark the commemorative acts at Powązki Cemetery and beyond. These texts often produced memory events of unusual originality and intensity. A fascinating example is a homemade radio programme from the early 1970s produced by Jerzy Cywiński. With no previous broadcasting experience, Cywiński created a seventy-five-minute documentary about Katyn based on secondary sources available in the Polish underground. The documentary employed basic technology and presented an articulate and well-researched account of the crime and its aftermath. The tapes were played initially in the Cywiński home and soon shared with selected friends and local church groups. Cywiński's widow, Dorota, estimates that the documentary was heard by several hundred people. The tapes were lost for many years before being located in the archives of the Polish Social and Cultural Association in London. A 2011 broadcast by Polish Radio 2 describes Cywiński's work as 'one of the earliest attempts to show the whole Katyn problem in all its complexity'. Expressing once again the need for memory hardware, the work concludes with the following words: 'As long as there is no monument in Poland [to Katyn], as long as there is no special train on All Souls' Day running from Warsaw to Smolensk, then in the space of this room let us pay tribute to those who fell at Katyn' ('Posłuchaj' 2011).

The circulation of the sources used by Cywiński was made possible by an increasingly emboldened Polish opposition movement, which in the 1970s began to distribute Katyn-related literature of its own. In 1977, the writer and politician Ryszard Zieliński published a concise, thirty-two-page brochure under the pseudonyms Jan Abramski and Ryszard Żywiecki – the first and last names on the 'Katyn List'. Zieliński's little book provides a brief overview of post-war developments related to Katyn, including the Nuremberg trial and the Madden Committee enquiry, and outlines the campaign of discursive cleansing in the PRL. Beginning with a discussion of Poland's horrific losses in the Second World War, it claims that, unlike German atrocities, the Stalinist crimes of 1939–41 and 1944 against the Poles had been forgotten by the world (Zieliński 1977, 4). Emphasizing the correspondence between the crimes of Nazism and the crimes of Stalinism has become a commonplace in Polish Katyn discourse and, more generally, in East European memory politics (see especially chapter 5). Zieliński concludes with the following address to PRL authorities: 'Accusations against the Hitlerite criminals will lose their moral ambiguity only when you start to condemn ALL perpetrators of genocide. Six million Polish citizens died at the hands of both German and Soviet criminals' (Zieliński 1977, 32).

Perhaps the single most significant work of the period was Jerzy Łojek's *The History of the Katyn Case* (*Dzieje sprawy Katynia* 1989), which was originally published in 1980.[14] Łojek was a leading Katyn activist whose work led authorities to undercut his career as an academic historian. Łojek places Katyn in the historical context of what he considers a Soviet tradition of 'genocide', which he traces back to the very beginnings of the USSR (Łojek 1989, 59). Much of his analysis constitutes an extended criticism of Polish military and political authorities for their failure to foresee the massacres and to respond effectively when the truth came to light. He is also critical of the British and American reactions (Łojek 1989, 41). Łojek calls for a UN tribunal to establish the facts of the massacres and to facilitate the transfer of all materials and all human remains to Poland. Implying a symmetry between Nazi and Stalinist crimes, he asserts that a future Katyn cemetery complex should have the same role as Auschwitz – namely, to reconcile divided peoples, commemorate suffering, and serve as a warning to the world (Łojek 1989, 68). He concludes with a powerful statement on memory:

> No people or state can cut itself off from its history; no state can build its traditions on falsified history, relying on fear as an instrument of the suppression of inconvenient elements of the past in the memory of society. The Russian people also cannot cut itself off from its Stalinist past (Łojek 1989, 66).

The increasingly organized activity of the Polish opposition led to the development of embryonic societies and institutions dedicated to the Katyn cause. In 1978–9, the Katyn Institute was formed in Krakow and the Katyn Committee in Warsaw. These groups emerged in the era of the Solidarity movement and the

---

[14] The brochure was written under the pseudonym Leopold Jerzewski; Łojek's father, who was murdered at Katyn, was named Leopold.

Committee for the Defence of Workers (KOR). Although it played a central role in underground publishing in Poland, KOR was initially reluctant to support the printing of Katyn materials for fear of jeopardizing future relations between Poland and the Soviet Union. Like KOR, Solidarity was at first wary of the Katyn issue and avoided the topic in its main weekly publication as part of its policy of 'self-limitation'. The issue of Katyn did appear, however, in some local, smaller Solidarity publications. Politically, Solidarity supported the initiative to erect a monument at Powązki, but counselled activists not to mention the date or identify the perpetrators (Wasilewski 2009, 63). By contrast, more nationalist oppositional groups like the Movement for the Defence of Human and Civic Rights (ROPCiO) and the Confederation of Independent Poland (KPN) were less passive and tentative (Macedoński 1996, 190). Later, Solidarity would change course and explicitly take up the Katyn cause. In the late 1980s, for instance, it issued a special commemorative postage stamp in a series on Polish history (Wasilewski 2009, 67) and, more significantly, gave the subject a prominent place on the agenda of the critical Round Table Talks (Sanford 2005, 212).

The Katyn Institute, led by artist and activist Adam Macedoński, produced leaflets and brochures about the massacres and translated and distributed key documents originating from émigré circles. The Institute published its own periodical, *The Katyn Bulletin (Biuletyn katyński)*, of which forty-five issues were produced (Juliański 2010). They also organized lectures for university students and encouraged priests to say masses for Katyn victims. Macedoński was repeatedly subject to repressions at the hands of the secret police and spent seven months in prison in 1981–2 (Macedoński 1996, 189–92).[15] The Katyn Committee, meanwhile, grew out of a group dedicated to uncovering obscured episodes of Poland's past, the National Memory Circle, which was formed in 1974 by activists associated with the Home Army, the Confederation of Independent Poland and the Catholic University in Lublin. The Katyn Committee, which included Stefan Melak, the moving force behind the cross erected in Powązki Cemetery in

---

[15] The first official Katyn Family was formed in Warsaw at the initiative of the Institute in 1987 and officially registered in 1989 (Macedoński 1996, 192).

1981, was instrumental in the commemorations that took place in Warsaw throughout the 1980s. Its activities focused on local churches, where members displayed posters, held lectures and organized masses (Wasilewski 2009, 61).

Figures from both the Katyn Institute and the Katyn Committee took part in the establishment of the Independent Historical Committee for Research into the Katyn Crime (NKHBZK), which was established in 1989 alongside the Polish Katyn Foundation (PFK). These two overlapping organizations, the NKHBZK and PFK, conducted historical research, gathered Katyn-related evidence and collected funds for memorials. They also produced a series of *Katyn Notebooks* (*Zeszyty katyńskie*) and pressed for judicial action against the perpetrators and for compensation for the victims' families. One of the most significant achievements of the Polish Katyn Foundation was the creation of a Katyn museum and library as part of the Museum of the Polish Military in Warsaw. The roots of the museum go back to the early 1990s, when the NKHBZK organized an exhibition dedicated to the massacre in a church in the capital. The work of the Foundation was supported by a coalition of relatives of Katyn victims, the so-called Federation of Katyn Families, which enthusiastically lobbied for a state-supported museum 'on the model of the museum at Auschwitz'. Here again, the correspondence between Nazi and Stalinist crimes is a discursive touchstone. The Katyn museum was unveiled within the Museum of the Polish Military in 1993, but it was later considered inadequate in size and scope. Its collections are to be transferred to a separate, modern Katyn museum in central Warsaw in 2012 (Łojek 2000, 144).

The Federation of Katyn Families has grown from a cluster of isolated cells of relatives dispersed around Poland into a powerful institution with influence in contemporary Polish politics.[16] The Families' first major wave of activity came in 1993, when they persuaded President Lech Wałęsa to declare 1995 the official 'Year of Katyn', with a major, international programme of events to mark the 55th anniversary of the tragedy. The mission of the Year

---

[16] In 2003, a poll asking whether and under what conditions the Poles could forgive Russia for Katyn included the question of whether forgiveness should come from the Sejm or from the Katyn Families. Opinions were evenly divided on the issue (Sanford 2005, 230).

of Katyn was to raise the international profile of Katyn, cultivate archival and historical work on the massacres, build cemeteries and memorials and improve relations between Russia and Poland through a revelation of the full truth of the crime. The programme of commemorations, which sought to produce a major memory event, turned out to be less socially resonant than hoped. Illustrating the cosmopolitan interdependency of national memories, the initiatives of the Year of Katyn fell flat largely because the Polish, Ukrainian and Russian sides failed to communicate and cooperate with one another effectively (Tarczyński 1996).

Today the Federation of Katyn Families arranges pilgrimages to the massacre sites, engages in Katyn-related education and public relations, and maintains the political profile of the Katyn issue in Poland and abroad. After first visiting Moscow at the invitation of Boris Yeltsin in 1992, the Families met with President Dmitrii Medvedev in 2010, when they declared that they would not demand reparative compensation from Russia (see chapter 6). Instead, they called for 'moral compensation' and the establishment of a 'living monument', such as a hospital or school, which would honour the victims. Having failed in Russian courts to exonerate and 'rehabilitate' their executed loved ones, who were condemned as criminally guilty by the Soviet Union in 1940, the Families have also taken the Katyn issue to the European Court of Human Rights in Strasbourg, pressing Russia to bring any living perpetrators to justice and to reveal all the details of the crime. Several of the Federation's members, including its president Andrzej Sariusz-Skąpski, were on President Lech Kaczyński's plane when it crashed near Smolensk in 2010. Their presence on the presidential plane – as well as Donald Tusk's remark only days before the crash that Poland was 'one big Katyn family' – testifies to the Federation's success in installing itself in the political firmament of the country.

In recent years, Polish governmental institutions have actively joined civil society to agitate for the Katyn cause. The Institute of National Remembrance (Instytut Pamięci Narodowej, or IPN), created by the Sejm in 1998, has organized public exhibitions and published regularly on the topic, particularly since 2005. It played a key role in the government-sponsored campaign, 'I Remember: Katyn 1940' ('*Pamiętam. Katyń 1940*'), which was organized by the Ministry of Culture and National Heritage and the National

Cultural Centre, among others. Combining memory hardware and software in an innovative way, the campaign produced so-called 'Katyn Buttons', replicas of the most common material traces of the massacre victims, and distributed them on the streets and by mail. The campaign also funded the publication of a high-profile graphic novel aimed at young adults entitled *1940 Katyn: A Crime on Inhuman Land*, which not only follows Czapski's account of the massacre in detail but also features a special 'appendix' dedicated to Lech Kaczyński and the victims of the 2010 crash (Gawronkiewicz et al. 2010, 107). As we shall see, such efforts to represent the Katyn tragedy in narrative and visual form are beset by challenges and controversies in Poland.

Representing Katyn

In 1994, Jacek Trznadel expressed the hope that the struggle to *know* Katyn – a struggle won through historical investigation and popular mobilization, both at home and abroad – would give way to a struggle to *understand* Katyn. In his view, the time had come for a deeper reflection on the meaning of the tragedy, a meaning that had 'not been properly described' (Trznadel 1994, 5) and marked a 'great absence' in Polish literature and culture (Lipowski 2005).[17] The massacres had been represented in 'a sea of documents' but not 'in high literature, except for a few poems'. Trznadel ventured an explanation for the lacuna:

> We live in the era of the document. [Literary] writers knew that it would not be easy to surpass the telling Katyn photographs, the excerpts from the last entries in the surviving diaries, or the accounts of those who stood over the uncovered pits of Katyn (Trznadel 1994, 128).

[17] The lack of a satisfactory literary treatment of Katyn was the motivation for émigré intellectual Jerzy Krzyżanowski to gather disparate works in various genres, some by famous literary figures but most by lesser-known writers, into the anthology *Katyn in Literature* (1995). Several writers and artists have touched on the topic of Katyn, such as the renowned poets Zbigniew Herbert and Czesław Miłosz, the experimental dramatist Tadeusz Kantor, and the contemporary writers Paweł Huelle and Paweł Demirski. They do so indirectly, by way of oblique, even hidden references.

Elsewhere in his work, Trznadel advocates a careful synthesis of documentary accuracy and imaginative, emotional power in literary representations of traumatic historical events (Trznadel 1995a, 33–4). Here he places the documentary and the imaginative as being in opposition to one another, yet needing to be skillfully combined. How should this be done with respect with Katyn?

In Polish literature we see two primary strategies of signification arise in response to this question, which we might call, borrowing from C.S. Peirce (1972), the iconic and the indexical. The *iconic* paints a picture of the tragedy, rendering it as fully and as directly as possible. It seeks to compensate for the witness-less nature of the Katyn tragedy. Mackiewicz's *The Katyn Wood Murders* (1951) stands as an example of this strategy; it employs a novelistic form to guide the reader through a meticulous presentation of the facts. The *indexical*, meanwhile, literally 'points' to something else. It reconciles itself with the witness-less nature of the tragedy. In the work of Włodzimierz Odojewski, this something else is often nothing at all – a void, a chasm, a suspension of understanding, a memory denied.

For Odojewski, who was forced to emigrate from Poland in 1971, memory is more than memory. 'Perhaps human memory is some kind of manifestation of God', he writes. 'Perhaps it even is God' (Odojewski 1984, 93). Literature is its apostle, making a 'lasting impression on the memory of the reader' by triggering the work of the imagination (Odojewski 1995a, 11). In Odojewski's prose, memory is not elicited involuntarily, by madeleine teacakes; it is constructed assiduously by the faculty of the imagination (Szczepkowska 2002, 92–4). It is human: vulnerable, fallible, even deceptive. In *Everything Will Be Covered by Snow* (*Zasypie wszystko, zawieje . . .* , 1995b), which was published in 1973 and stands as one of the most important novels of post-war Polish literature, Odojewski depicts the internecine violence that afflicted the *Kresy* (Poland's eastern borderlands) during the Second World War by way of a family drama of love, betrayal and reconciliation. The novel's protagonist, Paweł, embarks on a search for his missing brother, Aleksy, and visits Katyn during the German exhumations in 1943 in the hope of discovering his remains. Standing at the excavated pits, overcome by their sights and smells, Paweł confronts a physical and spiritual chasm, which Odojewski renders by way of a narrative stream of consciousness:

Once again he repeated, this time aloud, 'I must find him', and then
he found him, except this wasn't Aleksy at all, his own brother, it
wasn't even someone similar, it was some general Aleksy, it was him
and yet at the same time every other Aleksy, mutilated, unidentifi-
able, multiplied, close and yet far away, already buried in time, as
in the mud in which they all lay [. . .] (Odojewski 1995b, 127).

Pawel's abortive search suggests an aporia of Katyn memory. The
closer he comes to Katyn, the more disoriented, frustrated and
desperate he turns. He faints and stumbles into the pit, into the
'mud' of time.

In Odojewski's 'The Wood Comes to Dunsinan Hill' ('Ku
Dunzynańskiemu Wzgórzu idzie las', 1984), whose title alludes to
Shakespeare's *Macbeth*, memory is chimerical, hidden in a dense
labyrinth of hearsay, conjecture and incomplete testimony. The
story revolves around a journalist who listens to a recording of
an interview between a professor and a former Soviet partisan,
now a member of the Polish Communist militia. On the recording,
the militiaman recalls meeting a stranger during the war who
claimed to have escaped from the Katyn forest after his execution
was botched. The militiaman tells the professor what he remembers of the stranger's story, but the professor only manages to tape
half of the interview and recounts the rest from memory to the
journalist. All three interpreters – the militiaman, the professor
and the journalist – have doubts about the integrity of the stranger's
story. The more they endeavour to make Katyn present to memory,
the more it recedes out of their reach. The tragedy becomes a
narrative sinkhole.

Odojewski's penchant for the indexical – for a 'pointing elsewhere' that borders on infinite regress in 'The Wood Comes to
Dunsinan Hill' – met with criticism from Trznadel and Józef
Mackiewicz. In their view, Odojewski plays with the facts, sur-
rendering them to conjured plot details and parabolic narrative
form. 'Katyn does not have the good fortune to have been accu-
rately represented', writes Mackiewicz, who proceeds to survey
the inaccuracies in Odojewski's *Everything Will Be Covered by
Snow* and to remark that such inaccurate representations leave
'the impression that we actually know nothing about Katyn. Yet
in reality we know everything exactly' (Mackiewicz 1973, 179).
Declaring that he 'support[s] accuracy, because only the truth is

interesting', Mackiewicz considers the novelistic genre useful to the project of Katyn memory only to the extent that it 'expresses the spiritual side (*Geist*), the emotional side of the past events' (Mackiewicz 1973, 183). In other words, it should be a document that packages expression and emotion for the reader rather than a text that estranges the reader with what Wolfgang Iser calls *Leerstellen*, 'gaps' that the reader is meant to fill with the force of his imagination (Iser 1980).

For Trznadel, Odojewski commits a particular offence when he poses in 'The Wood Comes to Dunsinan Hill' the possibility of a Katyn survivor, who by his very existence understates the brutal, totalizing efficiency of the NKVD executioners in Katyn, Kalinin and Kharkiv. In Trznadel's view, if Odojewski wished to produce a 'fantasy' based on the massacres, he should have at least distanced it from the historical event itself and refrained from invoking the name 'Katyn' (Trznadel 1994, 19). For all this disapproval, however, Trznadel would later share Odojewski's interest in *Macbeth* as a fable about the Katyn Lie. In an essay of 1988 that speaks of combating the 'Orwellian furnaces of memory' of the PRL, Trznadel also alludes to the prophecy that 'Macbeth shall never vanquished be, until/ Great Birnam Wood to high Dunsinan Hill/ Shall come against him' (Shakespeare 1990, 174–5). In *Macbeth*, this strange prophecy is realized when Macbeth's enemies cut down and carry trees from Birnam Wood to disguise themselves as they approach his castle to avenge the murders he has committed. Both Trznadel and Odojewski imply that another forest will also rise to seek justice and vengeance against the guilty. 'We must after all fulfill the duty that is demanded of us by the dead, those unburied by the nation', writes Trznadel. 'Still the Katyn knights do not let the soul of the nation rest' (Trznadel 1994, 132).

Criticism did not dissuade Odojewski from returning to the subject of the Katyn massacres. In 2003, at the urging of filmmaker Andrzej Wajda, who wished to make a film about Katyn based on a suitable literary text, Odojewski published *Silent, Undefeated: A Katyn Story* (*Milczący, niepokonani: opowieść katyńska*). The novel's protagonist is the historical figure of Roman Martini, who led the official Polish investigation into the Katyn tragedy in 1945. As with the Soviet Burdenko Commission, the investigation was intended to confirm Nazi guilt and give another stamp of authority to the Katyn Lie. It is now believed that Martini insisted on carrying out a thorough and fair investigation, which led him towards the truth (Cienciala et al. 2007, 233). He was brutally murdered in 1946, allegedly by the jealous fiancée of a lover. Foul play on the part of the secret police is suspected by some historians today (Sanford 2005, 207).

Odojewski's Martini is not heroic. He is a naïve man who, after being interned in Germany during the war, walks blindly into collaboration with the Communist regime. Martini visits the Katyn graves to undertake his investigation, but the Communist authorities only permit him to travel to the site in the dead of winter, when the frozen ground makes exhumation impossible. Nothing is visible there apart from the modest Soviet monument that asserts Nazi guilt and mocks the memory of the dead with Polish-language text pockmarked with spelling errors. The only access Martini has to the site is by way of the experience of his niece Małgorzata, who travelled there in 1943 to recover her father's remains during the Nazi exhumation. As with Paweł in *Everything Will Be Covered by Snow*, the girl's experience is one of shock and horror. Overwhelmed by the gruesome sight and the smell of decomposing bodies, she faints and collapses, unable to bear witness. And as with the journalist and the professor in 'The Wood Comes to Dunsinan Hill', the recollection of her encounter with Katyn is highly mediated, available only through indirect discourse. Małgorzata will not speak of her visit directly to Martini; her mother Anna must do so on her behalf.

In the final scene of Odojewski's *Silent, Undefeated*, Małgorzata falls asleep and dreams of the Katyn forest. At first she envisions only darkness. Light slowly pierces the void, illuminating the excavated pits, filled with bodies:

> And then the bodies rose out of the depths of the pits, they were alive, they hauled themselves up onto the clearing, layer after layer, and formed rows, took up a formation, came to life, and moved forward in their rows, marching, row after row, in tens, hundreds of rows . . . They marched . . . And it seemed to last almost an eternity in that glittering light of the stars and the pale gleam of the moon among the constant, intensifying whisper of the pine trees, not at all surprised, but in fact expectant, calling, ordering them to set out on a many-year-long journey into the cold, indifferent world in order to move that world. And Małgorzata's eyelids

were still closed, they just trembled, giving away the fact that she sees (Odojewski 2003, 216).

Odojewski's visualization of the deceased victims of Katyn calls to mind Abel Gance's film *J'accuse* (1918–19), in which the fallen of the First World War rise again to march on the town where their wives and children now live with other men (Winter 1995, 15). Eighty years after *J'accuse*, visualizing the dead would become a preoccupation for filmmaker Andrej Wajda, who eventually passed on a cinematic translation of Odojewski's novel, choosing instead Andrzej Mularczyk's realist 'film-novella', *Katyn: Post-Mortem* (2007). As we shall see in the next chapter, Wajda makes the dead come alive once more – only to bring their death to the screen.

Chapter Two

Katyn in *Katyn*

Before 2007, no Polish film director had been able to complete a feature film about Katyn. Such a project was impossible during the years of discursive cleansing under Communism. Following the collapse of the PRL, however, something else seemed to impede a cinematic treatment of the tragedy for nearly two decades. According to director Andrzej Wajda, this obstacle was the lack of a suitable literary text on which to base a film.[1] He finally received this text in the form of Andrzej Mularczyk's 'film-novella' *Katyn: Post-Mortem* (2007). For Wajda, as for Odojewski and Mackiewicz, the challenge lay 'not in the subject itself, but rather in how it is portrayed' (Wajda 2008, 93). His feature film *Katyn* (2007) responds to this crisis of representation by choosing what we are calling an iconic strategy over an indexical one; that is, rather than reconciling itself with the witness-less nature of the massacres, it seeks to make viewers witnesses through a direct, relentless visual presentation of the killings themselves. This 'iconicity' has at once led the film to be received by many in Poland as both a work of memory, engendering mourning, and a work of history, offering a virtually unmediated portal to the past.

---

[1] Trznadel claims to have suggested the idea to Wajda as early as 1982 and to have passed him an idea for a script (Trznadel 1994, 18).

Beginnings

One of Poland's most prominent and revered filmmakers, Andrzej Wajda has made a long career out of exploring the nation's traumas and taboos through the cinematic medium, beginning with what has been termed the 'psychotherapeutic strand' of filmmaking about Polish experiences of the Second World War in the 1950s (Lubelski 2009, 182). Wajda has expressed his feeling that making *Katyn* was his personal 'responsibility' (Wajda 2008, 103): his father, infantry captain Jakub Wajda, was murdered in Kharkiv (see chapter 3), in one of the massacres that we designate now by the generic term 'Katyn'.

Katyn traces the journeys of four men captured by Soviet forces in 1939: a General, a Captain (Andrzej), a Pilot, and a Lieutenant (Jerzy). The first three are killed in Katyn, while the latter is spared and joins the Soviet-created Kosciuszko division before returning to Communist Poland. Most of the film's scenes, however, are dedicated to exploring the lives of the families that the men have left behind in German-occupied and post-war Poland. The General's wife, Róża, is shown footage of the mass graves at Katyn by Nazi officials but refuses to record a statement for propaganda purposes. The Captain's father is sent to Sachsenhausen at the beginning of the film and later dies, while the Captain's mother and wife, Anna, wonder about what may have happened to Andrzej. The Pilot's sisters are placed on opposing sides of the spectrum of survival in post-war Poland: Agnieszka attempts to erect a memorial tablet with the accurate date of her brother's death (1940 and not 1941), while her sister attempts to dissuade her. For fighting the Katyn Lie, Agnieszka is arrested and imprisoned. Then, in a sudden analepsis, the final twenty minutes of the film return us to the spring of 1940, showing the Polish prisoners being shot in prison cells and at the edges of mass graves. The film's most significant, and most powerful, scenes are those in which we see the murders taking place and 'witness' an event without surviving witnesses.

Katyn is unique in its sustained attempt to portray the massacres directly, a feat made possible by fictionalization. Much earlier in 1990, Wajda began a 52-minute documentary project entitled *Katyn Forest*, which was completed by Marcel Łoziński.

Divided into three parts, 'Journey', 'Politics' and 'Witnesses', *Katyn Forest* (1990) follows a group of family members of the Katyn victims as they retrace the journey to Kozel'sk. Archival images of the Katyn corpses are followed by interviews with leading politicians of the time, including members of the British Foreign Office. One of the family members is shown entering a village near the Katyn forest to question the elderly villagers about what they saw and heard in the spring of 1940. Most refuse to speak, but one villager eventually reveals that she heard shots fired through the night, and another that she saw the soldiers being transported to the forest. None admit to seeing the executions themselves.[2] In the film, the spoken memories of the family members and survivors of the Soviet camps are interspersed with lengthy shots of the countryside seen through the window of a train.

The frequent images of trains in *Katyn Forest* recall Claude Lanzmann's *Shoah* (France, 1985), which was made five years earlier and caused great controversy in Poland for what many saw as an anti-Polish stance. Like *Shoah*, *Katyn Forest* subscribes to an indexical strategy of signification; rather than reconstructing events, it dwells on their material and human traces and on the memories of those affected by them. The film also implicitly asserts that there is a limit to our ability to reconstruct the tragedy: we can view the landscape that the victims of the massacres gazed upon en route to their death, but nothing more. Because of its genre and also the time of its production, the documentary *Katyn Forest* left everything else beyond representation: the confrontation with the Soviet troops, the months of boredom and despair in the Ostashkov, Kozel'sk and Starobil's'k camps, and the very scenes of the massacres. When one of the family members does attempt to visualize the killings, claiming that 'one can retrace the steps' of the victims, we see only a forest heavy with fog through the lens of a handheld camera, which mimics the vision of a wandering subject. As in the work of Odojewski, *Katyn Forest* signals a blank spot in the mourning for the Katyn victims, an

---

[2] Several of the villagers also speak of their own experiences of losing family members, including those shot by the NKVD, and speculate on the vast scope of the victims buried in the Katyn Forest: Russians, Ukrainians, Romani.

inability to imagine their suffering and death. If *Katyn Forest* would not, or could not, construct a visual representation of the massacres, then *Katyn* would.

Wajda's feature film opens with a fog-shrouded frame that soon clears to reveal a landscape, signalling that the film itself will penetrate the shroud of the Katyn Lie and finally restore this atrocity to vision. But this is not yet the fog of Katyn. When it clears, we are presented with Poland's position in 1939, trapped between two totalitarian aggressors overtaking it from both sides. Two groups of Poles collide on a bridge, one escaping from the Germans, the other from the Soviets. The film aims for realism, offering viewers the sense that they are witnessing historical events as they occurred.

Yet there is more than historical authenticity at stake in the film's construction and reception. As Wajda stated, 'The whole truth about the event [. . .] had already been revealed in both its historical and political aspects [. . .] I avoid questions that have already been answered and conjure up images that have a much larger emotional capacity' (Wajda 2008, 97). The film addressed what was frequently described as a *need* that was fundamentally emotional and affective. Critics described the film as a national 'requiem' (Wakar 2007; Gajda-Zadworna 2007a), a filmic 'memorial' ('Filmowy' 2007), and a 'symbolic burial' (Sobolewski 2007; 'Katyń Wajdy' 2007).

History Lessons

Wajda developed the screenplay for *Katyn* with Władysław Pasikowski and Przemysław Nowakowski, basing it in part on Mularczyk's *Katyn: Post-Mortem*. The title *Post-Mortem* was originally adopted for the film, which reflected Wajda's desire to stage much of the action after the massacres, to conduct an autopsy, as it were, of Polish post-war society. In the screenplay, Wajda included episodes that he had found in individual recollections, diaries and other mementos, such that, as he wrote, 'most of the incidents depicted on the screen actually happened and were reported by eye-witnesses' (Wajda 2008, 5). The quest for absolute authenticity permeated all levels of the production. The consultant who oversaw the military paraphernalia of the film stated that it should be 'truth and nothing but', so that people could learn from it as they do from a 'well-written history book'. The costume designer asked for photographs from the Association of Katyn Families, so that, in her words, she 'authentically' had these people before her eyes (*Katyń* 2007).

At two junctures in the film, Wajda shows us authentic newsreel footage depicting the exhumation of the Katyn graves, once by the Nazis, and once by the Soviets. Yet this critical reflection on the manipulability of visual images is not extended to the film that *we* are watching; rather, it is anchored within the narrative of *Katyn*. At both points, a specific character, Róża, watches the footage and responds to the truth of the first newsreel (she faints) and the falsity of the second (she shouts at the projectionists). The inclusion of the archival footage increases what Anton Kaes has called the 'reality effects' of historical cinema, which 'appeal to the visual memory of the spectator' (Kaes 1989, 29). These include the 'authentic' costumes, objects and interiors of the film, as well as the newsreel footage, which is used to further the impression of the film's historical 'correctness'. Just before we see Róża setting the table for Christmas Eve, for example, we are shown black-and-white footage of people buying Christmas trees in a Krakow square. The sound of a crowd is heard on the soundtrack. This sound is not present in the newsreel footage itself but was recorded for the film.

Katyn tells its story in a way familiar to historical filmmaking, obeying the rules of classical realism and undertaking no self-reflexive experimentation. As Joshua Hirsch has written, classical realism in historical films is often employed 'in order to give the spectator the sense of experiencing not a particular narrative construction of reality but its authentic reproduction'. Realism presents the past 'un-self-consciously, drawing attention to the events represented, and away from the film's own act of presentation' (Hirsch 2004, 4). Historians have remained sceptical about films claiming to represent the 'truth' of historical events, accusing them of simplifying complex events in the interests of dramatic structure and emphasizing the spectacular rather than the analytic. In his defence of history on film, Robert Rosenstone has written that 'filmmakers can be and already are historians ... but of necessity *the rules of engagement of their works with the stuff of the past are and must be different from those that govern written history'* (Rosenstone 2006, 8; original emphasis). In Poland, however, these complex issues have largely been overlooked in the public discussion of the film.

Foregrounding the film's historical ambitions, Wajda changed its title from *Post-Mortem* to *Katyn* in April 2007. In May, the Polish government launched the educational and media campaign 'Katyn 1940. I Remember', which included TV adverts, billboards and multimedia projects designed for schools (Gajda-Zadworna 2007b, 13). The Minister of Culture and National Heritage, Kazimierz M. Ujazdowski, stated that he hoped the film would support his education campaign, as it constituted, in his view, 'an excellent history lesson' (Ujazdowski 2007). In fact, an exhibition entitled 'The Truth Cannot Be Shot. Katyn – A History Lesson' accompanied the film's premiere in the Kino Moskwa in Kielce. It contained objects related to Katyn, such as letters to and from the victims, exhumed buttons and photos of the victims and the places of their execution (Pawelec 2007). The film's premiere in Warsaw on 17 September 2007 was a major cultural and political event, attended by President Lech Kaczyński and Prime Minister Jarosław Kaczyński, high-ranking officials of the Catholic Church, members of the Katyn Families and representatives from the Russian 'Memorial' Society. The Director of the Polish Film Institute stated again that 'the film itself is a history lesson' ('Zakończyła' 2007).

Reviews of the film in the press were similarly inclined to accept the film as a work of history rather than a work of memory and mourning. One review used stills from the film to illustrate an historical article about the Katyn massacres, hardly referring to the film itself; these cinematic images replaced archival images that would normally accompany such historical scholarship (Pilawski 2007, 8–11). Another review seamlessly interwove examples of objects from the film with archaeological finds from the graves (Kiełpiński 2007). The film's perceived historical precision was further cemented by articles in which Second World War survivors recalled the events depicted in the film, such as the opening scene on the bridge (Mach 2007, 4). Stanisława Soja, who lost her father in Katyn, remembered how he had the chance to escape captivity in civilian clothing, like *Katyn*'s Captain Andrzej, but refused, as 'honour was the most important thing to him' (Kurzyńska 2007).

Perhaps the most strident voice in this literal reception of *Katyn* was journalist Krzysztof Masłoń. Disagreeing with Wajda's stated hope that other filmmakers would take up the subject of Katyn, he wrote: 'Wajda's vision opens and closes the topic of Katyn in Polish filmmaking. You cannot add anything to the last sequence of the film' (Masłoń 2007, 12). In an article entitled 'After *Katyn* one can only be silent', Masłoń gave viewers the sense that everything that is to be known about Katyn (let alone Kalinin or Kharkiv) can be seen in Wajda's film. While factual inaccuracies of historical films might be excused for reasons of poetic licence, a tendency to allow an historical film to foreclose the subject matter is a usual pitfall of their critical reception. Jacek Trznadel, who harshly criticized Odojewski for departing from historical fact in his prose, points out a number of inaccuracies in Wajda's film, accusing the director of misrepresenting in the dramatic final scene what must have been a banal, routine process (Trznadel 2007). Indeed, *Katyn* presents a picture that an historian would hardly recognize as comprehensive: only four Polish officers are offered to represent the many diverse victims of Katyn: the Jews, the policemen, the priests, the prisoners not sent to the camps at Ostashkov, Kozel'sk or Starobil's'k. That the film fails to chronicle the tragedy fully was rarely mentioned by critics, even those who faulted it as a work of art. One journalist wrote that *Katyn* was a 'paradocumentary vision of history' despite its aesthetic weaknesses, and that Wajda had evidently chosen to be 'faithful to History' rather than to the 'rules of filmic narrative' ('Fabryka' 2007). Whilst criticizing its weak characterization and posed dialogues, another journalist wrote that every history teacher should take their class to see the film (Lenarciński 2007, 19; also Dzierzbicka 2007, 23).

One of Wajda's concerns was to reach a young audience that he believed was forgetting its past. In this respect he was successful, as schoolchildren over the age of twelve were required to attend special screenings of the film. Published responses from younger viewers (including those of university age) suggest that the history lesson was duly received. Izabela Turek, 22, is reported to have stated that 'this is history . . . if you want to know the truth, I would recommend this film'. Zuzanna Chwiejczak, 15, is quoted thus: 'it brilliantly presents the whole historical truth. Such films are needed. They allow us to move away from mistaken beliefs and see what really took place' (Komar 2007). The film has become integrated into history lessons in schools. The educational publisher Nowa Era released a CD-ROM entitled 'The Lesson of Katyn', which was sent to every school in Poland. It consists of eight lessons about Katyn and its wider context and includes photographs from the set, the film's official poster, and interviews with the actors from Wajda's film and with Wajda himself. The advertisement for the CD-ROM announced that Wajda's *Katyn* is 'in a natural way a key part of didactic materials'. At the same time, the Polish press raised concerns about the suitability of the film for young viewers. Responses from parents and psychologists suggested that the execution scenes in particular had a damaging effect on teenagers, who were as yet unable to deal with the graphic representation (Rojek 2007).

Heroes and Villains

Given the general acceptance of the film as 'history', it is important to determine what kind of vision of the massacres and their aftermath the film presents and, accordingly, what kind of memory it packages for the viewer. As we have seen, the film does not offer a diverse picture of the victims killed: we see military officers, for example, rather than intellectuals or policemen, and one camp (Kozel'sk) and one killing field (Katyn Forest) rather than several. The Soviet figures in the film are also largely anonymous and interchangeable. Rather than offering up a particular villain deserving of the viewer's hatred, Wajda shows us human cogs in the hulking machine of Soviet totalitarianism and thus encourages a critique of 'the system' rather than specific individuals responsible for the massacres. In the final sequence, when the Polish prisoners alight from the train and enter the prison cars known as Black Marias, the sound of machinery is so loud on the soundtrack that we can only see the NKVD functionaries speaking to each other. We cannot hear them. Later, we see and hear machines at work preparing the ground for the mass graves. Underscored visually and aurally, such effects emphasize the mechanical, factory-like aspect of the Soviet deportations and massacres. The Soviet officers throughout this sequence consistently appear with folders, highlighting the methodically planned and bureaucratic nature of the killings.

Wajda also chose to include in the film a 'good Russian' character, Major Popov, who features in one extended scene in which he offers to marry Anna for her protection and reveals his knowledge of the death of her husband and the other Polish prisoners. He finally hides Anna and her daughter from NKVD officers who come to arrest and, presumably, deport them. The figure of Major Popov was inspired by 'two different sources found among the Katyn documentation', including the story of a Soviet officer who sent away the NKVD so that a Polish family could escape (Wajda 2008, 48). Wajda felt he had to include this scene 'if only to pay tribute to heroes unknown to us' (Wajda 2008, 48). Aided by the popularity of the Russian actor Sergei Garmash, who plays Major Popov, this effect parallels another successful film about socialist terror, *The Lives of Others* (von Donnersmarck, 2006), which presented the East German Stasi by way of the story of one good man in its ranks. While it may appeal to a transcultural audience, the sequence featuring Popov is disconnected from the rest of the film. His character is never alluded to again.

Wajda's film constructs a bleak vision of post-war Poland, largely through the fates of its characters, who are punished with death and imprisonment for attempting to speak the truth about Katyn and to defy the Communist regime's policy of discursive cleansing. Jerzy attempts to fit himself into the new order but eventually finds death preferable to existence in the PRL. When the General's wife tells him that he must testify to the truth that the Soviets committed the crime, he answers, 'I may as well shoot myself in the head'. He does so as Wanda Wasilewska (Communist Party activist and head of the Polish Provisional Government) is heard on the soundtrack condemning 'the German crime committed against the Polish nation'. Another character, Tadzio, a young man fighting in the Home Army, refuses to lie on his CV about when and by whom his father was murdered at Katyn. He is killed while being chased by the Polish militia, his death signifying that there is no room for the truth in post-war Poland. Agnieszka, who also refuses to capitulate to the Katyn Lie, is imprisoned. The gulf between pre-Communist and post-war Poland is also heightened in the tone, colour and cadence of the filmic frame. Production designer Magdalena Dipont wrote that, in the scenes set in post-war Poland, the pre-Communist 'world should disintegrate; become degraded, pale; fade away, turn grey. It should lose its colour and become ugly . . . because the world of our heroes has disappeared' (Wajda 2008, 167).

While reviewers largely accepted the film's claims to historical accuracy, this presentation of post-war Poland attracted some criticism (while the figure of the 'good Russian', Major Popov, largely did not). One critic suggested that according to the film 'the real Poland' was lost along with the officers at Katyn, the professors in Nazi camps and the dissenters killed or imprisoned in the PRL. This picture, he argued, does not reflect the reality of post-war Poland, which remained strong enough to eventually defeat the Communist system (Terlikowski 2007, 29).

The New Antigone

Katyn was intended to provide an historically accurate presentation of events and also, to recall Wajda's words, to 'conjure up images that have . . . [an] emotional capacity'. Theorist Anke Pinkert describes such a task as the mapping of the 'emotional fields forming around the historical experience of loss' (Pinkert 2008, 9). Wajda's history is an emotional one, and viewers are prompted to respond emotionally rather than critically. This is standard for historical filmmaking, which 'emotionalizes, personalizes and dramatizes history' in order to 'heighten and intensify the feelings of the audience about the events depicted onscreen' (Rosenstone 1995). Historical films frequently present the past as the story of individuals, and Wajda's film is no exception (Rosenstone 1995). Every scene emphasizes the inextricable connection between what we might think of as national history – invasions, military manoeuvres, war crimes – with the personal, the familial and the sentimental. This is only natural in a film that sets out to present the story of the families struggling with the loss of their loved ones. The scene of the deportation of the Polish men eastward at the beginning of the film, for example, is heightened emotionally by its explicit staging as a scene of separation of one man, Andrzej, from his wife and daughter, appealing to viewers' own familial attachments. We see the train pulling away from the young daughter's point of view, as she cries 'daddy . . . daddy'.

The film's characters function to a large extent as character-types embodying particular societal views and mythic traits, not 'figures of flesh and blood' (Nahlik 2009, 333). Their actions tend to showcase their loyalty and fidelity – to each other, to Poland and to the truth. Andrzej states that his sense of military honour forbids him from attempting to escape Soviet imprisonment; Anna refuses to enter into a beneficial marriage with Major Popov; Róza refuses to collaborate with the Nazis; and Tadzio and Agnieszka refuse to cover up the true dates and locations of their relatives' deaths. Shallow focus is often used to draw attention away from the background towards the character-types, who at times function like blank screens upon which viewers can project their own memories and familial ties.

The symbols and cinematic metaphors that condense many associations are good examples of the film's presentation of an emotive history. Towards the beginning of the film, we watch as Soviet soldiers tear apart a Polish flag, placing the red half back on the mast and using the white half to bandage a soldier's foot, thereby literally trampling on the symbol of Polish independence and statehood. Religious iconography and references proliferate in the film as well. At one point, we see wounded and dying sol- diers lying in a field under military coats. Anna recognizes her husband's coat and lifts it up to find a statue of Jesus. A priest, who has been giving the last rites to a dying soldier, approaches and begins praying over the statue, as though giving the last rites to Jesus himself. Crosses, either on the rosary given to the Pilot and his sister Agnieszka or in the graves themselves, are a key symbol in the film. In Poland, the cross joins both national and religious sentiments, politics and emotion; for some, it alludes to Poland's long-held self-perception as the 'Christ of nations'.[3] 'The cross for Christians symbolizes suffering, love and victory over evil. But it is also said to refer more specifically to Poland's Chris- tian heritage, to resistance against occupation under the partitions, during WWII, and under Communism . . . The cross represents the endurance of the Polish nation through the centuries, the resur- rection of the Polish state' (Zubrzycki 2006, 181). The setting of two of the film's scenes on Christmas Eve, one of the most important dates in the Polish Catholic calendar, also functions to

---

[3] The idea was famously formulated by Adam Mickiewicz in the third part of his poetic drama *Dziady* (1832). The banning of a production of the drama was the focal point for the opposition protests of March 1968 in Poland.

maximize sentiment. On Christmas Eve in Krakow, the General's wife pensively lays a plate for the absent General, while in Kozel'sk he makes an inspiring speech about the necessity for survival before leading the singing of a Christmas carol. As the prisoners sing, the camera gracefully rises above the men, as if suggesting a divine presence watching over them.

The material traces of Katyn in Wajda's film, such as the buttons, crosses and diaries exhumed from the graves, lend themselves to this emotive history by way of their dual status as evidence of the crime and as relics for the victim's families. The representation of the historical traces of Katyn within the film cues the viewer to conflate the actual evidence from Katyn with Wajda's represented evidence. In post-war Krakow, for example, we see a group of Poles in a laboratory gathering together envelopes containing individual victims' belongings and hiding them in a cavity in the wall. The camera lingers over military service books and crucifixes gathered from the mass graves. The character played by Krzysztof Głobisz, who appears to be directing this operation, is presumably Dr Jan Zygmunt Robel, whose team copied a cache of documents relating to Katyn (see chapter 1). The dialogue between the doctor and Jerzy, who comes to ask for Andrzej's belongings for Anna, makes it clear that these objects are not just historical artifacts: 'To you this is just evidence. But to her it may be relics.' This conflation of the historical and the memorial recalls Zbigniew Herbert's poem 'Buttons' (published in 1992), now a canonical text widely taught in secondary schools: 'Only buttons witnesses to the crime/ proved unyielding outlasted death and/ as sole memorial on the grave rise up/ from the depths of the Earth' (Herbert 2009, 477).[4] In the film, as in the poem, the buttons are both evidentiary and memorial, objects imbued with documentary authority and emotional affect.

---

[4] These buttons, bearing the Polish national symbol, the eagle, are among the most salient and poignant symbols of the tragedy. An album produced by Andrzej Wajda to accompany the release of his film features a two-page fold-out with a photograph of dozens of these buttons (Wajda 2008). In literature, buttons are a central motif in Kazimierz Orłoś' short story 'Second Entrance into the Forest' (1981–2), in which a group of three Poles and one Russian, who happen to be working near Smolensk, decide to visit the graves. They come across a boy collecting mushrooms, who produces a button. As the narrator states, 'the eagle shone, as though it had only just been torn from a uniform' (Orłoś 1995, 168).

Perhaps the most significant of these material traces is Captain Andrzej's diary, which is based on several texts written by Polish prisoners and exhumed from their graves, including the notebook of Major Adam Solski (Wajda 2008, 182). Our first glimpse of Andrzej towards the beginning of the film is accompanied by a voice-over as he writes in his diary the details of his capture, concluding: 'I'll try to write from time to time to let you know what happened to me if I die and don't return. Maybe this notebook will be sent to you'. The spoken 'you' is, as it were, Andrzej's wife; the unspoken 'you' is the viewer of Wajda's film.

A central symbol that transcends the Polish context revolves around the film's many intertextual references to Sophocles's *Antigone*.[5] Like the eponymous figure of the tragedy, the Pilot's sister Agnieszka attempts to fulfil proper mourning duties for her brother. Agnieszka cuts off her long, blonde hair in order to pay for a memorial tablet with the correct date of her brother's death. The hair is sold to a theatre, where a bald Auschwitz survivor, an actress who needs a wig, quotes from *Antigone*: 'Why live with so much evil around? It would be a true misfortune if my brother were left without a grave after his death . . .'. Wajda does not make it evident that the actress's dialogue is a citation from the play, which alludes to Agnieszka's plight; instead he incorporates it naturally into her speech. In case the viewer does not grasp the reference, a poster advertising *Antigone* is visible when Agnieszka leaves the theatre. Agnieszka's sister – her 'Ismene', as Wajda calls her – tries to dissuade her from mounting the memorial tablet: 'We can let them deport us, we can let them kill us, or we can try to build as much freedom as we can, or at least as much Polishness as we can' (Wajda 2008, 150). In defiance of the Katyn Lie, Agnieszka nonetheless installs the memorial tablet for her brother, but does so under the observation of the secret police, who then arrest her. The tablet is destroyed by anonymous hands.

Other Histories, Other Memories?

Overall, as we have suggested, Polish reviewers of the film tended to overlook the film's arguable weaknesses, from excessive symbolism

[5] Wajda chose to stage *Antigone* during martial law (1981–3) as it was 'accessible to a wide-ranging audience' (Wajda 2008, 168).

to typological characterization, and to herald instead the film's service to Katyn history and memory. In the words of one reviewer, 'memory, memory and once more memory about Katyn can never be lost' (Cichmiński 2007). Yet there were some in Poland who took issue with the form that Wajda's presentation had taken. Several writers were critical of the film's promulgation of the Romantic or martyrological tradition of Polish history, one that presents Poles as heroes or victims (or both) in a one-dimensional manner. Writing that the film was 'useful' for its clear presentation of the Katyn crime and its aftermath, Małgorzata Sadowska criticized it for being steeped in 'Romantic symbolism, as though there was no other language in which to present Polish history' (Sadowska 2007, 61). Lech Kurpiewski compared *Katyn* with Wajda's films of the fifties, remarking that while his earlier films also tackled 'History' with a capital H, they nevertheless tended to contest it. *Katyn*, by contrast, was a 'patriotic little story', presenting 'personifications' of historical issues rather than believable characters. Kurpiewski asked whether it was possible to pursue the 'noble mission' of presenting the truth about Katyn without turning such a presentation into 'a martyrological bazaar' (Kurpiewski 2007, 115). Wiesław Kot, meanwhile, was scathing about what he saw as the elements of the film that attempted to manipulate the viewer's emotions and play on patriotic sentiment. Kot wrote that '*Katyn* is not a film. It is a glorified television staging with elements of patriotic blackmail' (Kot 2007, 52). He continued: 'Poles need patriotism, but patriotism by choice, from an understanding of the challenges facing Poles, not from moral blackmail' (52). Kot claimed that it was almost impossible to criticize the film, as reviewers were expected to avert their gaze from its faults (53). Szerszunowicz criticized in particular the ending of the film and its manipulation of the audience: 'At the end of the film must come the obligatory shock. So [the audience] will react, be moved, feel proud and come out of the theatre with the sense that they have fulfilled a good obligation' (Szerszunowicz 2007). In Szerszunowicz's analysis, the depiction of the graphic nature of the massacres was cheap and calculating: 'Are cheap forms of expression, emerging from B thrillers, really the best way to express the tragedy of Katyn?' (Szerszunowicz 2007).

Related to this critique of the martyrological tradition was the contention that, according to several writers, the film was so steeped in pessimistic tragedy that it failed to convey what Allen Paul has termed 'the triumph of the truth' (Paul 2010). While praising the film, Paul expressed his surprise that Wajda had emptied it of optimism (Paul 2007). Rafał Stanowski, similarly, wrote of the film's lack of any sense of 'triumph' or 'hope' (Stanowski 2007, 12). This concern was shared by prominent film critic and writer Krzysztof Teodor Toeplitz, who wrote that Poles 'look for their pride in Katyn'. In the current political climate, he continued, 'Poland is not in a state to free itself from the adoration of misfortune' (Toeplitz 2007, 74).

'There is no end to Katyn', Trznadel (2007) has stated. Thirty-eight recent films collected under the title *Katyn Epitaphs* (*Epitafia Katyńskie*) testify to this observation. Produced in 2010 by Media Kontakt, each filmic 'epitaph' presents a three-minute description of the life of an individual victim of Katyn, Kharkiv or Mednoe. Each section is rich in visual and aural material: we see photographs, authentic newspaper articles, letters, exhumed objects, documentary footage and dramatic reconstructions of historical events. The images are continually in flux, overlapping with one another; images from Wajda's film are also reused in this project. Each section employs voice-over narration interspersed with the voices of actors reading from diaries and genuine letters to and from the men in the prison camps, as well as the spoken memories of family members. Each section ends with a digitally created memorial tablet, inscribed with the victims' name, rank and dates of birth and death: a virtual gravestone.

Massacre on Screen

Historical films, as Rosenstone has written, tend to leave you with 'a moral message and (usually) a feeling of uplift . . . The message delivered on screen is always that things are getting better or have gotten better or both' (Rosenstone 1995). An example is Roman Polanski's *The Pianist* (2000), in which Władysław Szpilman suffers horrifically during the Holocaust, but emerges at the end of the film as a successful pianist. Wajda's historical films rarely end on an optimistic note and *Katyn* is no exception. Its ending speaks to something more than the need for an historically accurate representation of a seminal, tragic event. Allowing us to finally *see* the murders in all their brutality, the film positions us as historical witnesses to an unwitnessed event.

Wajda initially allows the men at Kozel'sk to slip away in a temporal ellipsis. We last see them forty-four minutes into the film as they are being separated and led away, unknowingly, to their deaths. Towards the end of *Katyn*, Anna receives Andrzej's blood-stained diary. The image of the diary fills the screen and we hear Andrzej speaking in voice-over, 'Kozel'sk, 7th of April 1940.' In another flashback, the film then propels the viewer back into the past, showing Andrzej writing in the diary in a cell on a Soviet train. As he notes the precise times and locations, the hand-held camera, on the other side of the bars, scans the prisoners' faces. The Pilot etches his rank and the date on the wooden boards of the train, inscribing himself into memory.

In the pivotal concluding execution scene, the camerawork and editing aim for maximum shock value. Wajda's hand-held camera fragments the space of the frame to disorient the viewer. The length of the shots becomes progressively shorter, accelerating the pace of a film that, to this point, has been almost languid. The viewer first witnesses the murder of the General. Taken into a basement room, he is shot in the back of the head by an NKVD executioner whose point of view is simulated by the camera. The gun enters at the last moment from outside the frame. The camera then assumes the General's point of view, quickly swinging upwards to the ceiling light, and cuts back to the General as he falls forward, in a canted framing. Wajda shows the executioner passing the gun back and retrieving a loaded one, emphasizing the iterative, repetitive, mechanical nature of the killing. There is another sudden cut to a bucket of water thrown onto the blood on the floor. In quick succession we see this process take the lives of two more men.

After the General's death, the film returns to Andrzej and the Pilot being transported in prison cars. A lingering close-up of Andrzej's face is held as he writes in his diary and asks, 'What will become of us?' We then see his execution. With a rope tied around his neck and hands, he recites the Lord's Prayer as he is shot and falls into the mass grave beneath him. The use of deep focus during the execution scene ensures that the viewer sees other groups of men being killed in the background and grasps the scale of the massacre. Jumping from one perspective to the next, the hand-held camera gives us a series of disturbing views: panning shots over the corpses in the mass graves, the points of view of both the victims and the executioners. The film vacillates between shaking the frame wildly and tracking slowly and smoothly over the graves. The final shot shows us the Pilot's hand in close-up, clutching a rosary as dirt is heaped upon him and the camera lens.

The music heard over this sequence is Krzysztof Penderecki's 'Awakening of Jacob', whose title refers to Genesis 28:16, in which Jacob awakens after seeing a ladder ascending to heaven in a dream. Wajda uses Penderecki's music throughout the film. The strings unnaturally and repeatedly stretch one note before 'break-ing', perpetuating a feeling of dread. The music was previously used in Stanley Kubrick's psychological horror film *The Shining* (UK/USA, 1980), of which Penderecki wrote: '[I]t's scary how well it works in the movie, during very eerie moments. My music is rather abstract and maybe even strange-sounding for some people, so maybe that's why it has been used in so many horror movies and thrillers' (Filipski 2010). Suggestive of the feelings of the victims and the sheer horror of the crime itself, the effect of this piece encourages a sense of fear rather than sadness, trepidation rather than melancholia. Several Katyn Family members spoke of the execution scenes as if they were the actual executions them-selves. Ewa Gruner-Zarnoch, for example, stated that she and others who had lost relatives at Katyn would 'go to see the film as we would to the executions of our fathers' (Podgajna 2007, 2). Krystyna Brydowska said that 'when I watched the execution sequences, it was as if I was there where they shot my father' (Masłon 2007, 12).

At the very end of *Katyn*, we hear Andrzej, the Pilot, and two other men reciting a line from the Lord's Prayer before they are executed. Two of the lines continue directly on from one another, even though the men cannot hear each other. They leave us immersed in ritual even after the final image, the dead Pilot's hand clutching the rosary, fades to black. We hear male voices singing Penderecki's 'Polish Requiem', which was criticized for being 'per-fectly suited for a national funeral, but not for a film' (Lenarciński 2007, 19). Yet the film is meant, in effect, to serve as a national funeral, a cathartic event of mass mourning. As the credits roll in silence, testifying to the impotency of language in representing and responding to trauma, the film's graphic last scene resounds in the mind of the viewer.

Referring to the execution scene, a critic noted that 'we want to see it so as to say goodbye to it' (Sobolewski 2007). Such a statement echoes the temporal progression inherent in Freud's classic conception of the work of mourning. For Freud, mourning is a comprehensible response to loss which dissipates as the subject learns to detach his feelings from what is lost, whereas melancholia is the condition of remaining attached to it (Davis 2007, 132). As Alessia Ricciardi has emphasized, however, Freud's later writings retreat from this definitive distinction between mourning and melancholia: 'We see that [Freud] increasingly comes to regard mourning as an enigma to which neither the layperson nor the psychoanalyst possesses a ready solution'. In the twenty-first century public sphere, the enigma of mourning is continually returned to and re-inscribed in new genres, modes and constellations (Ricciardi 2003, 3–4, 32–3). In Polish visual media, mourning of Katyn continues not as a process that has its limits in time but rather as work that is 'interminable and impossible, already begun and never to be ended' (Davis 2007, 129).

Wajda's ambition was to make a film that would heal the 'open, festering wound in the history of Poland' (Wajda 2008, 5). His understanding of his own art was simultaneously mystical and therapeutic:

> We need to call up ghosts, not so that they will be with us always, but rather to dispatch them again, so they can go peacefully into our memories and let the living continue. We need a dialogue with the ghosts, to make things clear for them and with them. They will not rest and will continue to frighten us until they materialize ... Film 'materializes' its heroes in the most literal sense. Ghosts must stand before us and tell us their entire histories before we can emotionally come to terms with them and close them up within ourselves. And in the film they stand most forcefully. They look at us from the screen, and talk to us (Żakowski 2007).

There are echoes in Wajda's words with Jacques Derrida's observations on the spectre in culture and theory. For Derrida, ghosts are summoned to speak in order to be dispatched again: 'What seems almost impossible is always to speak *of* the specter, to speak *to* the specter, to speak with *it*, therefore most of all *to make or let a spirit speak*' (Derrida 1993, 32; see also Davis 2007; Etkind 2009). Wajda at one stage thought of including a scene of ghosts rising from the graves, as in Odojewski's *Silent, Undefeated*. He rejected the idea. What will the dead reveal when they are allowed to materialize and speak? For Derrida, the spectre 'does not return to deliver a message as such'; rather, it may reveal 'an essential unknowing which underlies and may undermine what we think we know' (Davis 2007, 11). In contrast, the execution scene in *Katyn* aspires to recreate the past in its certainty, to access the knowledge available only to the deceased and to the perpetrator. In the film's dramatic conclusion, the dead materialize not to speak, but to allow us to see. The images are meant to fill the void in our memory. Such is the draw and the novelty of Wajda's film: it offers the viewer the role of the witness that never was.

Chapter Three

Katyn in Ukraine

On 17 April 2008, Ukraine's President Viktor Yushchenko conferred the Order of Yaroslav the Wise upon Andrzej Wajda for *Katyn*. The award ceremony took place in Kyiv during the 'Days of Polish Cinema' Festival, which toured a diverse array of seven Polish feature films around Ukraine's major cities. *Katyn* was the festival's centrepiece, and Wajda's special commendation in the Ukrainian capital underscored its significance. The Order of Yaroslav the Wise is, after all, no ordinary distinction. It was established in 1995 in order to decorate individuals, primarily Ukrainian citizens, 'for significant personal deeds [performed] on behalf of the Ukrainian state' and for the 'strengthening of the international authority of Ukraine' ('Ukaz' 1995). In conferring the Order at the 17 April ceremony itself, President Yushchenko praised Wajda's film for shedding light not only on Polish history but on 'a part of our history too' ('Katyn'' 2008a). Yet *Katyn* features no Ukrainian characters, at least not explicitly, and makes no mention of Ukraine itself.

In one sense, the claim that the Katyn tragedy sheds light on Ukrainian history is a longstanding one. As we shall see, the Ukrainian émigré community in North America at times deployed Katyn as a metaphor for its own tragedies, particularly the 1937–8 mass killing of Ukrainian and other Soviet civilians at the hands of the NKVD in Vinnytsia. This 'Katyn' is the Katyn *for* Ukraine. Another 'Katyn', however, remains lesser known among Ukrainians today. This is the Katyn *in* Ukraine, the execution and mass burial of thousands of Polish prisoners from the Starobil's'k camp in and near Kharkiv and of thousands more from NKVD prisons throughout the country. To navigate Ukraine's literal and figurative 'Katyns' is to explore divergent regimes of remembering and forgetting, from émigré publications that sought to monumentalize suffering to newly-uncovered KGB documents that sought to obliterate its traces. It is also to explore the remarkable biographies of Ukrainian dissidents like Sviatoslav Karavans'kyi, whose work exposing the Katyn Lie in the Soviet Union came at great personal cost, and for whom the literal Katyn and the figurative Katyn were in effect one and the same.

The Katyn *in* Ukraine

The screening of *Katyn* on 17 April 2008 in Kyiv was not its Ukrainian premiere. The film had debuted three days before in Kharkiv, with Wajda in attendance ('Katyn'' 2008b). The setting in the city's central cinema was poignant, for nearly sixty-eight years earlier, the director's father had been executed only a few hundred metres away. Captain Jakub Wajda was shot not in Katyn Forest, but in the Kharkiv NKVD headquarters on Chernyshevskii Street with approximately 3,800 other Polish prisoners from the Starobil's'k camp (Cienciala et al. 2007, 193). Night after night, covered lorries transported their bodies along the Belgorod highway and then down a 'black road' into a forest abutting the village of Piatykhatky, less than ten miles away from the centre of the city (Zhavoronkov 2006, 104). The Poles were buried next to thousands of Ukrainians and other Soviet citizens executed in 1937–8, at the height of Stalin's Purges.

Only in the 1990s did the world come to know the details of this Katyn in Ukraine, the 'Kharkiv Katyn' (*Kharkovskaia Katyn'*). For half a century, the fate of Captain Wajda and his compatriots at the Starobil's'k and Ostashkov camps had been shrouded in mystery, confounding Katyn researchers and truth-seekers in Poland, Europe and North America (FitzGibbon 1975, 11). Were their remains uncovered in the Katyn Forest in 1943, as both the Nazi and Soviet propaganda machines had implicitly claimed (FitzGibbon 1975, 434)? Or were they killed and buried elsewhere? With respect to the prisoners of Starobil's'k, only one thing was known for certain: beginning on 5 April 1940, successive groups left the camp and travelled in train carriages to Kharkiv, over 150 miles away. Beyond this point, the trail went cold (FitzGibbon 1975, 439; Kola 2001, 119; Zawodny 1962, 113).

Two 'discoveries' in the 1970s and 1980s seemed to promise an end to the speculation. The first was the recovery of an 'official' NKVD report originally published in *7 Tage*, a West German tabloid (Sanford 2005, 148; Kola 2001, 119). Today dismissed as a forgery, the so-called 'Tartakov Report' made a reasonable – and therefore believable – claim about the final destination of the Starobil's'k prisoners. It identified Derhachi, a town less than ten miles to the northwest of Kharkiv, as the site of their 'liquidation' (FitzGibbon 1975, 441).[1] While ultimately misleading, the document fixed attention on possible execution and burial sites in the Kharkiv region. The second 'discovery', which was advanced in 1980 in the book *A Second Katyn?* by Solidarity activist Wiktor Kulerski, involved Ukrainian rumours of a mass grave of Poles *in* Starobil's'k itself – a possibility that, in the words of Józef Czapski, 'none of us had considered before'.[2] While ultimately false, the rumours convinced Kulerski of the need to recruit more 'Ukrainian friends' in the search for the truth (Rekulski 1980, 8, 28).

The truth finally emerged in a Kharkiv regional newspaper in 1990, weeks after the official announcement of 13 April that conceded Soviet responsibility for the 'crime' in the Katyn Forest (Cienciala et al. 2007, 345). 'A search has revealed another site of a mass grave' outside of Kharkiv, announced the press agency of the regional KGB on 3 June 1990, 'where over 1,700 Soviet citizens' lay buried alongside an unknown number of Polish 'military servicemen illegally executed in 1940' (Zavorotnov 2003, 122). The news initially reached a local readership in eastern Soviet Ukraine. Two weeks later, however, the journalist Gennadii Zhavoronkov pursued the story in the pages of the popular *Moscow News* (*Moskovskie novosti*). He reported that Kharkiv KGB Deputy Chief Aleksandr Nessen 'shrugged his shoulders' when asked about the discovery, remarking, '*net dokumentov, net svidetelei*' (Zhavoronkov 2006, 106). There are no documents; there are no witnesses.

[1] The document's assertions led Louis FitzGibbon to list 'Dergachi' alongside 'Katyn' in the subtitle of his 1975 book *Unpitied and Unknown*.
[2] Solidarity activist Wiktor Kulerski was writing under the anagrammatic pseudonym Rekulski.

Nessen was wrong. As we shall see, there were documents attesting both to NKVD perpetration of the Kharkiv Katyn and to shocking attempts to cover up the crime. And there were witnesses, of a kind. The voice of the first, Ivan Dvornichenko, reached millions of readers in Zhavoronkov's article:

> I, Ivan Dvornichenko, returned to Kharkiv in 1938 after being demobilized from the army. I took a job as a driver for the staff of the Kharkiv military district. Our garage was located at 41 Pushkin Street. Across [from us] was the NKVD garage. I often spoke with the drivers who worked there. Particularly with one of them, Oleksii. He was all of 30 years old, but he had already gone completely grey. Before the war, Oleksii told me that he transported the corpses of executed people to the Piatykhatky forest. People were killed in the NKVD building on Chernyshevskii Street, where Oleksii worked his covered lorry to death. They loaded the corpses in piles and covered them with a tarp. Among the executed were many Polish military servicemen (Zhavoronkov 2006, 106–7).

Here is the first reported memory of the Kharkiv Katyn, and it is given to us not only fifty years after the crime but also second-hand, through the perspective of a friend of an attendant to the perpetrator. It is hearsay, a trace of a lost source of testimony.

The voice of the second witness, Mitrofan Syromiatnikov, is more authoritative but less forthcoming. Syromiatnikov was an NKVD functionary interrogated by Soviet, Russian and Polish military prosecutors five times over the course of 1990–2 (Cienciala et al. 2007, 126–7). His is the only available, first-hand memory of the Kharkiv scene of the Katyn crime. And it is chilling. Here, in an exchange from a 1992 deposition, Syromiatnikov informs his incredulous questioners of the literal depths of the mass graves in Piatykhatky:

> Question: And the burial pit, was it deep?
> Syromiatnikov: Well, they usually made [the pits the size of] anti-tank trenches.
> Question: But you said here that one pit was so big that you could drive a lorry into it?
> Syromiatnikov: You could drive a lorry into it. It was the kind of pit you could drive a tank into.
> (Zavorotnov 2003, 102; Zinchenko 2011, 327–8)

Syromiatnikov's memory is distant, remorseless and not without cul-de-sacs and contradictions. It is a faded register of names, places and events with no reference to their meaning or significance. In abrupt, often exasperated sentences, Syromiatnikov coldly recalls the process of the executions as well as the identities of the men at the centre of them, including Timofei Kuprii, a commandant (*komendant*) in the Kharkiv NKVD (Zavorotnov 2003, 96, 99–103). Kuprii did not pull the trigger – such responsibility was likely left to a team of NKVD agents dispatched from Moscow – but he sat in judgement of the victims on Chernyshevskii Street and oversaw their burial at Piatykhatky (Zavorotnov 2003, 94). According to Syromiatnikov, he even sought to destroy the basement of the NKVD headquarters, where the murders took place, in advance of the Nazi occupation of Kharkiv in 1941 (Cienciala et al. 2007, 127–8).

Kuprii's name appears on one of the most important declassified documents about the aftermath of the Katyn crime. It is a top-secret letter released by the Ukrainian government in 2009 that sheds light on the institutional memory of the Soviet security apparatus. Dated 7 June 1969, the letter gives us Chairman of the Ukrainian KGB Vitalii Nikitchenko writing to KGB Chief Yuri Andropov about a 'mass grave' near Kharkiv. (An iteration of the letter is also addressed to Petro Shelest, Secretary of the Ukrainian Communist Party) (figure 3.1). Nikitchenko informs Andropov and Shelest that 'unknown persons' have uncovered a burial site in Piatykhatky, exposing human skulls and scattering 'bone fragments around the excavated pit' (Nikitchenko 1969, 1). He then makes this casual and macabre statement:

> It is established that in this location in 1940 the [NKVD] in the Kharkiv region buried a great quantity / several thousands / of executed officers and generals of bourgeois Poland, whose remains have been found by children in accidental circumstances (Nikitchenko 1969, 2).

Nikitchenko reveals that only eight men know about 'this location', among them the sixty-three-year-old Kuprii, residing in Poltava. He then also reveals, indirectly, that many significant details of the burial site are unknown to him. Nor are they available at the flip of a switch or the slide of a file drawer. To come

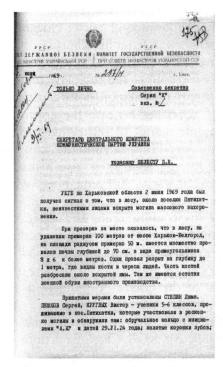

Figure 3.1 Letter dated 7 June 1969 from Chairman of the Ukrainian KGB Vitalii Nikitchenko to Secretary of the Ukrainian Communist Party Petro Shelest about the public discovery of the Katyn burial site in the Piatykhatky forest on the outskirts of Kharkiv, Ukraine.

to an understanding of the full significance of the Piatykhatky discovery, Nikitchenko must personally consult a pensioner named Galitsyn, one of Kuprii's underlings:

> KGB pensioner Galitsyn, who worked as a driver in the state security service and participated in the burial [at Piatykhatky], *explained that Soviet citizens could be buried in this site*, along with an array of personal effects confiscated by the NKVD during arrests in 1937–38 . . . (Nikitchenko 1969, 2; emphasis added).

That a high-ranking official in the Soviet security service has to refer to a retired driver for information about one of the largest NKVD killing fields is a striking revelation. Nikitchenko is perfectly aware of the Kharkiv dimension of the Katyn operation, but he does not seem to know that thousands of Soviet citizens lie buried in the same site, only miles away from his Kharkiv office. His ignorance demonstrates, in this case, that the institutional memory of the perpetrator is less a seamless and inviolate repository of the past than a closed system of disciplined forgetting. Uncovering the truth of who and what lies beneath the grounds of Piatykhatky forest is not a simple matter of retrieving, furnishing and citing documents. Documents disappear, and they can also be forged (see chapter 6). Even for the KGB, it is also a matter of recovering memory, of discovering who still remembers when they are conditioned to forget.

At the end of his communiqué, and in accordance with the Katyn Lie, Nikitchenko recommends that the burial site be explained away to local residents as a Nazi killing field. To dissuade them from visiting and exploring the site further, he suggests that the contents of the graves be publicized as the remains of victims with 'typhoid, cholera, syphilis, etc.', thereby posing a 'health risk to the public' that would require a restrictive cordon (Nikitchenko 1969, 3). KGB Chief Andropov and his staff in Moscow, however, devise a radically different solution. Responding to Nikitchenko at the end of June 1969, the Head of the Kharkiv KGB (and Hero of the Soviet Union) Petr Feshchenko relays orders from Andropov that the 'special objects' [*spetsob"ekty*] in the Piatykhatky mass grave be liquidated with a 'corrosive' chemical agent. This operation was to involve the construction of two buildings around the site – 'one to house security personnel, the other to store the chemicals' – and to take place over 'no less than four years' (Feshchenko 1969, 1–2). Whether Andropov's directive was fully carried out remains a lingering mystery of the Kharkiv Katyn. Exhumations of the site by Polish forensic scientists in 1994–6 revealed that the site was indeed damaged by mechanical drilling that frequently reached the bottom of the graves, most likely in the 1970s–1980s (Kola 2005, 317–18). Strangely, neither the corpses nor their personal articles were severely affected.[3] Apparently, as the journalist

[3] 'The intention of these activities is not entirely clear', wrote excavation leader Andrzej Kola in 2005, 'but traces of such drilling were also found in the graves of the other [i.e. Ukrainian and Soviet] victims of Stalinist repression, suggesting central decisions in this regard' (Kola 2005, 317–18).

Oleksandr Zinchenko (2011, 342) observes, 'the KGB was not very good at chemistry'.

The Katyn *for* Ukraine

Such was the literal Katyn in Ukraine, to a great extent: a series of orchestrated events in which NKVD officers from Moscow collaborated with local Ukrainian authorities like Kuprii to kill upwards of 260 Poles a day and bury them next to the remains of murdered Ukrainians and other Soviet citizens in a secluded wood (Zavorotnov 2003, 90). To those outside the Soviet Union, this Katyn in Ukraine was unknown for fifty years, consigned to hypothesis and conjecture; to communities in Piatykhatky and Kharkiv, it was known only intermittently after 1969, when it was labelled a place of Nazi evil; and to the Soviet security apparatus, it was both known and, to a degree, unknown before 1969, when it was remembered only to be targeted for forgetting under the din of drills.

A more figurative 'Katyn for Ukraine', however, circulated for decades before 1991, both in the public discourse of the Ukrainian diaspora in North America and in the underground *samizdat* (or *samvydav*, 'self-published') discourse of Ukrainian dissidents in the Soviet Union. This Katyn is not imagined to extend beyond the Katyn Forest; due to the Soviet campaign of misinformation and obfuscation, it remains more a denotation than a connotation. Among Ukrainian émigrés in Canada, working to assert a national identity in a 'new world' apt to overlook it, Katyn at first emerges in the 1950s as a unit of comparison by which to gauge the West's awareness of Ukrainian suffering under Stalin. In *The Black Deeds of the Kremlin: A White Book*, a collected volume of essays and testimonials published in Toronto in 1953 by the 'Ukrainian Association of Victims of Russian Communist Terror', contributing author Danylo Mirshuk complains that 'the Katyn story is discussed again and again' while 'the world is silent' about such Ukrainian tragedies as the murderous Terror-Famine, or Holodomor, of 1932–3 (Fedoriwsky 1953, 420).[4] What occupies Mirshuk

---

[4] Mirshuk, writing under the pseudonym Stepan Fedoriwsky, was a former member of the Ukrainian Insurgent Army (Potichnyj 2005, 464).

is not comparative or competitive victimhood, but comparative *recognition* of suffering on the international stage. He is concerned, in other words, with the way in which Katyn is remembered when other tragedies are, in effect, forgotten.

Such questions of differential recognition with respect to Katyn eventually give way to assertions of similarity and likeness in Ukrainian émigré publications. With its global resonance, Katyn becomes a valuable metaphor, a 'known' by which an 'unknown or imperfectly known is clarified, defined, described' (Whalley 1974, 490). The 'unknown or imperfectly known' in this transaction is most often Vinnytsia, the city in central Ukraine where in 1937–8 the NKVD tortured and executed over 9,000 Ukrainians and other Soviet citizens and built the 'Gorky Park of Culture and Rest' over their remains to conceal the crime. Beginning in 1949, Vinnytsia becomes known as 'The Katyn of Ukraine' (Seleshko 1949, 238). The metaphor is apposite. In 1943, only weeks after the exhumations of Katyn, Nazi occupiers unearthed over 90 mass graves in Vinnytsia, seeking another wartime propaganda victory. Once again they formed an international commission of forensic scientists and investigators – two of whom had also participated in the excavation in the Katyn Forest – and discovered thousands of corpses shot in the back of the head, their hands bound behind them. Of the 679 bodies identified, there were reportedly 490 Ukrainians, 28 Poles and 161 of 'uncertain' origin (Kamenetsky 1989, 27). Many victims were shot more than once, prompting British Katyn campaigner Louis FitzGibbon to surmise that the NKVD applied lessons from Vinnytsia to Katyn. '[In] many cases it had taken several shots to kill a man for the reason that the bullets used were less than 6mm caliber', he writes. 'Could it be for this reason that, at Katyn, the NKVD used 7.6mm German ammunition?' (FitzGibbon 1989, 87) In 1980, FitzGibbon declares Vinnytsia 'the forgotten forerunner' of Katyn, 'every bit as bad [. . .], but obscured by time and later tragedies' (FitzGibbon 1989, 86).

Katyn and Vinnytsia are thus discursively aligned in the West after 1949, but they are not, strictly speaking, connected. In his *Poetics*, Aristotle notes the importance of the 'foreign' [*allotriou*] in metaphorical transference, the way in which the known must be estranged from the unknown for a relation of likeness to obtain (Aristotle 1997, 150). Indeed, for all its similarities with Vinnytsia,

Katyn is essentially construed in Ukrainian émigré discourse as similar but *foreign*. It is remembered as a Polish tragedy, one that reflects and illuminates a Ukrainian tragedy, but from a distance. In the words of the late American-based scholar Ihor Kamenetsky (1989, 33), there is the 'Polish Katyn case' and the 'Ukrainian Vinnytsia case'. This distinction is of course an acknowledgement of the predominant (or, in the case of Katyn, exclusive) national identity of the victims in question, an identity that contributed to their condemnation as 'enemies' by the NKVD. Today, however, the distinction wavers upon closer scrutiny. As we have seen, the Katyn massacres were, in part, executed in Ukraine, and the Vinnytsia massacre included scores of Poles among its victims.

For Ukrainian dissidents in the Soviet Union, the lines between Katyn and Vinnytsia are not clearly drawn. The massacres do not mirror one another from a remove; instead, they are intimately connected in an archipelago of Soviet suffering. In 'The Despot's Smile' (1969), poet and philologist Sviatoslav Karavans'kyi foregrounds Vinnytsia and Katyn in a list of infamous crimes perpetrated by Soviet authorities with a twisted 'grin':

> You say: Friendship!
> > You do act holy.
> But Vinnytsia?
> > A city park built on corpses?
> And millions deported from their homeland?
> And cold-blooded murder in the Katyn Forest?
> > > > (Karavans'kyi 1980, 72)

Here Katyn and Vinnytsia operate less metaphorically than metonymically, as place-names connected to and designative of a more extensive landscape of Stalinist terror. Karavans'kyi does not divide them into known and unknown, native and foreign, Ukrainian and Polish. He casts them instead as Soviet crimes that call out for justice and action.

Karavans'kyi heeded this call very seriously. Like fellow Ukrainian dissidents Petro Grigorenko, Leonid Pliushch and Nadiia Svitlychna, he agitated publicly for the truth about Katyn. Yet Karavans'kyi's actions also bore, in the words of Jerzy Łojek, 'special moral import' (1989, 60). The remarkable, and often byzantine, story of his role in the 'Katyn affair' begins in May

1966 with a forceful letter to the Union of Soviet Journalists. Only months before, in late 1965, Karavans'kyi had been caught up in a wave of politically motivated arrests that attended the beginning of Brezhnev's rule. It was not his first confrontation with the Soviet regime. In 1945, he was sentenced to twenty-five years for his involvement in an Odesa youth group committed to the cause of Ukrainian independence. Karavans'kyi was granted an early release after serving fifteen years. He returned to Odesa to complete a prodigious dictionary of Ukrainian rhyme and to translate, among other works, Bronte's *Jane Eyre* (Jones and Yasen 1977, 145).[5] At the same time, he penned a series of letters to political authorities – never using a pseudonym, and always citing his home address – which protested the Soviet treatment of Ukrainian, Jewish, Crimean Tatar and Volga German national minorities, among others (Obertas 2010, 103). Like fellow poet-activist Vasyl' Stus, who endured seven years of imprisonment and exile only to return home and continue a vocal protest against the Kremlin, Karavans'kyi had an intimate understanding of the personal risks of such political activism. His letters promised, and delivered, another camp sentence.

His 1966 letter to the Union of Soviet Journalists, written from the Mordovian labour camps, mounts a vigorous defence of a mysterious Russian forest ranger named 'Andreev', who indirectly witnessed the Katyn massacre. For giving evidence to the German commission in 1943, Andreev had been condemned to twenty-five years of solitary confinement in Moscow's infamous Vladimir prison. Karavans'kyi thrust Andreev's name, which had circulated in whispers throughout the Soviet penitentiary system, into the wider public sphere.[6] His letter to the Union of Soviet Journalists was included in Viacheslav Chornovil's influential pamphlet *The Misfortune of Intellect* (*Lykho z rozumu*, 1967), published in

[5] Possession of Karavans'kyi's dictionary would contribute to the second arrest of prominent dissident Ivan Svitlychnyi in January 1972 (Kheifets 1971, 222; Tarnashyns'ka 2010, 72).

[6] He did so before Anatoly Marchenko, who wrote of encountering 'Andreev' in *My Testimony* (1967) (Cienciala et al. 2007, 134). According to Karavans'kyi, a prison guard had once mistakenly allowed Andreev, languishing in solitary confinement, to mix with other inmates in a courtyard and thereby relay word of the reasons for his imprisonment (Karawanski 1988).

English in 1968 under the title *The Chornovil Papers*. 'Twenty-five years of solitary confinement in prison!', exclaims Karavans'kyi. 'Is false testimony under duress really such a terrible "war" crime to justify twenty-five years in a stone grave?' (Karavans'kyi 1966, 207). Either ignorant of the truth at this point or careful not to add controversy to Andreev's story, Karavans'kyi kept his advocacy within the parameters of the Katyn Lie. Andreev, in his words, was only guilty of 'false testimony under duress'.

This is the last time Karavans'kyi would equivocate with respect to Katyn. In the summer of 1967, after months of abortive hunger strikes in the Gulag, he himself was sent to Vladimir prison, where he learned of other inmates whose only 'offence' was to have been caught up in the 'Katyn affair'. One was Boris Men'shagin, the former mayor of Smolensk during the Nazi occupation, who from 1951 had been condemned to solitary confinement within the walls of the prison. Like Andreev, Men'shagin was one of Orwell's 'unpersons'. Not only was he forbidden any form of human contact, but he was denied an official existence in the Soviet Union. He was a ghost. In state documents and press articles, Men'shagin was said to have 'fled to the West'. Outside of the Soviet Union, his fate had been a mystery. 'I have heard the name Meshagin [*sic*], who was head of the town of Smolensk during the German occupation', wrote Stanisław Rodziewicz, Chief Judge Advocate of the Polish Navy, in 1946, 'but I do not know what has happened to him. I imagine he also went with the Germans' (Maresch 2010, 73).

Men like Andreev and Men'shagin were the objects of a ruthless campaign of discursive cleansing. Their memories of Katyn, if spoken, posed a threat to the Soviet regime. Restoring their voice – and their memory – became Karavans'kyi's mission. It also became his misfortune. In May 1969, while searching his Vladimir cell, prison authorities discovered a number of encrypted texts written by Karavans'kyi in salicylic acid. Among them were two open letters addressed to the Red Cross and the United Nations in Men'shagin's name (Kolosov 1988, 139). They forcefully disputed the Burdenko Commission's narrative of German guilt and asserted that the NKVD was responsible for the Katyn massacres. Alongside these public appeals were also a number of poems alluding to Katyn, including 'The Despot's Smile' (cited above), 'There Is a God' and 'The Rhythms beneath Moscow' (Kolosov 1988, 140).[7]

These works strive to evoke the imagery, metre and tone of Taras Shevchenko, the great nineteenth-century artist imprisoned and exiled for his poetic indictments of the tsar. 'There Is a God' (1968), at once defiant and palliative in its affirmation of a divine presence in a world crippled by sin and suffering, casts the victims of 'the Katyn massacre' [*katyns'ka rozprava*] as God's 'prophets' who were 'annihilated [. . .] in cellars' (Karavans'kyi 1980, 26). It avoids explicitly naming the perpetrators. In 'The Rhythms beneath Moscow' (1968), a work endowed with the swift, abrupt cadence of a frenzied machine, Karavans'kyi avoids such ambiguity:

> O world!
>   You can heal such horrible wounds –
> The vanishings to Auschwitz, Buchenwald, and Majdanek . . .
> But why do you let Katyn and Iavas fester? (Karavans'kyi 1980, 66)

The poet connects Katyn and Iavas, the shorthand for the Mordovian labour camp, as wounds inflicted by the Soviet regime on the conscience of humankind without accountability. He also gives voice to Andreev, the Katyn 'witness' silenced by the Kremlin:

> From here [i.e. Vladimir prison] no one heeds this voice:
>   'I – I was a forest ranger in the Katyn Forest . . .
> And my wife?
>   Dead . . .
>   She could not survive this place . . .
> What am I guilty of? . . .
>   Of seeing hell. . .
> Was it truly against the law
> That I saw it, that I witnessed it?' (Karavans'kyi 1980, 66)

Karavans'kyi attempted to pass these texts to his wife, the prominent human rights activist Nina Strokata Karavans'ka, who was

---

[7]In 1980, only months after Karavans'kyi's release and emigration to the United States, these poems were published in Baltimore in a small collection of his verse entitled *Confronting the Typhoon* (*Sutychka z taifunom*).

to decode them for circulation into *samizdat* (Kolosov 1988, 139). Their interception in 1969, however, appeared to spell victory for the custodians of the Katyn Lie.

The victory was a pyrrhic one. The discovery of Karavans'kyi's documents unleashed an unusual series of disciplinary proceedings that drew the attention of increasingly mobilized and communicative Soviet dissident circles. Unspecified charges were levelled against Karavans'kyi, who was tried not in a municipal court, but in Vladimir prison itself. News of his closed trial introduced, for the first (and virtually only) time, the word 'Katyn' to the *Chronicle of Current Events* (*Khronika tekushchikh sobytii*), the seminal record of dissident activities in the Soviet Union. The date given for the massacre constitutes a direct engagement with the Katyn Lie:

> In 1969, a new case under Article 70 ('anti-Soviet agitation') of the Criminal Code of the RSFSR was brought against Karavans'kyi. This time the evidence against him [is . . .] a story of the execution of Polish officers in Katyn *in 1940*, recorded in the words of [. . .] former Soviet citizens Andreev (now deceased) and Men'shagin ('Eshche raz' 1970; our emphasis).

Not surprisingly, this brief reference to Karavans'kyi's case in Issue 13 of the *Chronicle* elicited particular interest in Poland. Only weeks after its appearance, the influential publisher of the journal *Kultura* Jerzy Giedroyc petitioned his Ukrainian colleague Borys Levyts'kyi for more details about Karavans'kyi's Katyn documents (Gedroits' 2008, 450). Very few could be provided, however. As the editors of the Ukrainian *tamizdat* periodical *Visnyk* would remark, 'Nothing specific about the content of [Karavans'kyi's case] is known. What is known is that the charges mention something about Katyn' ('Protses' 1970, 169–70).

Decades later, we now know that one of the men whom Karavans'kyi represented in these Katyn documents was brought as a witness against him. Boris Men'shagin, a figure more often mysteriously 'sighted' than substantively 'cited' in Katyn scholarship, finally appeared in the flesh in Vladimir prison in 1969, only months before his planned release from over two decades in solitary confinement. He was sixty-eight years old. According to court documents, Men'shagin testified that 'he did not have ties with the prisoner Karavans'kyi and did not instruct Karavans'kyi to write provocative statements about the so-called "Katyn affair" in his name'. He continued by stating that 'as the former mayor of Smolensk he did not know the details of the execution of the Polish prisoners of war in 1941, but was nonetheless convinced that [they] were shot by German fascists' (Kolosov 1988, 141). Karavans'kyi's fate was sealed. For fighting to remember a massacre of Poles witnessed indirectly by forgotten Russian prisoners, the Ukrainian poet was sentenced under Article 70 of the RSFSR Penal Code, 'Anti-Soviet agitation and propaganda', to another eight years in prison.

In characteristic fashion, Karavans'kyi refused to relent. He proceeded to bring his fight for the truth of Katyn directly to the Soviet Prosecutor, going so far as to call on the Kremlin to arrest the presiding judge and prosecutor in his case for 'concealing the bloody crimes' of Beria. In a letter dated August 1970, Karavans'kyi declares that the 'actions of the Vladimir district court cannot be qualified as anything other than the concealment of crimes against humanity, a concealment that now enables those who spilled the blood of the Poles to present themselves as friends of the Polish people and even to participate actively in Polish–Soviet friendship societies'.[8] As in 'The Despot's Smile', Karavans'kyi does not use national borders to define these crimes against humanity. He connects Katyn to other places where Beria's NKVD slaughtered thousands: Riga, Vilnius, Rostov-on-Don, Kyiv, 'and hundreds of other cities' (Karavanskii 1988, 144–6).

'Poor Yorickes'

Despite Karavans'kyi's intervention in the 'Katyn affair', the nationalization of Stalinist atrocities remains evident in some

---

[8] Many decades after his involvement in the 'Katyn affair', Karavans'kyi would publicly defend a highly controversial historical figure who is not remembered for cultivating Polish–Ukrainian friendship in the slightest. In 2010, at nearly 90 years of age, he enthusiastically declared Stepan Bandera (1909–59), the leader of the Organization of Ukrainian Nationalists, whose forces were responsible for massacring thousands of Poles during the Second World War, a hero and a 'genius' on a par with Taras Shevchenko (Karavans'kyi 2010).

poetic representations of the past in Ukraine. Two months after the discovery of mass graves in Piatykhatky in 1990, for instance, the late poet and literary scholar Yar Slavutych wrote a commemorative poem entitled 'To the Descendants of the Polish Officers', demarcating tragedies 'for you' and 'for us':

For you: Katyn, Ostashkov, and Kharkiv,
For us: Vinnytsia, and [Demianiv] Laz, and Bykivnia . . .[9]
Oh, how many mass graves each day
Were dug by Moscow in tranquil parks! (Hushchak 1998, 236)

As we have repeatedly seen, these sites do not discriminate according to nationality. The cold indifference of the ground would lead poet Vasyl' Symonenko to utter the following words while walking in the early 1960s through Bykivnia, the forest on the outskirts of Kyiv where the NKVD buried unknown thousands of executed Ukrainians during the Purges:

We tread on both friends and enemies,
O poor Yorickes, all of you in the same way.
In the cemetery of garrotted illusions
There is no longer room for graves (Hors'ka 1996, 162–3).

Recently archaeologists have confirmed that Bykivnia also contains the remains of Poles from the so-called 'Ukrainian Katyn List' (*Ukraińska Lista Katyńska*), a register of names of 3,435 Poles killed in the Katyn operation but buried somewhere beyond Piatykhatky in Ukraine. The list was compiled from NKVD records and given to Poland by the Ukrainian Security Service in 1994. The Bykivnia forest had long been suspected of concealing the mass graves of some of these victims, and to date at least nine Poles from the Ukrainian Katyn List have been identified among the bodies exhumed there. Their discovery has meant that the site remembered by Ukrainians as the largest single burial ground of their compatriots is now also remembered by Poles as a resting place of victims of their iconic national tragedy. These

---

[9] Demianiv Laz is a NKVD killing field outside of today's Ivano-Frankivs'k in western Ukraine.

memories met on a collision course in 2007, when the leadership of the Kyiv-based 'Memorial' Society of Vasyl' Stus wrote an open letter to Ukrainian President Viktor Yushchenko accusing Polish researchers and pilgrims of 'illegal' excavations in the Bykivnia forest.[10] 'The Polish side', wrote deputy head of 'Memorial' Stepan Kyrylenko, 'is attempting to turn Bykivnia into Katyn-2' (Kyrylenko 2007).[11]

By contrast, the Polish-led excavation of the 'Kharkiv Katyn' in the early 1990s witnessed no such political drama. In 1999, after the site was mapped and its contents catalogued, Presidents Leonid Kuchma and Aleksander Kwaśniewski laid in the forest a cornerstone for a cemetery complex, which was to be funded by the Polish government with additional support from private donors. To this point only a two-metre tripartite black granite memorial, erected in 1991 by local Kharkiv authorities, had marked the site and honoured the dead 'Soviet and Polish citizens'. The new cemetery, designed by architects Wiesław and Jacek Synakiewicz, opened on 17 June 2000, weeks before its counterpart in Katyn (Mackiewicz and Manowa 2007, 23). Prime Minister of Poland Jerzy Buzek marked the occasion by employing a narrative of common victimhood to cultivate Polish–Ukrainian solidarity:

> Ukrainian patriotism, like Polish patriotism, was a crime in the Soviet Empire, while Polish–Ukrainian friendship was a bad dream. But there is a symbolic message in the fact that it is on Ukrainian ground that we are opening the first of the cemeteries to the victims of the Katyn crime (Spanily 2000, 44).

Yet in Ukraine itself, the event of the cemetery's opening did not provoke vigorous public discussion of any 'symbolic message'. As Oleksandr Zinchenko explains, the act of speaking about the meaning of Kharkiv, Piatykhatky and other sites of Stalinist terror in Ukraine remains impeded by a 'peculiar metastasis of fear'

---

[10] The All-Ukrainian 'Memorial' Society of Vasyl' Stus is distinct from the Russian 'Memorial' Society, although there are links between the two organizations.

[11] The subject of a Polish memorial in Bykivnia has remained a matter of presidential politics. In 2010 Polish President Bronisław Komorowski called for a monument in Bykivnia to complement those in Katyn, Piatykhatky and Mednoe ('Komorowski chce cmentarza' 2010).

seizing much of Ukrainian society. In his view, the memory of Katyn among most Poles is 'alive', whereas the memory of Piatykhatky, Bykivnia and Vinnytsia among most Ukrainians is not. 'We are still too afraid', says Zinchenko, 'to discuss these things' ('Kharkivs'ka Katyn'' 2010).

The dull inertia of the Katyn Lie undoubtedly hinders the development of this public discussion in contemporary Ukraine. Karavans'kyi's efforts notwithstanding, sites like Katyn, Piatykhatky and Bykivnia were remembered in Soviet Ukraine for decades as Nazi killing fields, if they were remembered at all. Mourning their victims today, understanding who they were and why they perished, involves confronting the true identity of the perpetrators, the Soviet NKVD. In this respect, the name of the cemetery in Piatykhatky – 'Memorial to the Victims of Totalitarianism' – inhibits the mourning it seeks to engender (figure 3.2). *Whose*

Figure 3.2   Sign for the 'Memorial to the Victims of Totalitarianism' in Piatykhatky forest on the outskirts of Kharkiv. Photo by Rory Finnin.

totalitarianism? Within the gates of the cemetery, there is precious little to clarify explicitly that these victims were put to death by the Stalinist, not the Nazi, totalitarian regime.

This aetiological minimalism, which consigns the historical origins of the mass graves to the background, is to be contrasted with what might be called the cemetery's semiotic maximalism. Polish eagles and Ukrainian tridents keep vigil at the gate; the Star of David and the Crescent line an entry path that follows the 'black road'; red-and-white and yellow-and-blue flags flit between pine trees; and crosses – Latin, Orthodox and military (particularly Poland's Grand Cross of Virtuti Militari) – mark the graves and the ground with quiet solemnity (figures 3.3 and 3.4). The site abounds in iconic symbols and engages in meaning-making both metaphorical and metonymical, at once enabling and

Figure 3.3   Entrance to the 'Memorial to the Victims of Totalitarianism', Piatykhatky. Photo by Rory Finnin.

Figure 3.4 Interior of the 'Memorial to the Victims of Totalitarianism', Piatykhatky. Photo by Rory Finnin.

undermining straightforward national readings. At one end of the cemetery complex stands a copper-coloured wall inscribed with thousands of names of the Polish deceased; on the other, a wall inscribed with thousands of Soviet names written in Ukrainian. Both structures mirror each other in size and position, but from a distance (figures 3.5–3.8). Like the state flags that fly in tandem nearby, they bring the Polish and Ukrainian victims into 'a sphere of similarity' while asserting an essential difference between them. At the same time, the seventy-five convex mounds of basalt stones that mark the surrounding mass graves constitute a literal 'concatenation of signs along a string of contiguity' (Ricoeur 1986, 427) (figure 3.9). They connect all of the victims to one another anonymously. There is no discernible pattern to their placement. While they are adorned either with a Latin or Orthodox cross, and often with a Polish eagle, the graves resist enforced 'native-foreign', 'ours-theirs' distinctions. Their sheer number, their very omnipresence, speaks quietly but profoundly to a unity of fate.

Figure 3.5 Wall of Ukrainian and Soviet victims at the 'Memorial to the Victims of Totalitarianism', Piatykhatky. Photo by Rory Finnin.

Figure 3.6 Close-up of wall of Ukrainian and Soviet victims, Piatykhatky. Photo by Rory Finnin.

Figure 3.7   Wall of Polish victims at the 'Memorial to the Victims of Totalitarianism', Piatykhatky. Photo by Rory Finnin.

Figure 3.8   Close-up of wall of Polish victims, Piatykhatky. Photo by Rory Finnin.

Figure 3.9 Burial mounds in the 'Memorial to the Victims of Totalitarianism', Piatykhatky. Photo by Rory Finnin.

Figure 3.10 Plaque honouring Polish victim Jan Gumułka ('Teacher'), Piatykhatky. Photo by Rory Finnin.

Figure 3.11   Plaque honouring Polish victim Jakub Wajda, Piatykhatky.
Photo by Rory Finnin.

Between the two walls is a lane lined with 3,794 epitaph
tablets listing the rank, name and birth date of the Polish victims
of the 'Kharkiv Katyn'. On important dates of pilgrimage –
particularly 1 September and 17 September – Polish families come
to Piatykhatky to honour the dead and to use these plaques, if
only for a short while, as shrines. Some plaques are set off with
lanterns, while others bear old photographs frayed by the elements
that testify to pre-war lives, occupations and aspirations (figure
3.10). One of these plaques is for Captain Jakub Wajda, the father
of Andrzej Wajda (figure 3.11). In 2008, in connection with the
Ukrainian premiere of his film, Wajda visited this cemetery for the
first time. He found it 'beautiful and noble' (Pasiuta 2008). 'I
promised myself that I would come to Kharkiv to visit my father's
grave only after I made *Katyn*', he said. 'I waited a long time.'

Chapter Four

Katyn in Belarus

After the transfer of the 'Ukrainian Katyn List' to Poland in 1994, questions abounded about the existence of an analogous 'Belarusian Katyn List' containing the names of 3,870 victims who were imprisoned in the former Polish eastern borderlands and killed in Belarus, far from Katyn, Kalinin and Kharkiv. Indeed, a compelling body of evidence points to Belarus as a resting place of the Katyn dead. On 21 March 1940, NKVD Commissar Lavrenty Beria wrote to Stalin's henchman Lazar Kaganovich about an urgent need to transport 3,000 prisoners from West Belarus to Minsk, requesting over 150 train cars for the operation (*Katyń* 1998, 81–2). The following day, Beria ordered the NKVD heads of the Belarusian and Ukrainian SSRs to dispatch 3,000 prisoners from West Belarus to Minsk (*Katyń* 1998, 83–4). Whilst neither of Beria's documents contains a direct reference to his 5 March Katyn execution order, the coincidence of the dates, itineraries and prisoner numbers strongly suggests that the killings and the transportation memoranda were directly related and that a site in or near Minsk contains the remains of victims of the Katyn operation.[1]

---

[1] The numerical discrepancy between the 3,870 victims and the 3,000 transported to Minsk may be explained by an 'excess' of 870 Polish prisoners who could have been imprisoned in the capital already (Kalbarczyk 2008, 136).

The Belarusian Katyn List is, in the words of one Polish expert, 'the missing element of the truth about Katyn' (Kalbarczyk 2008). Unlike Ukraine and Russia, the Belarusian state has never given Poland archival documents pertaining to the repressions in Soviet-occupied West Belarus between 1939 and 1941. Its security archives remain closed. Polish requests to help sift through primary source documents and search for the Belarusian Katyn List have been repeatedly ignored.[2] Polish appeals have also been directed to Moscow, where a copy of the original list would have been filed in accordance with Soviet protocol. In April 2010, rumours circulated that the list had been found in a Moscow archive and that Russian Prime Minister Vladimir Putin intended to offer it to Poland during the seventieth anniversary commemorations of the Katyn massacre. Putin, however, did not furnish the list ('Putin nie przywiezie' 2010).[3] Without this documentary evidence, the story of the Katyn operation in Belarus remains a sodden field of hypothesis and informed conjecture. At the centre of this field is Kurapaty, Belarus's own 'Road of Death' (*Kurapaty* 1993).

Katyn, Khatyn, Kurapaty

In Belarus, Stalin's terror claimed the lives of the intelligentsia, the clergy, and the military leadership of the country, effectively 'decapitating' the nation, as in Poland, Ukraine, the Baltic States (see chapter 5), and elsewhere. The Second World War caused

[2] Belarusian authorities have also ignored Polish requests to carry out excavations of the mass graves discovered under a town church in Hlybokae in northwestern Belarus in 2009. The material remains appear to be those of Polish victims executed by the NKVD in or around 1940.

[3] Leading Russian expert Natal'ia Lebedeva believes that even if the original list in Minsk was destroyed during the Red Army's retreat in June 1941 and the archival copy in Moscow destroyed at a later date, its contents should nonetheless be available in other documents held in military archives in Moscow ('W Rosji' 2010). Members of the 'Index of the Repressed' project conducted by the Polish KARTA Centre Foundation are reconstructing an annotated list from the fragmentary evidence available and compiling a growing database of information on approximately 500 Katyn victims believed to have been killed in Belarus (personal interview with project member Anna Dzienkiewicz, conducted by Simon Lewis, 14 September 2011).

further losses, especially of the Jewish population, and changed the demography of the country forever. In the words of historian Timothy Snyder, 'In Belarus, more than anywhere else, the Nazi and Soviet systems overlapped and interacted [. . .] By the end of the war, half the population of Belarus had either been killed or moved. This cannot be said of any other European country' (Snyder 2010, 249–51). In the post-war period, however, the memory of these losses went underground, both figuratively and physically. The Kremlin suppressed historical truth and engaged in selective mourning, commemorating the sacrifices made by Soviet citizens during the Second World War while concealing the fate of the individuals it executed *en masse* during Stalin's reign.

This strategy of simultaneous commemoration and concealment may have been behind Moscow's decision to foreground as an important site of Soviet memory and mourning the Belarusian village of Khatyn, where German soldiers and their collaborators in March 1943 massacred 149 people, including 75 children. In July 1969, Soviet authorities inaugurated a memorial complex on the site to honour the two million Belarusian citizens killed during the Second World War and the hundreds of Belarusian villages eviscerated during the Nazi occupation. The concerted Soviet promotion of Khatyn has been read by some as a smokescreen, a cynical ploy exploiting a phonetic and orthographical similarity to obscure the crime of Katyn. According to Norman Davies, for instance, Khatyn was part of the Kremlin's 'calculated policy of disinformation' related to Katyn (Davies 1996, 1005; see also Przewoźnik and Adamska 2010, 385).[4] Soviet authorities had apparently first planned to construct the memorial complex in another vanished village called Vel'ie, before Piotr Masherau, First Secretary of the Belarusian Communist Party, decided to move it to Khatyn, and thus closer to Minsk ('Narodny khram pamiatsi' 2009, 5). Whether Moscow ushered him towards this decision remains unknown. 'Every citizen of Belarus and every visitor to the country', Masherau remarked, should 'have access to the memorial and understand what kind of tragedy the Belarusian

---

[4] As one Polish student from Gdańsk remarked, 'I have met many people in Moscow, Smolensk, Minsk and Warsaw who visited Khatyn and were convinced that they had been to Katyn' (Przewoźnik and Adamska 2010, 385).

people have lived through' ('Narodny khram pamiatsi' 2009, 5). One of these visitors was US President Richard Nixon, whose state visit to the Soviet Union in May 1972 included, in the words of one American newspaper, a visit to 'Katyn [sic], where 149 Russians [sic] had been forced into a barn and burned alive by Nazi troops on 22 March 1943' (Cienciala et al. 2007, 241).[5] The Soviet policy of selective and strategic memory was revived by Belarusian President Aliaksandr Lukashenka, who assumed power in 1994 (Lindner 1999; Sahanovich 2001, 2009). As a result, today many thousands lie in Belarus in unmarked graves, unidentified and consigned to oblivion. The largest and most iconic of these sites is the Kurapaty Forest, which could be a burial ground of the Katyn victims executed in Belarus. Among the materials exhumed at a small fraction of the site include boots of Polish manufacture, a comb with a message etched in Polish, and medallions bearing images of Our Lady of Częstochowa, a national symbol of Polish Catholicism (Gorelik 1996, 54–5; *Kurapaty* 2002, 19–22; Kalbarczyk 2007; Przewoźnik and Adamska 2010, 553). Yet no military relics and no personal documents have been uncovered at Kurapaty, making a direct, substantive link to Katyn impossible to assert (Gorelik 1996, 60–1).

The history of the Kurapaty site nonetheless bears some striking resemblances to that of Katyn. In both cases, the initial charges of Soviet responsibility for the mass graves were countered by rival Soviet reports that blamed the Nazis for them. In both cases, Soviet officials in the late 1980s finally admitted that they were NKVD killing fields, only to see these concessions spark more counter-allegations and conspiracy theories. These correspondences have led Belarusian émigré writer Sakrat Ianovich to employ the Katyn metaphor and remark that '[Kurapaty] is our Katyn. It is our memory and our participation in the tragic history

---

[5] This discussion of Khatyn's propagandistic instrumentality can lose sight of the fact that the village is a genuine site of Belarusian mourning. The museum was designed by Belarusian architects and artists, and its content has retained a specifically national focus since its inception. Indeed, Khatyn occupies a central place in Belarusian culture, inspiring literary works by such prominent writers as Ales' Adamovich (1927–94), whose 1971 novella *The Khatyn Story* (*Khatynskaia apovests'*) was the basis for the heralded late Soviet film *Come and See* (*Idi i smotri*, 1985).

of Europe. It is our conscience and our pain' ('Nasha sumlenne' 2005). In one significant way, however, Kurapaty does not resemble Katyn at all. Kurapaty has yet to be memorialized by the state.[6] No monument commissioned by Minsk stands at Kurapaty; no museum or research institute funded by the Belarusian government educates citizens about its legacy and significance. Acts of vandalism at the site go unpunished. An unofficial commemorative procession held every year since 1988 on *Dziady*, the traditional feast day commemorating the dead, is never mentioned in the mainstream state-controlled media.

The existence of mass graves at Kurapaty was first made public on 3 June 1988. Writing in the newspaper of the Belarusian Writers' Union, *Literature and Art* (*Literatura i Mastatstva*), archaeologist Zianon Pazniak and historian Iauhen Shmyhaleu exposed Kurapaty as a site of 'genocide'. They lamented the sanctioned forgetting of Stalinism's victims and issued a powerful imperative to remember, warning that 'if this memory is lost, if it is suppressed, it will all start happening again' (*Kurapaty* 1993, 69).[7] As part of their reportage, Pazniak and Shmyhaleu conducted a series of interviews with residents of the villages of Zialiony Luh, Tsna-Iodkava and Drazdova. According to these respondents, victims were brought to the Kurapaty region and shot day and night from 1937 to 1941. A 10–15 hectare area in the forest was cordoned off with a tall barbed wire fence, and covered lorries carrying the condemned carved a passage through the wood. All of the respondents were certain that the perpetrators were uniformed agents of the NKVD. When asked 'Did the Germans do any shooting here?', they responded that the Nazis had shown no particular interest in the area (*Kurapaty* 1993, 69–77).

---

[6] Memorials have been erected at Kurapaty through private initiative. Hundreds of crosses, as well as a small number of Jewish and other religious dedications, stand in the forest, many in memory of specific victims. In January 1994, US President Bill Clinton visited Kurapaty during an official visit, placing a stone bench at the site with the inscription 'To Belarusians from the American People'. Both 'Clinton's bench', as it has come to be known, and the memorial crosses have been repeatedly vandalized, but it was not until 2008 that the first suspected vandals were arrested ('Vpervye v Kuropatakh' 2008).

[7] This theme would develop into a fundamental guiding principle of the organization 'Martyrology of Belarus', a Belarusian equivalent of the 'Memorial' Society in Russia.

Pazniak and Shmyhaleu's article immediately caused a sensation in the Belarusian SSR and spurred the government in the late summer of 1988 to form an investigatory commission. The commission was led by Pazniak and staffed by both state officials and well-known Soviet Belarusian dissidents (Marples 1994, 515; Gorelik 1996, 19). Pazniak and his colleagues exhumed eight out of an assumed total of 510 mass graves and uncovered human and material remains in seven of them. Their preliminary report to the State Procurator's Office, dated 1 August 1988, concluded that civilians had been executed by a single revolver shot to the head, fired from Nagan firearms of Soviet manufacture. Markings on material items from the graves suggested that the victims had been buried in some sites no later than 1937 and in others no later than 1939, offering decisive proof that Kurapaty was an NKVD killing field. Pazniak speculated that a total of approximately 250,000 victims were buried at Kurapaty (*Kurapaty* 1993, 66–8). The final estimate was subsequently lowered to 'at least 30,000 people' (Marples 1994, 515; Kuzniatsou 2002, 30).[8]

The case was hardly closed, however. In August 1991, news spread of 'eyewitness reports' by a former partisan named Mikhail Pozniakov who claimed to have seen the Nazis execute Jews in the area (Pozniakov 1991; Sanich 1991). In 1993 a 'Civic Commission for the Investigation of Crimes at Kurapaty' successfully campaigned to have the investigation re-opened, arguing before the Belarusian State Procurator that the Kurapaty site contained the remains of Nazi victims. After reviewing the findings of the Pazniak investigation, the State Procurator Valerii Komorovskii sent queries to Yad Vashem in Israel and to German institutions, all of which responded that Kurapaty was not a site of Holocaust violence. Komorovskii ultimately concluded that there was no basis for carrying out more exhumations, but by this point, doubt and uncertainty about the identity of the perpetrator had already crept into public discourse (Kuzniatsou 2002, 40). By 1994, the government contended that the mass killing at Kurapaty had been perpetrated by the Nazis in 1941 (Marples 1994).[9] The 1997

---

[8] See also Tarnavskii et al. 1990, 182–98, and Gorelik 1996, 52 for criticism of Pazniak's estimates.

[9] Critiques of this version of events are provided in Marples (1994) and Kuzniatsou (2002, 36–44).

edition of the *Historical Encyclopedia of Belarus* reflected the official turnaround (Lindner 1999, 642).

Initially, Belarusian activists like Pazniak overlooked the 'Katyn factor', but Polish activists did not overlook the 'Kurapaty factor'. In August 1991, an organization called 'Vigil for Polish Graves' erected the first Polish monument at Kurapaty, a metal cross from Wrocław with the inscription 'To the Eternal Memory of the Poles Shot at Kurapaty'. In June 1993, President Lech Wałęsa laid a wreath at this monument on an official visit to Minsk. A year later, Belarusian authorities reported the results of the Pazniak investigation to a visiting Polish delegation, officially acknowledging the possibility of a link between Kurapaty and Katyn (Przewoźnik and Adamska 2010, 553–6).

In Belarus, a connection between Katyn and Kurapaty has been frequently asserted by Ihar Kuzniatsou. A prolific and uncompromising historian of Soviet terror, Kuzniatsou is a leader of a nascent Belarusian campaign to remember Katyn and honour its victims. Framing the relation between Katyn and Kurapaty as a metonymical one, he writes that 'Katyn and Kurapaty are links in the same chain' (Kuzniatsou 2002, 40). In recent years, a Belarusian Katyn initiative has joined Kuzniatsou and worked to commemorate both Katyn as a site of Belarusian suffering and Kurapaty as a site of Polish suffering. On 23 August 2009, the European Day of Remembrance for Victims of Stalinism and Nazism, a contingent of Belarusian activists from fifteen grassroots organizations made their first pilgrimage to the Katyn memorial site, flying the unofficial white-red-white Belarusian flag.[10] In addition to paying homage to the victims of the Katyn massacre of 1940, they also placed crosses in remembrance of the Soviet victims of the terror of the 1930s buried in the Katyn Forest ('Prosti, Bat'ka' 2009; see also chapter 7).

That Katyn is a place of Belarusian victimhood is a point made by a documentary film produced and screened by BELSAT, the

[10] When Belarus gained independence in 1991, the national flag was restored to the white-red-white banner of the short-lived Belarusian People's Republic of 1918. In 1995, however, Lukashenka put in place a modified version of the BSSR's green-red flag, with a new emblem featuring a five-pointed red star. The white-red-white flag has remained active as a symbol of the Belarusian opposition.

Polish-funded satellite television channel for Belarus. Entitled *Katyn – 70 Years Later*, the film premiered in October 2010 and cited a claim made by Kuzniatsou that approximately one quarter of the 4,421 victims officially commemorated at the Katyn site were natives of West Belarus (*Katyn'. Praz 70 hadou* 2010). These numbers have been adapted to claim that a quarter of all the 21,857 victims executed in the Katyn operation came from within the current geographical borders of Belarus ('Istorik' 2010).

Indeed, a large proportion of the Polish soldiers captured by the Red Army during the invasion were ethnically Belarusian and Ukrainian, but most of them were released in October 1939, unlike their commanding officers (Cienciala et al. 2007, 26, 62–3).[11] According to NKVD documents, there were approximately fifty persons of Belarusian nationality among the officers incarcerated in Kozel'sk, Ostashkov and Starobil's'k (Grzybowski 2006, 210; Cienciala et al. 2007, 119). The Polish-Belarusian historian Yuri Hrybouski (Grzybowski in Polish publications) argues that 'this number, however, only accounts for those who declared Belarusian nationality in official documentation' (Grzybowski 2006, 210–12). In practice, argues Hrybouski, many Belarusians, especially Roman Catholics, were likely recorded as Poles. Two such cases involve Franciszek Umiastowski (*Bel.* Frantsishak Umiastouski) and Franciszek Kuszel (*Bel.* Frantsishak Kushal'), Belarusian military commanders who continued their careers in the Polish army and represented an oft-forgotten non-Soviet Belarusian military and political legacy.[12] It is also believed that among the victims buried at Katyn (and Kurapaty) were members of the Communist Party of West Belarus, a branch of the Communist Party of Poland, which campaigned for Belarusian minority rights in the interwar period ('Belorusy v Katyni' 2010; 'Katyn' – Kurapaty' 2010).

---

[11] Their fate was not enviable, of course. Many were sent into forced labour, while others subsequently perished under arduous conditions (Grzybowski 2006, 199–207).

[12] Umiastowski was shot and buried at Katyn. Kuszel was interned at Starobil's'k, but survived and later wrote a memoir in Belarusian entitled *The Road to the Katyn Forest*. Both were active members of the independent Belarusian Military Commission during the Russo-Polish war and committed Belarusian activists in later years.

Despite their crucial importance and poignant resonance, both Katyn and Kurapaty remain largely confined to the margins of national memory in Belarus. There are no books about them available for purchase, even in specialist academic bookshops. Only the internet offers a 'public' venue to discuss them.[13] The film *The Road to Kurapaty* (*Doroga na Kurapaty*, 1990) has never been broadcast on public television in post-independence Belarus; a shorter television documentary produced for BELSAT, *Kurapaty: The Path of Conscience* (*Kurapaty: Shliakh sumlennia* 2008), meanwhile, has reached only a small audience. For Ihar Kuzniatsou, this enforced marginality is unsustainable when, in effect, hundreds of Kurapatys wait to be exhumed across the country. He posits that there are at least eight locations containing Soviet mass graves and at least forty other areas where executions took place in and around Minsk alone (Kuzniatsou 2008, 29).

Lukashenka vs. Mourning

Judith Butler has written that 'the differential distribution of public grieving is a political issue of enormous significance. It has been since at least the time of Antigone, when she chose openly to mourn the death of one of her brothers even though it went against the sovereign law to do so' (Butler 2009, 38). As we have seen, the Belarusian state has often played the part of Creon with respect to Katyn and Kurapaty, sanctioning forgetting and inhibiting public remembrance. The few Katyn monuments extant in Belarus, for instance, have been installed by Polish activists, and one of them was declared illegal by the authorities and forcibly removed ('Białoruś' 2010). As recently as 2009, a widely-used school history textbook entertained the possibility that Nazi Germany was responsible for the Katyn crime, claiming that there was no documentary evidence that the NKVD had carried it out (Novik 2009, 151).

While state authorities give cover to the Katyn Lie, they bury the Kurapaty truth. In a remarkable editorial published on 29

---

[13] Every publication about Kurapaty referenced in this book was printed outside Belarus. By contrast, numerous publications about Khatyn, Belarus's officially recognized site of mourning and martyrdom, are easily available inside the country.

October 2009, the festival day of *Dziady*, the largest state-owned newspaper *Soviet Belarus* (*Sovetskaia Belorussiia*) asserted that the victims of Kurapaty were indeed killed by the Stalinist regime but better left concealed and interred in a sepulchre of silence and forgetting. 'Why drag the dead out of their graves?' asked the editors. They claimed that the current government bears 'no responsibility' for the crimes committed and that Stalinism had 'long ago become history'. Continued 'speculations' about the tragedy of Kurapaty, the editors argued, would only divide society and eventually lead to 'new Kurapatys' (Yakubovich 2009). The Belarusian authorities would now prefer to avert their gaze from the tragedy and diminish its profound significance. In fact, in early 2009, Minsk refused to nominate Kurapaty as a candidate for the UNESCO World Heritage List. Kurapaty, said Belarusian state authorities, represents a 'monument to Belarusian history' but is 'not of world significance' ('Minkul't otkazalsia' 2009).

In 2010, Minsk began to assume something of a more constructive role with respect to Katyn. In June, a temporary exhibition entitled 'We Remember Katyn' opened in the State Museum of the Great Patriotic War, with Andrzej Wajda's *Katyn* featured prominently on the programme ('U Mensku pomniats'' 2010).[14] In July, the documentary film *Katyn: The Belarusian List* (*Katyn'. Belorusskii spisok* 2010) aired on ONT, a state-run television channel. The film places a strong accent on the Belarusian origin of many of the victims and posits that one-third of the slain came from West Belarus. Notably, it makes no mention of Kurapaty and offers no speculation as to the location of the Belarusian Katyn List. Directed specifically at Belarusian audiences and emptied of 'dangerous' key facts, the documentary seeks to cultivate a national identity loyal to Lukashenka's state.

In November 2010, six weeks before the presidential elections, Lukashenka gave his first interview to Polish journalists in over ten years. He pledged to deal with the issue of the Belarusian Katyn List personally, but tempered expectations by warning that many key documents had been taken to Moscow ('Polacy mogą'

---

[14] Andrzej Wajda was also awarded an honorary doctorate by the Belarusian Academy of Arts in April 2010, a few days before the Smolensk catastrophe ('Andzhei Vaida' 2010). The film was aired on Belarusian state television for the first time two weeks after the tragic accident involving the Polish presidential plane.

2010). Yet when Lech Kaczyński's plane crashed near Smolensk in April 2010, Belarus was for seven days the only country in the region not to observe a period of official mourning. After complaints and critiques from diplomats and journalists, a six-hour period of state mourning was instated on 18 April 2010, the day of Lech Kaczyński's funeral ('No Official Mourning' 2010; 'Usio zhe adzin dzen' 2010; ' "Zhaloba" u Belarusi' 2010).

'The Belarusian pages of the history of the Katyn tragedy have still not been fully written', writes the historian Ihar Mel'nikau. '[I]t is vital that each of us relates to this part of Belarusian history with appropriate respect' (Mel'nikov 2011b). Mel'nikau helps to write these 'Belarusian pages' by appealing online for public information and compiling a makeshift Belarusian Katyn List until the real one is recovered. The information originates in Belarus, from descendants of wartime Polish officers who are today Belarusian citizens (Mel'nikov 2011a, 2011b). If the Belarusian Katyn List is ever found, thousands of descendants in Poland and Belarus will discover that they are personally linked to one another by the Katyn massacres, which Kuzniatsou calls 'the pain of both the Polish and the Belarusian people' ('Historyk Ihar Kuzniatsou' 2011).

Silencing discourse about Katyn means silencing discourse about Kurapaty and vice versa. Jay Winter has distinguished three types of silence: 'liturgical' silence, which is bound to ritualistic mourning and grief; 'political' or 'strategic' silence, which seeks to mask violence and conflict; and 'essentialist' silence, which dictates who has the right to speak (Winter 2010b, 4–6). In Belarus the silence over Katyn and Kurapaty is clearly political and strategic. This silence is also a form of denial. According to Eviatar Zerubavel, there is a meaningful difference between an 'elephant in the room', which is wilfully ignored by a collective, and a 'skeleton in the closet', which is unknown and waiting to be disclosed (Zerubavel 2010, 40–2). In Belarus, enthusiasts of memory like Zianon Pazniak and Ihar Kuzniatsou have sought to bring out the closeted skeletons of Kurapaty and Katyn. Rather than denying their existence, the Lukashenka regime has embarked on a different strategy. They now acknowledge the elephant, but keep the skeletons concealed. The dead are remembered, but not mourned.

Chapter Five

Katyn in the Baltic States

In August 2008, months after Ukraine's President Viktor Yush-chenko bestowed state honours upon Andrzej Wajda for *Katyn*, his Estonian counterpart Toomas Hendrik Ilves presented the Polish director with the Cross of Terra Mariana, which is given to foreigners in recognition of service to the Estonian state ('President Ilves' 2008). When *Katyn* was first screened in Estonia later that year as part of the Dark Nights Film Festival, critics immediately embraced the film as an historical document and called for its incorporation in school curricula, as others had done in Poland (see chapter 2). 'The film is indirectly about us', wrote one reviewer. 'One of our duties to the youth [is not to] let the memory of the periods of [Soviet] occupation become hazy or be wiped out. The screening of this film in schools is very necessary [. . .] because memory cannot be allowed to become murky. We cannot let the noise of information obfuscate it' (Maimik 2009). According to another critic, *Katyn* was not 'indirectly about us' at all; rather, it spoke *directly* to Estonia's past. 'If one were to claim that the tragedy of Katyn could very well have taken place in Estonia, he would be right to do so. [Katyn] did happen here too, if in a somewhat more dispersed manner' (Kommel 2009).

In Estonia, Latvia and Lithuania,[1] the Katyn massacres are subject to the rhetorical push and pull of such 'direct' and 'indirect' reference. Directly, Katyn figures in various relations of similarity and comparability as a prominent counterpoint and complement to wartime Baltic tragedies, from the Rainiai and Tartu massacres to the mass deportations of the Lithuanian, Latvian and Estonian political and social elite in 1941. Indirectly, as an original sin of what Timothy Snyder calls 'Molotov-Ribbentrop Europe' (Snyder 2010, 119), Katyn binds together Poland and the Baltic States as partners in victimhood, as 'states of a commonly held fate', in the words of a former Estonian deportee (Toom 2010; see also Kärk 2008; Donskis 2010). The cover of the Estonian translation of Andrzej Mularczyk's novel *Katyn: Post-Mortem*, upon which Wajda's film was based (see chapter 2), foregrounds this conjunctive function: 'This is the story of a nation and a people caught between two totalitarian states and a story about two totalitarian states that do not differ greatly from each other. [It is therefore] very familiar to Estonians' (Mularczyk 2008). In other words, Katyn represents for Latvia, Lithuania and Estonia a devastating symbol of the collusion between the Nazi and Stalinist regimes and, as such, serves as an admonitory 'memorial to our [i.e. Baltic] freedom' (Laasik 2008). As we shall see, this symbol exercises significant political force in the consolidation of a new geopolitical alliance of central and eastern European Union member states – the so-called 'new Europe' – which demand that their wartime experiences be included in the traditional European understanding of the events and the afterlife of the Second World War (Mälksoo 2009).

---

[1] These three states are generally referred to as 'the Baltic States' in contemporary political discourse. Even though this reduction (which is definitional as well as geopolitical) tends to conflate the differences between these three distinct sovereign states, it is nonetheless commonly used as shorthand in policy and academic discourses. It should be noted, however, that the concept of 'the Baltic countries' has been subject to fluctuations in the past. Originally, what is only today's Estonia and Latvia (the former provinces of Estonia, Livonia and Curonia) composed the Baltics (*das Baltikum*). In the beginning of the twentieth century, Finland and even Poland were sometimes regarded as 'the Baltic countries' besides the now common 'Baltic Three' of Estonia, Latvia and Lithuania.

Catalysing Memory

As in Ukraine, Katyn has at times served as an instructive and illustrative metaphor for lesser-known tragedies in Lithuania. In May 2010, Speaker of the Lithuanian parliament Irena Degutienė travelled to the villages of Kaušėnų and Ablinga, where the Nazis killed a total of nearly 2,000 Jews and other civilians during the Second World War. Although these 'wounds of the Lithuanian land' were German killing fields, Degutienė spoke of them as 'Lithuanian Katyns' (*lietuviškosios Katynės*) (' "Dėkoju jaunimui ir visiems" ' 2010). Her use of the Katyn metaphor in this case was less an allusion to Katyn as an historical event perpetrated by the NKVD than an allusion to Katyn as a powerful catalyst of communicative memory. Just as the memory of Katyn in Poland had helped consolidate the Polish nation, Degutienė implied, so too should the memory of Kaušėnų and Ablinga in Lithuania shape the identity and mobilize the activity of the national collective for generations to come. News reports of Degutienė's memorial trip accordingly ran with the headline, 'Speaker of the Parliament Pays Homage to the Victims of the Lithuanian Katyns' ('Seimo' 2010).

In Estonia, Katyn is cast in direct relation to the NKVD's mass deportations of the Baltic political and social elite to the Noril'sk prison camp north of the Arctic Circle in 1941 (cf. Kaasik 2006, 781; 'Kolme Balti' 2011; Estam 1996, 70–2). Former US Ambassador to the United Nations Jeane J. Kirkpatrick likens this event to a 'decapitation'. 'On a single "night of terror" – June 14, 1941 – the Soviets deported almost the entire Baltic intelligentsia to Siberia where most of them perished', she writes. 'The Baltic nations were decapitated, very much as the Polish nation was decapitated at Katyn' (Kirkpatrick 1988, 51). The execution of the Polish prisoners in the Katyn massacres has prompted some Estonian historians to entertain counterfactuals about an alternate fate of the deported elite (Uluots 1999, 75; Arumäe 2010). Ülo Uluots, for instance, has speculated that the Baltic officers would have been executed like their Polish counterparts near Smolensk, if the war had not begun so unexpectedly for the Soviet Union. After all, as he remarks, '[t]here was still enough space left in the Katyn Forest' (Uluots 1999, 76).

In the documentary film *The Soviet Story* (2008), which was largely well received in the West but widely condemned in Russia, the Latvian director Edvīns Šnore plots Katyn on an arc of Soviet evil alongside the Ukrainian Terror-Famine, or Holodomor, of 1932–3 and the NKVD's mass deportations during and after the Second World War (cf Luik 2008).[2] These three tragedies figure centrally in the politically charged discourse of victimization in the region. The Estonian parliamentarian Silver Meikar (2010) has maintained that the Katyn massacres have been for Poles as tragic an event as the Holodomor for Ukrainians or the mass deportations for the Baltic nations. In Meikar's view, the comparison between these three events can be made despite the disparity in the number of victims – tens of thousands in Katyn vs. millions in the Holodomor, for example – because they each entailed not only the 'inhuman brutality' of Soviet state-sponsored violence but also sanctioned deception. 'For decades one was not allowed to speak of these issues honestly', says Meikar. 'Even now, twenty years after the collapse of the Soviet Union, these crimes have not been unanimously condemned' (Meikar 2010).

Memorial Militancy

In 2011 Irena Degutienė made a pilgrimage to the village of Rainiai, where the NKVD tortured and executed scores of Lithuanian civilians in 1941. In honouring the victims buried at the site, she remarked: 'When the Soviet occupiers understood that they could not deport everyone before retreating from Lithuania [. . .], they simply began killing. And when [we reburied these] martyrs of freedom, [we discovered] horrible sights reminiscent of the Polish Katyn tragedy or the concentration camps' (Degutienė 2011). Once again Degutienė does not restrict her Katyn reference to the realm of Soviet terror. In her formulation, Katyn resembles both the NKVD crime of the Rainiai massacre and the Nazi crimes

---

[2] *The Soviet Story* won the Mass Impact Award at the Boston Film Festival of 2008, and Šnore has been decorated with state honours by Estonia and his native Latvia. In Moscow, however, the director's effigy was hanged and burnt outside the Latvian embassy by the pro-Kremlin youth organization *Rossiia Molodaia*.

of the 'concentration camps'. Indeed, among various influential constituencies in Latvia, Lithuania and Estonia, the crimes of Nazism and Stalinism are frequently compared, and their interactions and mutual influences hotly debated. Invariably these debates allude to an uneven historical playing field. According to political figures like Jüri Luik, the Estonian ambassador to NATO, Europe has thoroughly investigated and roundly condemned Nazi atrocities, but it has yet to confront the full extent of Communist crimes, particularly in a juridical setting. 'While the philosophical and legal bases for the condemnation of Nazi crimes and the respective punishments are clearly defined in the Western legal sphere', Luik (2008) writes, 'the issue of the penalties imposed for Communist crimes has mostly been viewed as an internal matter' for the countries of Central and Eastern Europe.

Luik calls for an international commission to investigate the crimes of Communism and to forge a new European consensus on its legacy. In his conception, the commission should not be a witch hunt but an 'honest self-examination':

> The commission should evaluate all the events on the basis of legislation governing the condemnation of crimes against humanity, from Nuremberg to the ICC . . . [It] should focus its attention mainly on bigger cases that affect large sections of society and public opinion, for example the Ukrainian famine induced by the Communists, the fate of the Polish officers [at Katyn], the deportation of the Baltic peoples, the [development] of the Gulag system of slave labour camps in order to boost the economy, the exploitation of psychiatric hospitals as repressive instruments, mass executions [. . .], and [intentional] environmental catastrophes (Luik 2008).

Advocating a process akin to the German *Vergangenheitsaufarbeitung* ('a working through and coming to terms with the past'), Luik posits that a forthright historical and moral clarification of Communist crimes has the potential to ameliorate the collective trauma in the Baltic States and beyond. As long as these crimes are not thoroughly examined, he argues, there would be 'dark areas in the collective psyche of ex-Communist countries. These societies will start to function normally only if their pain is brought into the open, analyzed and universally accepted' (2008).

In a joint declaration of 18 March 2008, Polish President Lech Kaczyński and Estonian President Toomas Hendrik Ilves similarly called for an international assessment of the Communist crimes of the twentieth century. They appealed to the international community to respect the victims of Communist atrocities as well as 'the children of the victims who today, as citizens of Europe, see their plight treated as a secondary "historical" issue, better left untouched' (Ilves and Kaczyński 2008). As they argued:

> Crimes like the Katyn killing of Polish officers, mass deportations from the Baltic States, the creation and operation of the Gulag or the man-made famine in Ukraine, the imprisonment of people who today are leading citizens of Europe, the denial of fundamental rights of freedom, of expression, speech, movement and many others have been neither properly investigated nor internationally assessed (Ilves and Kaczyński 2008).

In contrast to Kaczyński, who frequently employed a narrative of Polish suffering and martyrdom over the course of his political career (see Coda), Ilves has cautioned against depicting one's own national trauma as unique and unprecedented. While a member of the European Parliament in 2005, for instance, he emphasized that Estonia's sufferings during the Soviet occupation were not remarkably different from those of the other Central and East European nations. Ilves strongly objected to Estonian attempts to stake out a position as 'exemplary victim', because 'to become the greatest sufferer is not an achievement – nor is it the truth' (Ilves 2005). In his view, even if Estonia's historical suffering and injustice were proved singular and unique, it would pay few dividends in foreign policy. Here Ilves leverages Katyn as an event of the past that should direct Estonians to a new future:

> Our suffering is our own business [. . .] No one cares about it except us, just as no one except the Poles cares about the mass murder in the Katyn Forest. Finding justifications for our current behaviour [. . .] in the injustice of the past and the remaking of [the past] does not help us. We need a modern 'narrative'. And if this [narrative] is our belonging to the West [. . .], then we have to behave accordingly (Ilves 2005).

Ilves's comments notwithstanding, Lithuania, Latvia, Estonia and Poland have nonetheless proceeded to forge an alliance in 'memorial militancy' (also Wood 1999, 30) and to advance a common foreign policy agenda that dwells, to a significant extent, on 'the injustices of the past'. At the centre of this policy agenda is the criminalization of the legacy of Soviet Communism, which constitutes an ontological security challenge for contemporary Russia (e.g. Mihkelson 2010, 122).

Katyn as Litmus Test

Many Baltic political elites, from Latvian politician Ģirts Valdis Kristovskis to Lithuanian politician Vytautas Landsbergis, are particularly critical of the narrative of the Soviet 'Great Patriotic War' as a defence solely against Nazi aggression, a narrative that invariably ignores or discounts the significance of Nazi–Soviet collaboration under the auspices of the Molotov-Ribbentrop Pact. They seek to assert, *inter alia*, that (i) the Soviet invasion of Poland on 17 September 1939 was an act of 'aggression'; (ii) the occupation and annexation of the Baltic States by the Soviet Union were illegal acts; and (iii) the Katyn massacres constituted a Soviet war crime. They disagree with the Russian legal position that, in the context of the Second World War, more was permitted to the party whose war could have been considered just in terms of *jus ad bellum*. Pavel Laptev, Russia's former official representative at the European Court of Human Rights (ECHR), expressed the discriminatory concept of war crimes directly in an interview with *Kommersant"* (2010). Responding to the question '[Could one have used] any means to fight Nazism?', Laptev said, 'Within the limits of reason – of course' (Bartul 2010). In the controversial case of *Kononov v. Latvia*, which was tried before the ECHR, the divergence in this politico-juridical interpretation led the Russian Federation to intervene as a third party in support of Vasilii Kononov, who was convicted of war crimes by a Latvian court, and Lithuania to intervene as a third party in support of Latvia (cf Mälksoo 2011).

Russia's position on historical events like the 1939 invasion or Soviet crimes like Katyn is perceived by many in the Baltic States as a litmus test of its democracy, as a sign of its commitment (or lack thereof) to atone for the past and not repeat it in the future. In the words of a conservative Estonian politician, 'it is precisely Katyn . . . that sets a test [for Russia] to repent for its sins' (Mihkelson 2008). If Russia fails this test, according to Mart Laar, Estonia's Minister of Defence, then it would in effect perpetuate the 'unbelievable success of Soviet power in hiding their crimes from the world for decades, even in cases where there was sufficient proof established about their perpetration' (Laar 2009b). Laar claims that the Soviet Union was not alone in concealing these crimes; in his view, the West aided and abetted Moscow's obfuscation and falsification. 'Communist lies would never have been so well-spread', he argues, 'if the West's silent complicity had not enabled them' (Laar 2009a). Laar speculates that, had the Western leaders made Stalin's crimes public in due course, informed European and North American publics could have pressed for a more effective foreign policy vis-à-vis the Soviet Union, which in turn could have prevented the Sovietization of Central and Eastern Europe (Laar 2009a).

For Lithuanian politician Vytautas Landsbergis, a musicologist who became the first leader of post-Soviet Lithuania, Katyn is similarly a symbol of 'memory work' still yet to be done in Russia, which remains a country enslaved 'by the lack of the truth' (Landsbergis 2007, 2008, 2010). And 'without truth', he writes, 'Katyn has no end' (2008). Russia's aversion to acknowledging Soviet crimes like Katyn 'is a result of the moral weakness not only of Russian society, but of European society as well', which has become the 'indirect inheritors of Stalin' (Landsbergis 2009). Landsbergis exposes a double standard in the way Europe treats the past of its Western and Eastern parts:

> [C]rimes committed anywhere in Europe by Europeans are our common European heritage. Denying them is our European fault [. . .] If tens of thousands of French officers had been executed in Katyn [in 1940], President Sarkozy would hardly keep silent about it in his dealings with President Medvedev (Landsbergis 2009).

Landsbergis concludes that not much has changed in Russia since the Communist era: in his view, the political approaches and mentality of the governing elite remain Soviet. He reserves no suspicion for today's Kremlin. Believing that the Smolensk crash of

2010 served Russia's interests by eliminating the Polish president and dividing Polish society (see Coda), Landsbergis is the only senior politician in the Baltic States who seriously considers conspiracy theories that blame Moscow for the catastrophe (Landsbergis 2011).

The late Polish President Lech Kaczyński had close relations with the Baltic States, and their leaders repeatedly acknowledged after his death that they had lost 'a friend' (e.g. 'Baltic Leaders' 2010). In Lithuania in particular, the Smolensk crash was accorded extraordinary importance by the political elite and public alike. The Cabinet of Ministers in Vilnius held an extraordinary session and announced three days of national mourning (12–14 April) after the plane crash and another day of national mourning on the day of Kaczyński's funeral. By comparison, the EU and Russia officially observed only a day of mourning in response to the tragedy.[3] Putin's reconciliatory approach towards the Katyn issue before and after the plane catastrophe in 2010 was followed very carefully in the Baltic States, as it seemed to promise that long-awaited repentance. In the words of Lithuanian Prime Minister Andrius Kubilius (2010), 'Prime Minister Putin [is] trying to change his attitude to historical issues'.

Yet the nature of this reconciliation has been doubted in the Baltic States, given the reality of Moscow's closed archives and adamant refusal to rehabilitate Katyn's victims or compensate their families. The tendency has been to read any movement on the Katyn issue on the part of the Kremlin as a tactical, rather than a substantive, shift. The prominent Estonian foreign policy magazine *Diplomaatia* ('Soojem aastaaeg' 2010), for instance, labelled the new line in Russia's official memory politics 'a charm offensive', questioning whether it truly signalled 'substantive and

---

[3] By comparison, Algirdas Brazauskas, the former president of Lithuania who died on 26 June 2010, was 'awarded' three days of mourning. The famous Lithuanian poet Justinas Marcinkevičius, sometimes called 'the conscience of the nation', received two days of mourning. The deceased Polish President Lech Kaczyński was therefore essentially honoured as if he were the president of Lithuania. The current Lithuanian President Dalia Grybauskaitė paid her respects to the late Polish president by deciding to travel to Poland by car (c.800 km trip), when the eruption of the Eyjafjallajökull volcano complicated air travel at the time of the funeral. Valdis Zatlers, the president of Latvia, was also present at the funeral.

sustainable strategic cooperation' with its former East European satellites. Yet those who see the glass as half-full draw some encouragement from the Russian Duma's 2010 decree recognizing Katyn as a Stalinist crime (e.g. Donskis 2010). To be sure, potential for reconciliation is great, and the stakes are high. In the words of Erkki Bahovski (2010), a media consultant for the European Commission in Estonia: 'If the Polish-Russian account of the history [of the Second World War] changed such that the Katyn issue was no longer obscured or silenced, the overall European account of history would change as well.'

Chapter Six

Katyn in Russia

On 18 June 1943, Sir Alexander Cadogan, Britain's Under-Secretary for Foreign Affairs (1938–46), responded to a confidential memorandum about the Katyn massacre of Polish officers. He wrote:

> I confess that in cowardly fashion, I had rather turned my head away from the scene at Katyn – for fear of what I should find there. [. . .] On the evidence that we have, it is difficult to escape from a presumption of Russian guilt. This of course raises terrible problems, but [. . .] on the purely moral plane, they are not new. How many thousands of its own citizens has the Soviet regime butchered? And I do not know that the blood of a Pole cries louder to heaven than that of a Russian (Paul 2010, 306).

Cadogan's remarks would resonate for many around the world who came to believe that Stalin was responsible for Katyn. They knew that the Soviet regime had killed 'many thousands', as Cadogan put it, or rather millions of its own subjects in 'class warfare', which involved the liquidation of the bourgeoisie, dekulakization, artificial famines, ethnic cleansings, mass deportations and other kinds of 'repressions'. Most of Cadogan's peers on the left and the right of the political spectrum likely agreed that, in absolute terms, the Soviet killing of the Poles was no worse and no better than the Soviet killing of Russians, Ukrainians, or anybody else. The state terror unleashed upon the newly annexed territories of Western Ukraine and Western Belarus was of the same character but 'significantly more intensive' than elsewhere in the Soviet Union (Lebedeva 1999). In several waves of ethnic cleansings of the resident Polish population before 1940, the Soviet regime had killed many more Poles than it killed in Katyn (Snyder 2010).

It is the memory of Katyn, however, that has become emblematic of Soviet terror. The Poles executed by the Soviet regime were not its citizens, but neither were they legally its prisoners-of-war. They were foreign nationals who were to become Soviet subjects when the USSR annexed Eastern Poland according to the Molotov-Ribbentrop Pact of 1939. They were also prospective allies. Indeed, only a year after the Katyn massacres, Stalin authorized the formation of what would become popularly known as 'Anders' Army', the Polish armed forces mobilized on Soviet territory and led by Władysław Anders. During the Second World War, the Soviet Union made many strategic alliances with the bourgeoisie, including the almost 100,000 Poles who were recruited to fight under Anders' command. They were mainly conscripted from the camps of the Gulag where they had been sent because of their 'class nature'. There was no explanation as to why some Polish officers and soldiers were murdered in Katyn in 1940 while others were armed to fight the Nazis in 1941.

One of many non sequiturs in Soviet politics, the Katyn crime has evolved into an all-embracing political symbol. A seasoned diplomat who directed British foreign policy through some of its most turbulent years, Cadogan was admirably honest in admitting his desire to avert his gaze from the truth of Katyn. Weighing both 'the purely moral plane' of the massacre and its political implications, he wrote: 'The ominous thing about this incident is the ultimate political repercussions. How, if Russian guilt is established, can we expect Poles to live amicably side by side with Russians for generations to come?' (Paul 2010, 306). Even though he sheepishly called the Katyn murder an 'incident', Cadogan predicted the pivotal role Katyn would play in the unfolding of the complex, long-term, multi-causal dynamic of Polish–Russian relations.

From Shelepin to Medvedev

In 1944, cinemas from Moscow to Siberia screened a documentary film that blamed the Nazis for the massacres and featured the

Soviet Burdenko Commission at work in the Katyn Forest, explaining, *inter alia*, that the bullets unearthed at the site were German-made (*Tragediia* 1944). As we have seen, the conclusions of the Burdenko Commission would become the basis of the Katyn Lie and a crucial lynchpin of Soviet propaganda. Fifteen years later, KGB chief Aleksandr Shelepin would argue that the truth should be destroyed in order to protect this propaganda. Writing to Communist Party boss Nikita Khrushchev, Shelepin acknowledged that the 'operation of liquidating the [Polish prisoners] was carried out on the basis of the decision of the CC CPSU [Central Committee of the Communist Party of the Soviet Union] of 5 March 1940' and subsequently proposed the destruction of all individual files related to this 'liquidation' and, moreover, 'all the records of the operation' (Cienciala et al. 2007, 332–3). According to Shelepin, these files and records had no 'historical value' because they contradicted the 'official version' of events formulated by the Burdenko Commission. In 1992, Shelepin confirmed the authenticity of this document, although it is still not clear which documents were actually destroyed, if any (Iazhborovskaia et al. 2001, 395).[1]

Despite this internal recognition of the truth about the massacres in 1959, Soviet authorities continued to deny responsibility for Katyn until 1990. Surveying the seventy-year-long history of the mass murder in Katyn, one cannot escape surprise at the amount of effort invested in both concealing and revealing the crime. Generations of Soviet officials not only destroyed relevant evidence but also fabricated a full-scale alternative history of the event, a feat that they did not attempt for many other atrocities. With the demise of Soviet socialism, the pendulum swung in the other direction. Following Mikhail Gorbachev, who in 1990 announced that the Soviet Union was responsible for Katyn, every leader of the Russian Federation, one after the other, has admitted the guilt of the Soviet government in the massacres. President Yeltsin did so in 1992, President Putin in 2002 and President Medvedev in 2009. This series of acknowledgments built to a crescendo after the crash of President Lech Kaczyński's plane

---

[1] According to Valerii Kharazov, Shelepin told him that Khrushchev (or in other versions, the Politburo) rejected his request to destroy the documents and that they were preserved. Shelepin thought that preservation of this evidence was a major mistake ('Valerii Innokent'evich Kharazov' [undated]; see also Mlechin 2009).

in 2010 (see Coda). While many critics of the Russian position on Katyn claim that Russia has not done enough to apologize to the Poles, we would like to reverse the argument and ask a different question: what has forced Russian leaders to acknowledge this guilt repeatedly, although always inconsistently and incompletely?

A tentative answer is that, having failed to disentangle themselves from the Soviet and Stalinist legacies, leaders from Gorbachev to Medvedev have been trying to explain the crime to themselves. They have sought to interpret the massacres in terms understandable to them and compatible with their political identities. The more tightly these identities are connected to their Soviet genealogies, the more difficult it is for them to 'apologize' for Katyn. The very senselessness of the Katyn massacres, meanwhile, obstructs efforts to give them a believable, intuitively acceptable explanation. Explaining Katyn is an impossible task, but it seems necessary for the Russian political authorities. Partially true explanations and partially effective apologies make it necessary to give still another explanation and still another apology, while the very idea of combining apology with explanation undermines these efforts.

Deniers and Interpreters

Rather than confronting the crime itself, Russian officials have often submerged Katyn in the long and tortured history of the Polish–Russian feud, which has caught fire in the Russian cultural memory of the new century. For instance, when in 2005 the Putin administration decided to replace the 7 November Soviet-era public holiday marking the Bolshevik revolution of 1917 with a different holiday, it conjured 4 November as the commemoration day of the emancipation of Moscow from Polish invaders in 1612. This living anti-Polish mythology is conveyed by Valentin Falin, who prepared Gorbachev's statement of 'deep regret' for the Katyn massacres in 1990, in a documentary of 2010 entitled *The Polish Cross of Russia*:

> I always tell the Poles: what do we start with? They say, let's start with 1918. I say, why? You hate Suvorov [an eighteenth-century

Russian commander]; so let's start with Suvorov. Or let's start with your march to Moscow with Napoleon. Or let's start from the False Dmitrii [the seventeenth-century impostor who was supported by the Poles]. Or we can start with the first Crusaders' attack on the Orthodox Church in 1348. Or we can start with [the rule of] Khan Batyi [in the thirteenth century], when you robbed all the western provinces of Russia. We have a choice (*Pol'skii krest Rossii* 2010).

Falin worked for Soviet leaders who engaged in the difficult task of de-Stalinization, from Khrushchev to Gorbachev. His words should be taken seriously. But his logic is questionable. The same Soviet institutions that murdered over 20,000 Polish prisoners in 1940 killed in a similar way huge numbers of Ukrainians, Jews, Kazakhs and others who had different histories of relations with Russia. Why, in that case, should the history of Russian–Polish relations have mattered for the Katyn massacres? If we agree for a moment that a millennium of Russian–Polish relations does indeed matter to Katyn, then we lend weight to the argument that the massacres were an act of genocide, a crime directed against Poles as Poles. Falin would hardly subscribe to this argument.

In the tortured history of the Russian acknowledgement of responsibility for Katyn, three streams of power clash with one another: executive, judicial and archival. The degree of discord between these streams in the case of Katyn is striking. Indeed, it is often assumed that law enforcement and the management of the archives are contingent on the vicissitudes of government in Russia, but either due to inability or lack of political will, the executive does not always dictate the direction of the judicial and archival with respect to Katyn. Russian presidents and prime ministers have acknowledged the crime, but the Russian courts refuse to recognize it. The archival policies of preservation, destruction, fabrication and publication of documents often follow their own mysterious agenda.

Gorbachev, for instance, admitted Soviet responsibility for the massacres and passed the first file of documents from his presidential archive to the Polish leadership in 1990, after which point the Chief Military Prosecutor of the USSR started a legal investigation. With the collapse of the Soviet Union in 1991, the prosecutors had to split the case into three, in accordance with new Russian, Ukrainian and Belarusian jurisdictions. Arguing that the decisions that led to all of these murders were made in Moscow, the office of the General Prosecutor of the Russian Federation then took over the case, which was closed in 2004 after fourteen years of investigation. Out of 183 volumes of documents pertaining to the case, 67 were given to the Polish side. The other volumes were withheld because the Chief Military Prosecutor claimed, amazingly, that they contained military secrets from 1940. The Prosecutor, however, agreed with the identification of the remains of 22 bodies as Polish officers and recognized that 14,542 Poles had been convicted and sentenced to execution by Soviet authorities.

This sentence still stands, though Katyn families have appealed to Russian courts to exonerate and 'rehabilitate' their loved ones (see also chapter 1). Under Russian law, only direct descendants can mount this appeal, but because exhumed corpses have only rarely been positively identified, very few relatives can do so. Thirty-four claims by the descendants of Polish victims of Katyn have been considered by Moscow courts; all have been rejected on technicalities. Appeals went as far as the Supreme Court and the Supreme Military Court, both of which rejected the claims of the victims' relatives, arguing that there was no way to identify the victims or the murderers because the crucial archival documents had been destroyed. The Katyn Families have gone on to appeal to the European Court of Human Rights at Strasbourg.

We wish to underline the logic of mourning behind Polish hopes that the murderers who did all that they could to destroy the traces of their victims in the grave preserved the traces of their victims in the archive. In fact, we now have a great deal of information about the victims, the perpetrators and the procedures of the Katyn massacres, but most of this information has come from sources far from Soviet officialdom. The crucial evidence about the massacres from Moscow has been preserved not in the regular archival system of Soviet and post-Soviet Russia, but in a special 'presidential file', the so-called 'File No. 1', which appears to have been passed down through generations of Party leaders. Ironically, the most damning source of information about the massacres contained in the presidential file is Shelepin's handwritten note of 1959, which proposed the destruction of all archival documentation related to Katyn and its victims.

At some level, the difficulty of finding justice in legal institutions and truth in the archives was part of the very design of Soviet power. Orders tended to be given orally, with few witnesses. Archives were moved, merged and purged (see, for example, Petrov 2001); during the Second World War and afterwards, they sometimes rotted, burned or disappeared without a trace. Security officials were often strategically rotated; many of those close to secret operations such as the Katyn massacres were liquidated. Some of the Katyn executioners were arrested and shot in the 1940s, while others committed suicide in the 1950s; virtually none of them was still alive in the 1960s (Voronov 2010). When the Soviet and Russian authorities began to investigate the Katyn murder in the 1990s, witnesses were largely unavailable. There were no memoirs. Archives remained classified, while an unknown part of them had been destroyed. Many Poles still feel that there is some truth in the former Soviet archives that Russia is keeping secret. As a general principle, there is no reason to expect truth from the Soviet archives any more than there is to expect justice from the Soviet courts. But if you cannot rely on archives, what can you rely on?

To this question, many would answer 'national interest'; others, 'popular fears'. Viktor Iliukhin, a Communist member of the Russian parliament where he served as the vice-chair of the Committee for Security until his death in 2011, alluded to both in the following remark:

> I always pose one question to my Polish counterparts: what do you want to accomplish? What do you want? It seems that our presidents have apologized to you. But the Poles say again and again: we want the truth. Which truth? Truth does not matter for them. The Polish side is going to present large financial claims – now to the Russian Federation, not the Soviet Union (*Pol'skii krest Rossii* 2010).

Iliukhin led a small but active group of Katyn deniers, which also featured a prominent diplomat, Iulii Kvitsinskii, who headed the Soviet delegation on Nuclear Arms Limitation talks in 1981–5. They argue that the Polish officers in question were killed by the Germans elsewhere and that the Katyn Forest was used for many years by both the Soviet secret police and the Nazis for various executions. Kvitsinskii explains his position thus:

The Katyn affair was a German provocation, in which the purpose was to poison our relations with Poland, to prevent the development of the partisan, pro-Soviet and pro-Russian movement against the German occupants in Poland (*Pol'skii krest Rossii* 2010).

In contrast to the infamous Holocaust deniers in Western Europe who are mostly academics, these Katyn deniers are mostly former high-ranking bureaucrats. There are, however, several trained historians in this group as well. Together and separately, they have published several books, maintained an internet site and produced *The Polish Cross of Russia* (2010). In further contrast to Holocaust deniers in Western Europe, these Katyn deniers are not roundly condemned by the international community. After the release of Wajda's *Katyn*, the Polish daily *Gazeta Wyborcza* published an angry editorial by Adam Michnik, who was responding to a critical review of the film in *Le Monde*. He denounced a global 'conspiracy of silence' related to the massacres that constituted 'a great victory for Stalin and his propaganda' (Michnik 2009). According to Michnik, while in Central and Eastern Europe this 'hypocritical silence' was enforced by terror, in Western Europe it was imposed by ideological dogmas. Even in 2009, wrote Michnik, these massacres were 'still the skeleton in the cupboard of the French Left that has shown such understanding for Stalin [. . .] Sadly, stupidity is just as international as it is incurable'.

Katyn deniers produce a number of critical arguments in order to question the validity of the central archival documents related to the Katyn massacres. On one document, they argue, there is no date of issue. Another document was typed by two different typewriters, appending an authentic signature to fraudulent pages. Yet another document makes glaring mistakes in geography. Most of these documents, they continue, are not available in the original. These Katyn deniers revere the Soviet bureaucratic process so much that they cannot imagine that the documents issued when Stalin and his henchmen executed one of the most disastrous decisions in twentieth-century history were simply a mess. The disordered character of the available documents does not prove that enemies of the state forged them. If anything, it demonstrates instead the slipshod, inconsistent and unreliable character of

Soviet documents, as state archives preserved them.[2] The case that the Katyn deniers have tried to build is an instructive lesson in archival fetishism, a belief that the truth about the past is hidden in the archives and what is not available there did not happen at all (Kotkin 1998).

The Katyn deniers repeatedly allege that the Polish appeals for Soviet documentation are part of a grand design to level retributive claims against the Russian Federation. No such claims, however, have ever been made by parties in Poland despite repeated acknowledgements of responsibility by Soviet and Russian politicians. Wildly exaggerating the financial estimates of these potential claims, Iliukhin stated in the Russian Duma that they could go as high as one hundred billion dollars. There is absolutely no precedent for such an amount. The Katyn Families have publicly insisted, moreover, that they have no intention of seeking financial compensation in any case (see also chapter 1). If 'rehabilitated' under the Russian law of 1991 like millions of Soviet 'victims of political repressions', the Polish descendants of the Katyn victims would be able to claim a state pension and a return of confiscated property. The state pension is miserable. As for compensation, the potential ramifications of rehabilitation are unclear: since most of the victims lived in Poland or in what is today Ukraine and Belarus, their lost property would not be located in Russia, save the personal items in the mass graves in Katyn and Mednoe. Since 2005, the prominent Russian civil society organization, the 'Memorial' Society, has led legal efforts directed towards the 'rehabilitation' of the Katyn victims with no success, even though other high-profile cases of 'rehabilitation' evidently pregnant with financial implications have been successful. (In 2008, for example, the Supreme Court of the Russian Federation 'rehabilitated' Nicholas II and his family, who were murdered in 1918.) In February 2011, the Russian Ambassador to Poland promised the 'rehabilitation' of the Katyn victims in the near future; the 'Memorial' Society lawyers responded to this statement with scepticism (Gur'ianov 2011).

---

[2] For an excellent analysis of the pseudo-historical arguments that Iliukhin and his team of historians use in their writings, see several essays by Aleksei Pamiatnykh and Sergei Romanov on their site, http://katynfiles.com.

From Détente to Catastrophe

Since 1944, monuments to the victims of the Katyn massacre have replaced one another, materializing in memory hardware the changing narrative propagated by the Soviet state. After the infamous Burdenko Commission completed its work, a temporary sign and then a stone monument in the Katyn Forest stated that the Nazis killed Polish citizens at the site; these monuments bore inscriptions exhorting, 'Soldier of the Red Army, Take Revenge!' In 1978, a new bilingual monument was erected; two inscriptions – one in Russian, the other in broken Polish – said 'To the Victims of Fascism, the Polish Officers Who Were Shot by the Hitlerites in 1941'. In 1988, the Poles erected a tall Catholic cross behind this monument; they also laid a stone nearby with an inscription that promised to erect new monuments. In 1991, the inscriptions on the Soviet-era monument were changed so that 'Fascism' and 'Hitlerites' were no longer mentioned, although no new information about the actual perpetrators appeared. The Poles also sponsored bilingual memorial plaques on other sites of the massacres, such as the monastery Optina Pustyn near Ostashkov. The new Polish–Russian memorial in Katyn was opened in 2000 (see especially chapter 7), featuring a museum and an impressive construction with several large crosses, Catholic and Orthodox, symbolically marking the Polish and the Russian areas. The museum fully acknowledges the Soviet responsibility for the massacre. It also emphasizes that Russian and other Soviet citizens were killed and buried at this site along with the Poles, especially at the height of the Purges. While the memorial names all the murdered Poles whose identities are established, it fails to do so for Soviet victims executed at the site.

In the spring of 2010, on the eve of the symbolic anniversary of the massacres, Russian Prime Minister Vladimir Putin and his Polish counterpart Donald Tusk devised a pragmatic solution to the long-standing tensions between their countries. They agreed to orchestrate a joint pilgrimage to Katyn, exchange archival materials and facilitate more collaboration between Polish and Russian historians. On 2 April 2010, an elite Moscow TV channel, *Kul'tura*, broadcast Wajda's *Katyn*. On 7 April, Putin and Tusk went to Katyn to perform a memorial rite together. They arrived three days before the scheduled visit of President Lech Kaczyński, essentially in order to leave him in the shadows. It would have been Kaczyński's second visit to the site; his first took place on 17 September 2007.

Lech Kaczyński died on 10 April when his airplane crashed in the fog, killing him together with many Polish officials and public figures. On the very next day, Wajda's film was shown again on Russian television, this time during primetime on the national Channel One, by far the country's largest. Russian authorities were visibly concerned that they would be blamed for the catastrophe and demonstrated unusual transparency in the investigation of the crash. As in Poland, Russian newspapers and websites responded with a panoply of conspiracy theories and transhistorical analogies. According to one publication, Lech Kaczyński repeated the fate of another Polish leader, General Władysław Sikorski, whose airplane crashed in the sea near Gibraltar in 1943 allegedly en route to Katyn, where he was invited by the Nazi leadership to inspect the traces of the massacre. As one commentator remarked, there was a mystical force in these repeated punishments imposed on Russia's enemies (Andriukhin 2010). While the former Polish President Lech Wałęsa immediately called this loss of life 'the second Katyn', Russian Prime Minister Putin emphasized the unprecedented character of the event. Nothing like this has ever happened before, said Putin, trembling in his first televised statement after the catastrophe. Wałęsa chose to include the presidential crash in the broad context that the Katyn massacre of 1940 symbolized for him, while Putin, as if anticipating this contextualization (which would connect him to Stalin), proclaimed the exceptional character of the crash.

Putin and Tusk later returned to the airport near Katyn and embraced one another. Though the crash of Kaczyński's presidential plane has changed the story of Katyn in a most dramatic way (see Coda), the fact is that the new and warmer relations between the Russian and Polish prime ministers, not to mention the change in the Russian official attitude towards Katyn, all preceded the crash. Several explanations have been given for this rapprochement. Historian Andrzej Nowak emphasizes the 'internal cold war' between Kaczyński and Tusk over the issue of the Polish myth of victimhood, which the latter disavowed publicly as an historian in 1987 (Nowak 2011a). A high-profile Russian journalist, Iuliia

Latynina, focuses on Putin rather than Tusk and explains the new tone of Russian politics towards Katyn as driven by the recent discovery of shale gas in Poland, which would potentially eliminate Polish dependency on Russian gas (Latynina 2010). Historian Timothy Snyder, meanwhile, explains it by way of the memory politics of the Polish-Russian-Ukrainian triangle (Snyder 2011). In January 2010, Ukrainian President Viktor Yushchenko posthumously bestowed the country's highest award, Hero of Ukraine, on Stepan Bandera (1909–59), the controversial leader of the Organization of Ukrainian Nationalists whose forces were responsible for massacring thousands of Poles during the Second World War. Both the Russian and Polish governments condemned Yushchenko's move. (The award was later annulled by Yushchenko's successor and one-time rival, Viktor Yanukovych.) The Bandera affair cooled relations between Poland and Ukraine, which in turn may have led to a warming of relations between Poland and Russia. To be sure, all three factors – psychological, economic and memorial – contributed to this major development.

In August 2010, President Medvedev announced that he would decorate Wajda with the Order of Friendship for his contribution to the development of Polish–Russian relations. In November 2010, the State Duma of the Russian Federation, the lower chamber of the parliament, declared that the Katyn massacre had been committed at the direct order of Stalin. The Duma also stated that there were thousands of Soviet citizens, victims of Soviet terror, whose remains lay alongside those of the Polish victims. Issued to commemorate the 70th anniversary of the massacre, the statement expressed solidarity with all victims of 'unjustified repressions' independent of their nationality. In speaking of 'unjustified repressions', the Duma continued the terminological tradition of Khrushchev's so-called 'Secret Speech' to the Twentieth Party Congress in 1956, which exposed many of the crimes of Stalinism (but not, of course, Katyn). The Duma, however, shunned its legal responsibilities and stated that 'history itself has rehabilitated the victims of Katyn'. A large part of the Duma declaration addressed archival issues. 'The published materials, which have long been kept in the secret archives, reveal the scale of the tragedy and testify to the fact that it was organized by the direct order of Stalin and other Soviet leaders' ('Zaiavlenie' 2010). The Communist faction of the Duma voted against this Declaration. One of its leaders, Viktor Iliukhin, stated that Joseph Goebbels, the Nazi Minister of Propaganda, was applauding the Declaration from his grave.

Among more liberal politicians, the Katyn massacres have also taken a prominent place on the public stage. In February 2011, President Dmitrii Medvedev expanded the Presidential Council for the Development of Civil Society and Human Rights, which developed an unusually radical new 'de-Stalinization' programme in cooperation with the 'Memorial' Society. If realized, this programme would create memorial centres across Russia to enlighten the public about Stalinist crimes and prohibit by law the denial of these crimes by state officials. Sergei Karaganov (2010), a member of the Council, introduced the programme by stating that, while Russia had 'completely and unreservedly recognized Katyn' and 'displayed nobility and sympathy for Polish grief', the country had not yet found 'the strength to admit that the whole of Russia is one big Katyn, strewn with the mostly nameless graves of the millions of victims of the [Soviet] regime' (see also Coda).

In response, Iliukhin launched a new round in the archival war in May 2010. In a letter to President Medvedev and in a number of public statements, Iliukhin claimed that the major documents that prove Soviet responsibility for Katyn were forged in the early 1990s by his former colleague, a prosecutor with connections to the Russian security services. According to Iliukhin, the forgery was commissioned by the Yeltsin administration, which manufactured the two most important documents on the Katyn massacre, Lavrenty Beria's 1940 memorandum and Shelepin's 1959 note to Khrushchev. Iliukhin's 'informant' revealed a number of technological aspects of the forgery and even presented him with samples of old stationery and seals ostensibly used in the process. A law enforcement official with decades of experience, Iliukhin (2010a, 2010b) personally testified to the veracity of his informant's claims. Moreover, in a televised interview, Iliukhin stated that some other crucial documents from the Stalin era, such as the secret protocols of the Molotov-Ribbentrop Pact, were also fabricated by Yeltsin's 'anti-Russian' government. Iliukhin concluded, dramatically, that 'all our archives are discredited by this discovery'. In February 2011, Iliukhin played a leading role in a public trial organized by a group of retired officers, who accused Vladimir Putin of high treason. Immediately afterwards, in March 2011, Iliukhin died of a heart attack, still a deputy of the Duma. There was no lack of conspiracy theories surrounding his death.

Quo Vadis?

Following its screening of Wajda's *Katyn* on 2 April, the *Kul'tura* channel organized a debate in its studio. High-profile historians discussed the film together with a prominent politician and a celebrity. From Poland, Wajda warmly addressed the group by videolink. The debate started with a remarkable statement by the Head of the Russian Federal Archival Agency, Andrei Artizov, who authoritatively stated (pace Jacek Trznadel: see chapter 2) that every aspect of Wajda's film was historically accurate: 'Every fact of this film finds confirmation in the archives that I oversee' (Artizov 2010). If this is the case, it is not clear what has prevented Artizov from releasing these confirmatory documents. The key issue in this televised debate, however, was this: had the post-Soviet Russian people chosen to be a new nation that claimed no continuity with the Soviet past and therefore could condemn it in an objective way, as other post-Soviet republics have done? Historian Aleksandr Chubar'ian, the eighty-year-old Director of the Institute of Global History, formulated the issue thus:

> We should be thinking about historical reconciliation. Our relations with Germany are the best example. We lost many millions there. But do we have anti-German feelings in Russia? No, we do not. . . . It is very important to draw the conclusion that the tragic events of the past should not be brought to the present. It evokes mutual distrust and hostility. Our Russia is an entirely different country now. It has changed completely (Chubar'ian 2010).

If Russia is now a different nation, culture and people, it should be able to look at the crime of Katyn like any other nation in the world and condemn it outright. The problem is that this solution – Chubar'ian's distancing – is not acceptable to those in Russia who celebrate and hold fast to the Soviet legacy. You can disavow your ancestor who was a criminal, but if you keep him in your family history, you need to explain his crime again and again.

Troubled by this problem, the filmmaker Nikita Mikhalkov, also present at the debate, made the following remark:

> Wajda is a great film director. His film is very powerful, but it is also a film of resentment. Evil is faceless in the film . . . It is just evil . . . This facelessness troubles me, because I want to know why they did it. I want to know who did it (Mikhalkov 2010).

Several days later, Prime Minister Putin announced his 'personal opinion' on the matter in Katyn on 7 April. According to Putin, the massacres were Stalin's revenge for the deaths of Soviet prisoners-of-war in the Polish–Soviet war of 1920. According to Putin, more than 32,000 Soviet POWs died in Polish camps, and as former Commissar on the war's South Western Front, Stalin exacted vengeance for these losses twenty years later at Katyn. A trained lawyer, Putin needed to understand the criminal motive in order to judge the crime. Revenge was the motive that Russia's leaders consistently employed in their attempts to understand and explain the doomed policies of their predecessors. But Putin's explanation does not address the fact that in the early spring of 1940 the prospective victims of Katyn could have joined the Red Army or that in 1941 thousands of Poles joined Anders' Army on Soviet territory with Stalin's authorization. Now that Russia has acknowledged Soviet responsibility for Katyn, it struggles with a compulsive need to explain the crime. These explanations offer little solace.

Chapter Seven

Katyn in Katyn

The history of the Katyn memorial in Russia is a barometer of fluctuations and changes in the memory of Soviet terror. While the victims mourned at the site are both Polish and Soviet, the Polish graves in Katyn Forest occupy less than 1.5 per cent of the estimated total area of mass graves; the vast majority contains the remains of Soviet citizens who were shot and buried by other Soviet citizens. Paradoxically, it was Poland's campaign to give a decent burial to its victims in Katyn that prompted Russia's federal government to back, for the first time, the construction of a monument to the victims of Soviet terror. The result is the most developed, impressive and informative site of memory for the victims of Stalinism anywhere in Russia.

Successive Russian leaders have declared sacred the memory of the victims of Soviet terror. In 1992 Boris Yeltsin swore to preserve this memory upon meeting with Lech Wałęsa about Katyn and its aftermath; in 2009 Dmitrii Medvedev made his own vow via video-blog. Yet to translate this rhetoric into reality – to design and construct memorial complexes, to develop new public rituals – presents an array of challenges. What form should an official monument to the victims of Soviet state terror take? What messages should it convey? What lessons should a group of children from Smolensk, Moscow or Warsaw receive from a museum visit? The story of the Katyn memorial is a story of competing attempts to answer these questions.

Origins – and Problems

There are more than 1,000 monuments and memorial plaques marking the sites of the Gulag across the former Soviet Union, but the international nature of the Katyn crime has made the case of the Katyn memorial distinctive. Indeed, the vast majority of Russian monuments to victims of Soviet terror have been initiatives undertaken by individuals or civil society groups, local authorities, or (more rarely) regional authorities. Today scores of 'temporary memorial emblems' and foundation stones placed by local authorities in the late 1980s and early 1990s to mark sites for future monuments stand abandoned. By contrast, the Katyn memorial has been granted federal status by the Kremlin, the only monument to the victims of terror guaranteed a right to state protection and preservation in Russia.[1] It stands as a rare instance of the 'hardware' of cultural memory with respect to the Stalinist legacy on the Russian memorial landscape; its construction testifies to a 'crystallization' of memory made possible by a sufficient consensus about the past (Etkind 2004, 47).

Founded jointly by Russian and Polish state institutions – the Russian Ministry for Culture and the Polish Council for the Preservation of Struggle and Martyrdom Sites (ROPWiM) – the Katyn memorial is the largest of the three Polish–Ukrainian and Polish–Russian complexes devoted to the Katyn tragedy.[2] A belated product of a honeymoon in Polish–Russian relations in the early 1990s, it opened on 28 July 2000, one month after its counterpart in Piatykhatky on the outskirts of Kharkiv (see chapter 3) and two months before the one in Mednoe. The memorial project was borne out of the goodwill generated by the gestures made by Yeltsin when, in 1992, he handed Wałęsa documents confirming Soviet responsibility for the Katyn massacres and, in 1993, knelt down before the Katyn cross in Warsaw, asking Poles: 'Forgive us, if you can'. Yet Polish–Russian relations deteriorated later in the

---

[1] The website of the Katyn Memorial presents it as Russia's 'first international monument' to the victims of Stalinist repressions.

[2] A diptych memorial plaque, inscribed in both Russian and Polish, can also be found in the monastery of Nilova Pustyn, near Ostashkov, where a number of Katyn victims were held before the massacres.

decade, a process closely bound up with periodic conflicts related
to the memorialization of Katyn.

There were a number of contested issues at stake. Many in
Poland hotly debated the idea of building the cemetery on Russian
soil in the first place. Some families of the victims were strongly
in favour of bringing the remains home to Poland, where they
could be re-buried in individual graves (Przewoźnik 1997, 11).
Others took issue with the proclaimed 'international' status of the
site (Tarczyński 1996, 173). Initially, the Polish side had come
under considerable pressure to agree to a joint memorial whereby
the national borders separating the different groups of victims
would be downplayed. According to a key negotiator on the
Polish side,

> On many occasions our interlocutors underlined the 'necessity' of
> building joint 'memorials', making the argument [. . .] that one
> cannot separate victims after death. Because all the victims of the
> Soviet NKVD had been made equal by death. This view clashed
> with the position of the Polish negotiators who asserted that this
> crime in particular [. . .] had a special significance and symbolic
> dimension for us Poles (Przewoźnik 1997, 8).

In Russia, the plans for a shared memorial also prompted criticism
that the Kremlin was attempting in effect to 'dissolve' the Polish
tragedy into the broader Russian one (e.g. Krotov 1995). Others
opposed the idea of giving up Russian land for a Polish memorial,
and at one point, the Polish Embassy in Moscow was forced to
deny rumours circulating in Smolensk that the Poles were intent
on renting or purchasing the land at Katyn (Pushkar' 1995).

The result of compromises on both sides, the Katyn memorial
complex commemorates both Polish and Soviet victims of Stalinist
terror without conflating them. It contains a Polish component,
rendered as a military cemetery, which is at once connected to and
set off from the rest of the site.[3] As at Piatykhatky, the cemetery
features individual plaques giving the rank, name and birth date

---

[3] The cemetery was called upon to 'fulfil the function of cemetery-sanctuaries
whose rank would be equal to the Grave of the Unknown Soldier on Józef
Piłsudski Square in Warsaw' (Przewoźnik 1997, 12). It is widely acknowledged
to have successfully met these demands, and the high expectations of the
victims' families (*Katyń: Księga Cmentarna* 2000, LIII).

of each of the 4,421 victims at Katyn as well as a 'wall of memory' also inscribed with their names. Its design draws on a national Polish Katyn narrative strongly inflected by Roman Catholicism, as we saw in chapter 1. The wall, for instance, symbolizes a monumental 'portal' shifted into the depth of the burial ground 'by the power of human faith in justice'. The weight and power of the wall are meant to evoke Christ's tombstone, pushed aside 'by the power of hope and faith in the revelation of truth'. An underground bell mounted under the wall symbolizes a truth that cannot be hidden, even underground; its voice may be muffled but never silenced (Przewoźnik and Adamska 2010, 511). Most of the elements in the cemetery are rendered in red-coloured cast iron, representing the blood spilt in the forest. When the cemetery opened to the public on 28 July 2000, the widow of one of the Katyn victims, Irena Kalpas, said of the ceremony: 'For me [this] was the day of my husband's funeral. His real funeral. We Katyn families were dressed in black. The bell rang, we wept. I felt then that my husband had finally been buried not only symbolically but in actual fact [*naprawdę*]' (Hałacińska 2010).

The Polish decision to commemorate the victims with a military cemetery meant that the designers could draw on the established symbols and practices traditionally associated with similar sites in Poland and elsewhere in the Western world. It also reinforced Poland's classification of all the Polish deaths at Katyn as official military casualties, which was made despite the fact that there had been no formal declaration of war between Poland and the Soviet Union in 1939 and that many Polish civilians were also executed at Katyn. Under this classification, both the civilian and military dead were to be re-buried with full military honours. For the civilian Soviet victims of state terror buried in the same forest, however, there was no possibility of a similar distinction.

The Russian Memorial

The process of agreeing upon what form the Russian component of the Katyn memorial should take was more fraught and contentious. Whilst the Polish deliberations over the cemetery and its placement, function and design were conducted with a high degree of transparency, the Russian discussions were held behind closed doors at the eleventh hour. Long periods of stalling and deadlock were punctuated by bursts of frenetic activity, which generally preceded major ceremonies at the site, most notably when President Wałęsa laid the foundation stone in 1995 and when the memorial was officially opened to the public in 2000. International attention provided the additional impetus needed to push the project to fruition. Both the Russian and Polish sides expressed awareness that their actions were being observed by a global audience at the time. They compared Katyn to a stage on which memory was being performed 'under the spotlight' (Przewoźnik 2010) and 'on display before the entire planet' (Russian Deputy Prime Minister Yarov, cited in Krasnovskii 2006). Even in these conditions, it was necessary to fight for the release of the promised state funding at every stage of construction. In 1997, the head of the committee overseeing the Russian project complained of a 'complete absence of financing obstructing the whole process of the immortalization of the memory of the Russian victims of totalitarian repressions' ('Protokol' 1997). According to the architects, only 20 per cent of the promised funds actually materialized (Nevskaia 2002).

A team of Moscow architects headed by Mikhail Khazanov and Nikita Shangin designed the Russian component of the Katyn memorial and Mednoe memorial. Both are prominent figures whose assignments have included the reconstruction of the Bolshoi Theatre and other major state commissions, including Moscow government buildings. Shangin considers the Katyn memorial to be his most significant project. He undertook it with the conviction that a confrontation with the history of Katyn was more important for Russia than for Poland (Bukharina 2006). Shangin and the entire team of Russian architects were nonetheless mindful of the international character of the complex, which includes both separate spaces for private mourning and shared 'ritual grounds' for joint ceremonies. Two pilgrimage routes – one leading to the Polish Military Cemetery, the other to the Russian burial sites – branch out from the first ritual ground, where there stands a memorial stone similar to the Solovetskii Stone in Moscow (Iuzbashev 2004, and Katyn memorial website) (figure 7.1). These paths then reconverge south of the Polish cemetery, leading to an amphitheatre used for joint Russian–Polish ceremonies. A shared exit from this space spills out onto a raised 'Avenue of Memory', which symbolically separates the living from the dead and reminds visitors of

Figure 7.1 First ritual ground, Katyn Memorial. Photo by Julie Fedor.

the graves beneath them. It also helps facilitate the ongoing excavation of the site, most of which still remains uncharted.

The memorial in its current form represents, in the words of Shangin, 'only a drop in the sea' compared to the one originally conceived (Bukharina 2006). The vast majority – 85 per cent – of the plan was discarded after the conclusion of the opening ceremony. The project was to include, for instance, a 'Road to Eternity', a partially underground memorial in the form of a corridor lined with steel walls riddled with bullet holes and framed by mirrors and candles. Intended to allude to the boundlessness of Stalinist terror, to the unknown number of its victims, the corridor would rise up to ground level and then towards the sky before breaking off in mid-air (Bukharina 2006). That the original plan has not been realized in its entirety may be read as symptomatic of Russia's abortive mourning for the victims of Soviet terror. As Shangin remarks, 'The state does not want to deal with this [subject] in a genuine way. This theme is unpleasant for the state' (Bukharina 2006).

The memorial that has been built, its limited ambitions notwithstanding, represents an attempt on the part of Russian architects to depart from traditional Soviet models and to find new symbolic forms for memorializing the victims of state terror. In the words of architect Mikhail Khazanov, it is 'no customary

Mother-Motherland monument, no fraud, no soap bubble' (Nevskaia 2002). Before the official opening, a journalist commended the site for its lack of 'grieving mothers, bronze warriors, stone columns or eternal flames' (Novikova 1999). Indeed, the architectural team led by Khazanov and Shangin emphasized that the memorial was not a monument to heroism. It resists redemptive narratives, mythologizing gestures and reductive typologies. The glass doors of the entrance pavilion create a visual effect that breaks down the boundary between past and present, the dead and the living (figure 7.2). More generally, the memorial is, as it were, 'insiteful': it enlists and engages the earth where the dead lie and the forest that grew over their bones in an act of meaning-making (Iuzbashev 2004). In the absence of living human witnesses, it casts the forest as the 'mute witness' to the massacres (Przewoźnik 1997, 12). In 1997, the Polish and Russian architects attached to the project were all 'called upon to take exceptional care' to preserve the forest and acknowledge its importance as 'an essential substance of the memorial complexes', an entity 'uniquely and independently forming the emotional atmosphere of the memorial zones' (Bragin 1997, 2). As architect Khazanov acknowledged, 'For many people this language is incomprehensible. Many would prefer to see a monument to the unknown prisoner in the middle of a concrete square. But we could not cover over this soil with concrete. There are people in it' (Revzin 2001).

Figure 7.2   Entrance pavilion, Katyn Memorial. Photo by Julie Fedor.

Leading Russian architecture critic Grigorii Revzin praised the memorial's design for successfully introducing a new 'language' of memory to Russia:

> We have a huge tradition of memorial complexes in Russia. We have developed a language for talking on this theme. [The war memorials in] Volgograd, the Brest Fortress, the Piskarev Cemetery [for the victims of the Leningrad siege]. They combine grief, glory and the lessons to be learned from the feats that were accomplished for the sake of a great country. The problem is that all these monuments were built by the Soviet regime. They are memorials to deaths in the name of the Motherland, and in the name of the Soviet regime. [. . . In the case of Katyn,] we are dealing not with a monument to this regime but with a monument to those who were destroyed by this regime. And it is simply impossible to convey this meaning using the very same language in which that state glorified itself (Revzin 2001).

Writing in a popular newspaper, Revzin observed that the architectural style of this monument, which he defined as neomodernist, was significantly different from comparable examples in the West or East. Elsewhere, he said, neomodernism was a joyful aesthetic approach that celebrated the human connection to the natural world. The Katyn memorial translated this humble respect for nature in a new way: 'The same dirt, grass and trees – this is what the murdered have become'. In Revzin's view, this tragic note was a powerful response to both international neomodernism and the Soviet architectural tradition. He approved of the fact that the architects had not attempted to solve the problem by simply throwing money at it and building an ostentatiously spectacular monument: 'It would be unacceptable to say that [these people] died but we have spent a huge amount of money to immortalize them and now our debt to them is settled' (Revzin 2001).

A peculiar feature of the memorial is the random form of the mass graves, which are set off by jagged fences. Khazanov views the arrangement of these scattered execution pits as a 'document' in its own right, a riposte to the dearth of other forms of documentary evidence related to the Katyn massacres (Andreenkova 2009, 26). The design constitutes a refusal to derive comfort through recourse to redemptive narrative (Langer 2006) and to invest a sacrificial meaning in the mourned deaths (Etkind 2009).

It pays homage to the improvised and informal mourning practices that had previously arisen at Katyn and other sites of Soviet mass killing (Merridale 2000). Khazanov remarks that his architectural team was inspired by the ad hoc personal memorials created by visitors to the Katyn Forest before 2000: 'When we saw Katyn for the first time, this was a forest with evenly spaced trees, a cross and photographs that relatives had brought to attach to the trees. This was more powerful than any memorial, more powerful even than what the Poles later did [at the site]' (Nevskaia 2002). In an allusion to such personal practices of mourning, Khazanov and Shangin mounted icon lamps on the fences encompassing the mass graves. They evoked the form of a crust of bread placed over a drinking glass, items traditionally placed at Russian graves to feed the dead in the afterlife. Facilitating private grief was in keeping with the aspirations outlined in 1997 joint guidelines on the aesthetics of the Katyn memorials, which stipulated that the designers should create a space operative on both the individual and the official levels, capable of moving in equal measure 'the solitary pilgrim as well as the numerous participants of official solemn funereal ceremonies' (Bragin 1997, 2).

Khazanov and Shangin's opponents were horrified by the plans for the memorial. As members of one local history community club remarked, 'It is difficult to say what the authors were guided by, but it is hard to call this draft anything other than a mockery of the memory of the dead' (Krasnovskii 2001). Some families of the victims complained that, by stylizing the lamps to resemble crusts of bread and drinking glasses, the architects had turned the deceased into 'alcoholics'. Eventually a number of locals decided to take matters into their own hands and smashed the offending glasses, which were then replaced with more generic decorations (figure 7.3). These grievances and assaults were provoked in part by the secular character of the memorial's design.[4] The architects

---

[4] Some other instances of resistance to the monument can be read as indications that the effects of the old method of blaming the victims of Soviet terror have yet to dissipate fully. The architect Khazanov has said that there was 'very strong resistance' in Smolensk both to the Polish and the Russian memorials. Locals told him, 'we don't know who lies in these Katyn graves. Maybe they're all Smolensk prostitutes, or maybe thieves, robbers, crooks. That is, if they shot them, maybe there was a reason to shoot them?' (Nevskaia 2002; cf. Diukov 2011).

Figure 7.3   Russian graves, Katyn Memorial. Photo by Julie Fedor.

were opposed to introducing religious symbols at the site, but a ten-metre high steel Orthodox cross was nevertheless erected at the site, reportedly at the insistence of local authorities (Iuzbashev 2004).

The Russian Orthodox Church hierarchy has taken a somewhat ambivalent stance on the issue of the memorialization of the dead at Katyn. In 1994, the local Smolensk clergy cautioned not to disturb the dead by exhuming their remains (Grachev 1994). This position has since changed to accord with the emergence of the Orthodox discourse of 'new martyrdom', which has sought to displace the secular memory project advanced by such organizations as the 'Memorial' Society over the past decade (Bogumił 2010). This transhistorical discourse of martyrdom, notably, places no emphasis on the culpability of the perpetrators and re-casts Soviet terror as a Russian national trial. Speaking at Katyn in May 2005, the future Patriarch of the Russian Orthodox Church Kirill described Katyn as a 'Russian Golgotha', emphasizing that the only repentance possible was 'before God [. . .] not before other peoples':

> One can only repent before God. Our people have things to repent for: destroyed churches, for example. After all, walls were not only destroyed, but the life of people was destroyed as well. And the fact that we do not know how to preserve memory is our national sin. It is for this that we must repent (Krasnovskii 2006).

While it is not a part of the Katyn memorial complex, a new forty-metre-high Orthodox church, currently under construction nearby (and sponsored by the Rosneft petroleum corporation), will infuse more of the religious and ecclesiastical into the spatial and ideological horizons of the Katyn Forest.[5]

The Soviet Victims

A fundamental lack of knowledge about the precise location and number of the Soviet mass graves at Katyn has been perhaps the most daunting obstacle to the memorialization of its victims. Whereas the Polish victims are known, the Soviet victims remain almost completely anonymous. Their precise number remains unclear. This tragic lacuna presented a series of problems for the Russian architects. A great deal of flexibility had to be built into the design, with a view to enabling the memorial complex to evolve in response to ongoing archival and field research. When the authors created the original draft design in spring 1998, for instance, they were forced to construct five symbolic 'dummy' graves and then adapt the design when more information about the location of the sites came to light later that year (Gurskaia and Koneva 2010, 67). Last-minute changes also had to be made to the Avenue of Memory after builders uncovered more graves during construction; the Avenue now curves in places to avoid these sites.

By the time of the memorial's opening in 2000, nine Soviet 'fraternal' graves had been put forward for remembrance. These graves form the heart of the Russian part of the memorial complex (Andreenkova 2009, 26). Eight of these graves were discovered in the course of exploratory works in November 1998, while the ninth was uncovered accidentally during the memorial's construction. Together they constitute roughly only two per cent of the uncovered Soviet burial sites (Lapikova 2002). The vast majority

---

[5] Vladimir Putin has lent his support to this intermingling of the religious and the memorial, accompanying Patriarch Aleksei II on a 2007 visit to another Soviet mass grave, at Butovo near Moscow (a site which was officially handed over to the Orthodox Church in 1995) and visiting the site of the future Orthodox Church at Katyn together with Donald Tusk as part of the official Katyn commemoration ceremonies on 7 April 2010.

of the Soviet graves are located in the so-called Valley of Death, which is adjacent to the memorial site. Polish excavators discovered 150 burial sites here in 1994–5, and a local search group set up by the Smolensk Regional Administration's Committee for Youth Affairs uncovered another 277 in the autumn of 1995. The staff at the memorial complex are determined to transform the Valley into a place of pilgrimage and to ensure that visitors are informed about its history. As a first step, they inscribed the following on a memorial stone in the Valley in 2009:

> In the '30s–'40s of the twentieth century this part of the territory of the former dachas of the UNKVD for the Smolensk region became the site of the secret burial of many thousands of Soviet citizens – victims of the political tyranny of the Stalinist regime. Eternal memory to the innocent victims (Andreenkova 2009, 27–35).

This inscription was laid over a plaque dating to the stone's installation in 1995 and reading only that 'At this site a memorial in memory of the victims of political repressions is to be erected'. The additions to the text may appear minor, but they are heavily loaded and hard-won (figure 7.4). Advances in knowledge about the Soviet victims buried at Katyn have come slowly and in fits and starts. Only in 1991 did Soviet authorities first concede the actual presence of the remains of Soviet citizens at Katyn. A major breakthrough occurred in early 1995. In the lead-up to a visit by Wałęsa, the regional branch of the security services (then called the FSK, now the FSB) provided written confirmation that, based on their archival holdings, there were 'sufficient grounds' to assert that victims of political repressions were buried at the site. Nearly fifteen years later, on the eve of the high-profile seventieth anniversary of the Katyn massacres in 2010, the regional FSB also provided a list of the names of 2,997 executed Soviet citizens whose remains were believed to be beneath the forest ground. According to the staff at the memorial, the list represents only a fraction of the total number of victims. Nonetheless, its appearance was a milestone (Wojciechowski 2010). Sadly, FSB officials have seemingly since distanced themselves from the list and now claim to be unable to verify, confirm or provide any further information about it. Meanwhile, the memorial staff have placed both

Figure 7.4   Monument in the 'Valley of Death', Katyn Memorial. Photo by Julie Fedor.

FSB documents in prominent positions near the memorial entrance, using them as a wedge to prevent a half-open door to the truth from slamming shut.

Even when and if the doors to the Russian state archives are fully opened, an underlying problem related to both Katyn history and memory will still persist. This problem is the strategic 'ellipticism' endemic to NKVD recordkeeping. In the Stalinist period, the NKVD expended great effort to ensure that the burial sites of Soviet citizens – either those summarily shot or condemned to the camps – were not registered in documentation related to their sentencing or execution. As we saw in chapter 3, this practice led to selective holes in the institutional memory of the KGB many years later. To ascertain the precise location of a given individual's grave today is virtually impossible. The execution list provided to the memorial by the FSB, for instance, indicates the name, year of birth, nationality, profession and date of execution of the victims – but not the place of burial. The impotence of archival evidence in this regard undermines the petitions of citizens and activists seeking an official status for candidate burial sites and increases the likelihood that such sites will fall into disrepair.

This problem is particularly acute in documentation related to the Smolensk region, which was subjected to intense scrutiny and oversight due to the violent events of the war and German occupation (Andreenkova 2010, 9) and to the sensational discovery of Katyn in 1943. In general, one can make educated guesses about the burial sites based on the place and timing of sentencing (Khachaturova 2009, 101), but beyond such conjecture, little certainty is possible (Kornilova 2004, 9). Whilst methods have been devised for identifying remains in mass graves by cross-referencing execution lists with the estimated age of the exhumed bones, they remain prohibitively expensive and time-consuming. The lack of detailed archival evidence in the case of Katyn means that, whilst the presence of corpses at this site is undisputed, questions about their identities and provenance remain.

'Fictional' Victims

Alongside the thousands of Polish and Soviet citizens buried and now mourned in the Katyn Forest, the memorial also honours a third category of victims, a group of 500 Soviet POWs allegedly executed at Katyn by the Nazis in 1943. Local authorities erected a memorial plaque to these men in the 1980s (Gurskaia and Koneva 2010). They are, however, likely figments of propaganda. The POWs emerge as incidental characters in the Katyn cover-story produced by the Burdenko Commission in 1944, which claimed that in the spring of 1943 German authorities took Soviet prisoners from a nearby concentration camp to excavate the mass graves at Katyn and to falsify the evidence by removing exhumed items bearing dates later than April 1940, among other things. According to the Burdenko Commission, the POWs were then executed by the Nazis in a cover-up operation.

On the one hand, it is true that in April–June 1943 the Nazis used Soviet POWs, together with local residents, to carry out the Katyn exhumations. On the other hand, the claim that they were subsequently executed and buried at the site rests exclusively on the report of the Burdenko Commission, which was officially repudiated by the Soviet Union in 1990 (Lebedeva 2001, 428, 529–31). Given that the Burdenko Commission report is a tissue of doctored evidence and coached testimony, the story of the POWs must be considered unreliable at best. Early sceptics, for instance, noted that the Burdenko Commission report contained no information about the location of the alleged execution and burial of the POWs (Mackiewicz 1951, 224–5). Recent efforts by the Katyn memorial staff to find evidence confirming these shootings have all failed.

These Soviet POWs were in fact the first Soviet 'victims' of Katyn mentioned in official discourse during the Gorbachev era. In April 1988, when the Kremlin called for a joint Polish–Soviet memorial to be built on the site in response to growing Polish pressure, it was the 500 Soviet POWs who were to be commemorated there, not the thousands of Soviet victims of the NKVD buried at the site, who were still unmentionable and 'ungrievable' (Butler 2009). In September 1988, during the visit of a Polish delegation, foundation stones were indeed laid for the future memorial complex to Polish officers and for a monument to the Soviet POWs killed at Katyn. Even after the Soviet Union claimed responsibility for Katyn and acknowledged the presence of its own citizens in the mass graves, Russian state officials continued to foreground the Soviet POWs. In May 1994, the head of Russian counter-intelligence Sergei Stepashin briefed Prime Minister Chernomyrdin on the situation surrounding the Katyn memorial, warning that 'the accent has completely shifted to the re-burial and immortalization of the memory of the Polish prisoners-of-war'. Stepashin noted that his agency's archives held data indicating that, alongside the Poles buried at Katyn, 500 Soviet POWs had been shot there by the Germans. He recommended that it was of 'fundamental importance' that memorials to the Soviet victims be built simultaneously with the Polish constructions, not only in order to fulfil the debt to the memory of the dead, but to 'facilitate the raising of Russia's prestige' (Krasnovskii 2006).

In the summer of 1994, the Kremlin announced that recent archival findings had made it possible to establish the precise location of the burial site of the 500 Soviet POWs. The announcement was made simultaneously with the admission that the Katyn Forest also contained the remains of 'many hundreds of Russians who perished during the First World War and during the years of the Stalinist repressions' (Ermolovich 1994). One year later, Boris Yeltsin also invoked the Soviet POWs in his written address to Lech Wałęsa on the occasion of the Polish president's high-profile visit to Katyn. The relationship between the two leaders had frayed at this point. Yeltsin was conspicuously absent at the ceremony held to mark the laying of the foundation stone at the Polish Katyn memorial, and his address to Wałęsa frostily emphasized the non-Polish suffering associated with the site:

> We understand the feelings of the Poles well. After all, it was not only their fellow countrymen who were touched by the totalitarian terror. In the Katyn Forest alone, according to incomplete data, apart from the remains of Polish officers, around nine thousand victims of political repressions are buried, people of various nationalities. There is reliable information on the shooting by Hitlerites at this site of over five hundred prisoners-of-war, exploited during the war years in the construction of secret military installations. Therefore we view the Katyn Forest as a site of memory of the victims of totalitarianism and Nazism, where a monument to all those who suffered innocently ought to be created (Lebedeva 2001, 582).

Yeltsin's address introduced several changes to the Russian side of the Katyn story. The number of Soviet victims was raised from 'many hundreds' to 'nine thousand', and the assertion made by the Burdenko Commission that the Soviet POWs were forced to falsify evidence at Katyn was replaced by the claim that the prisoners had been used 'to construct secret military installations during the war'. In official Russian documents from this period, these two categories of Soviet Katyn victim – civilian, executed by the NKVD, and military, executed by the Nazis – are presented in tandem. Mentioning one category nearly always involves mentioning the other. The trope of the Soviet POWs in this way could be deployed conveniently and effectively in both foreign and domestic policy. Abroad, and particularly in relations with Poland, it offers a symmetrical, wartime Katyn victimization narrative. At home, it clouds public awareness of the identity of the Katyn perpetrator, the NKVD, with references to the dead as 'victims of totalitarianism and Nazism'. It also transforms the victims into meaningful sacrifices made for the sake of victory over fascism, a victory whose traditional narrative is threatened and undermined by remembering Katyn.

The alleged discovery of archival documents identifying the precise location of the mass grave of the Soviet POWs involved re-positioning the 1988 memorial plaque onto the route leading to the Polish section of the memorial. To date, no document has materialized to confirm this location or substantiate Stepashin's more general claims. Given the propaganda value of the issue, it is possible that the location was chosen for a purely political purpose, namely, to ensure that visiting dignitaries first pause to commemorate the Soviet POWs before proceeding elsewhere. This order was followed not only during President Wałęsa's visit to the site to lay the foundation stone in the summer of 1995 but also during the opening ceremony itself in 2000. The official procession began with a laying of wreaths at the Soviet graves and the memorial plaque to the 500 Soviet POWs, and only then, the local press noted, did ceremonies at the Polish military ceremony commence (Orlov 2000).

While some relatives of the victims are in favour of dismantling the Soviet POW memorial, the staff at the complex argue that it

Figure 7.5 Monument to Soviet POWs, Katyn Memorial. Photo by Julie Fedor.

should be left in place to testify to the history of the project. Indeed, this particular monument speaks eloquently to the relentless and contested conversation between the history and the memory of Katyn (figure 7.5). The grave is still visited during official rituals on anniversaries related to the war (e.g. Pavlova 2010, 4), but it does not feature in the excursion routes offered by the memorial staff. Guides pass it by without comment; if asked about it directly, they describe it as a 'political' monument. They might also explain to the site's Polish or Russian visitors that the mourning and remembrance of the Katyn dead is complicated not only by evidence purposefully contaminated or destroyed by their murderers, but also by the elaborate legacy of fabrications of the historical record.

Coda

'Katyn-2'

On 10 April 2010 the Polish presidential plane went down in the forests of Smolensk, killing all 96 members of a delegation on its way to a ceremony commemorating the seventieth anniversary of the Katyn massacres. Although the Smolensk crash was an accident, the tragic result of a combination of adverse weather conditions and human error, the impulse to read the catastrophe in the light of Katyn was a powerful one. In one stroke, the crash immediately called forth seventy years of mourning for the victims of Katyn. During the initial period of shock that followed the tragedy, Lech Wałęsa was only the most famous voice in a chorus labelling the disaster 'Katyn-2' (Kublik 2010). Indeed, the crash would bring in its wake a new wave of encounters with the memory of Katyn.

Unintended Sacrifice

The crash took place in what former Polish President Aleksander Kwaśniewski called a 'cursed place' situated a few miles away from Katyn Forest but at the very centre of Poland's historical mythology of sacrifice and martyrdom. For Polish historian Andrzej Nowak (2011a), this mythology is behind the political rivalry between President Lech Kaczyński, who perished in the crash, and Prime Minister Donald Tusk over the years 2007–10. Their rivalry marked, in a sense, a dramatic 'return' of history and memory to Polish public life at the turn of the twenty-first century. Both politicians *nolens volens* turned their gaze to the socialist past, diverging from the positions adopted by their predecessors Prime Minister Tadeusz Mazowiecki (1989–91), who sought to draw a 'thick line' between past and present, and President Aleksander Kwaśniewski (1995–2005), whose electoral slogan 'Let's Choose the Future' called upon Poles to look ahead, not back. In the wake of a series of historical controversies, from the debates over the 1941 Jedwabne pogrom to periodic scandals connected to documents uncovered in the archives of the Communist security service, such positions became untenable.

Alongside his twin brother Jarosław, Lech Kaczyński was one of the most politically active proponents of this historical mythology of sacrifice and martyrdom, which imagines Poland as the 'Christ of nations' and its suffering at the hands of Russia and Germany as a national 'Golgotha'. Their Law and Justice (PiS) party – which won both parliamentary and presidential elections in 2005 – has called for active state intervention in defence of Polish collective memory (Brier 2009) and, to some degree, cultivated a sense of moral panic around the idea of a crisis of Polish memory. A group of conservative historians and philosophers provided the ideological underpinnings for this platform (e.g. Cichocki *Power and Memory* 2005; Merta *Memory and Responsibility* 2005; *Polish History Policy* 2004) (Tokarz 2011). Lech Kaczyński had a keen sense of a mission to restore Polish memory and to educate the world about Polish history (Niżyńska 2010, 472–4). This mission was made manifest in one of his projects as Mayor of Warsaw (2002–5), the Museum of the Warsaw Uprising, which is noted for, among other things, its willingness to draw upon popular culture, from rap music to comic books, in order to make history more appealing to Polish youth (see, for instance, www.1944.pl). Similarly, the 2004 commemorations of the Warsaw Uprising that he organized had a significant resonance in Polish society. Focusing on the sacrificial heroism of the Poles and blaming the Soviet Union for neglecting to help this major anti-Nazi rebellion, these commemorations convinced many Polish politicians and intellectuals of the need for a robust memory policy that would be a cornerstone not only of domestic policy, but of foreign policy as well (Gawin and Kowal 2004). As president (2005–10), Lech Kaczyński took issues of memory to the international stage, condemning the Putin regime for a creeping rehabilitation of the Stalinist and Soviet legacies. In September 2009, he hosted a ceremony in Gdansk to commemorate the onset of the Second World War. Among the heads of state in attendance were Vladimir Putin and Angela Merkel. In opening the proceedings, Kaczyński emphasized the symbolic role of Katyn and compared it to the Holocaust. 'What is the comparison between the Holocaust and Katyn?' he asked. 'Jews died because they were Jews. Polish officers were killed because they were Polish officers' (Day 2009). Putin, of course, did not pursue this idea in his own remarks, emphasizing instead the number of Soviet losses during the war (Mal'gin 2009; Etkind 2009).

Once Donald Tusk became premier in 2007, however, Polish policy towards Russia bifurcated. Tusk is, after all, a trained historian who in 1987 ridiculed the Polish 'Romantic-imperial-messianic' tradition as a 'pathetic-grim-grotesque theatre of unfulfilled dreams and ungrounded longings'. In his view, Poland's national task is to find its place in 'the end of history' and, more specifically, to play the pragmatic role of mediator between the European Union and its trading partner Russia (Nowak 2011a). His minister for culture and national heritage, Bogdan Zdrojewski, once proclaimed that Poland should not become 'a country of necropolises and museums' (Smolar 2008, 61). The remark was a thinly veiled reference to Lech Kaczyński's politics of memory, a politics driven, in the view of Tusk and his allies, by a morbid fascination with victimhood and bloodshed (Romanowski 2010b).

Tusk's Civic Platform party (PO) – which was elected to government in 2007 and, as of November 2011, also holds the presidency – has sought to depart from the Romantic model of Polish memory and identity, viewing it as an obstacle to Poland's development and European integration, on the one hand, and an obstacle to the creation of viable economic relations with Russia, on the other. Tusk has framed this cleavage in terms of modernity vs anachronism (Nowak 2011a). Historians in this camp – such as Paweł Machcewicz, the director of the planned Museum of World War II, which Tusk announced in late 2007 would be built in his home town of Gdansk – argued that the time had come to correct the Kaczyński government's excessive focus on

Soviet crimes against Poles. Kaczyński had created a 'completely false image' of the Second World War in Poland whereby the German crimes were pushed 'into the shadows . . . as somehow less deserving of memory'. Writing in the wake of the Smolensk crash, Machcewicz (2010) asserted that the real state of Polish collective memory was closer to historical truth than the version propagated by PiS.

This deep ideological and memorial bifurcation in Polish politics was clearly manifested in Tusk and Kaczyński's duelling commemorations of the seventieth anniversary of the Katyn massacres in 2010. They were scheduled three days apart from one another: Tusk flew to Katyn on 7 April, Kaczyński on 10 April. (The discrepant timing of their trips is, to an extent, a legacy of the Katyn Lie: for decades, the precise dates of massacre were unknown. In Poland, for instance, the nationwide commemorative date observed by decision of the Polish parliament is 13 April, when the Germans announced to the world their discovery of the mass graves in 1943.) Only on 3 February 2010, well after his itinerary had been confirmed, did Kaczyński become aware of the plans for Tusk and Putin's preemptive meeting. Despite the divisive political posturing around the event, Kaczyński prepared a conciliatory speech for his commemoration ceremony on 10 April. Still speaking of 'the Polish Golgotha of the East' and framing Katyn as the 'most tragic station [of the Cross]', the Polish president nonetheless expressed the wish that 'the Katyn wound [would now] finally heal and cicatrize'. Typically a memory hawk, Kaczyński even wrote in this last text that 'we' – by which he meant both Poles and Russians – 'are already on the way' towards such healing. He was killed before he was able to give this speech, which also praised the Russians for 'what they have done in the past years' with respect to Katyn (Kaczyński 2010).[1]

It is in the context of Kaczyński's sacrificial discourse that his own accidental death became so meaningful. The magnitude of the disaster and its extraordinary location made the crash at Smolensk-Severnyi airport on 10 April a memory event of unique intensity. Adam Michnik (2010) described the powerful outpouring of

---

[1] Kaczyński also planned to decorate Russian activists from the 'Memorial' Society during his stay in Smolensk ('Katynskii rok' 2010).

emotions released by the disaster: 'The Smolensk catastrophe broke something in our Polish and Russian hearts. In the hearts of the leaders and of regular people. It was as if a gigantic dam opened – a dam behind which unexpressed words and gestures were piled up'. Polish Minister for Foreign Affairs Radosław Sikorski likewise announced an 'emotional breakthrough' in Russian–Polish relations (Kulish and Levy 2010). In this way, the last station of the 'Golgotha of the East' offered redemption and freed both sides from their entrenched positions. Rather than cicatrizing the wound, the crash opened it once more, but in this opening it promised the possibility of healing.

Russia Responds

The spontaneous outpouring of grief on the Russian side was perhaps the most striking consequence of the crash. Traffic routes surrounding the Polish Embassy in Moscow had to be closed off because so many mourners had rushed there to lay flowers and sign the book of condolences (Kolesnichenko et al. 2010). Similar scenes were witnessed in other cities throughout Russia (Rogoża 2010). This mass public performance of grief was also an act of mourning for the victims of Russia's own traumatic past. One Russian newspaper headline, 'A Doubling of Grief', played on the repetitions at work: not only had Smolensk 2010 amplified the echo of the Katyn of 1940 and provoked an outpouring of Polish grief, but it had unlocked and unleashed Russian grief as well (Kolesnichenko et al. 2010). For Russian journalist Ol'ga Allenova, these events seemed to indicate that Russian memory had entered a new phase, which might one day make it possible for her to find and visit the unknown grave of her great-grandfather, a victim of Stalinist terror (Allenova 2010). As a journalist at the influential Polish daily *Gazeta Wyborcza* remarked, 'Today Russia is weeping together with us. In Russia things are happening which Poles are looking at in amazement . . . Russia has opened up to Poland, but also to itself, to its history and to a coming to terms [*na rozrachunek*] with Stalinism' (Kurski 2010).

A key motif in the Russian commentary on the new tragedy near Katyn was the feeling of release engendered by the sense that something deeply significant had happened: something had 'shifted' [*sdvinulos'*] after the crash, in the words of Russian poet, journalist and scholar Lev Rubinshtein ('Posle tragedii' 2010). It was the uncannily iterative nature of the event – a 'Katyn-2' – that was at the core of its perception. A Polish public address to the Russian people issued shortly after the crash acknowledged this strange metaphysical doubling: 'Both these events are united by location and by pain, and if the first was the result of Stalinist terror, which also affected Russians themselves, then the second proved to be a misfortune for which we cannot blame the masters of the Russian land' (Miasnikov 2010). In effect, this time around, things could be done differently. The victims and the bereaved would be treated with care and respect. The newly dead would be given a decent burial. In so doing, perhaps the Katyn dead might also be laid to rest. The Russian authorities and the Russian public assumed the role of friend to the victim, recognizing and acknowledging pain and showing respect for suffering and grief.

The response on the part of Russian authorities was marked by strong expressions of empathy and solidarity. Pledges were made to ensure a swift, transparent investigation of the crash, and extensive support was provided to the victims' families. In an unprecedented gesture, President Medvedev declared 12 April a nationwide day of mourning, and the Russian parliament observed a moment of silence. Even more importantly, Wajda's *Katyn* was broadcast for the first time in a primetime Sunday evening slot on Russian state television on 11 April. (As noted in chapter 6, before the crash the film had been shown only on the *Kul'tura* arts and culture channel.) Polish academic Włodzimierz Marciniak interpreted the decision to re-screen *Katyn* as a desperate move aimed at warding off suspicions of Russian involvement in the crash ('Marciniak' 2010) and to send 'a signal to the world that the [Katyn] problem had been solved' ('Rosja' 2010). Whatever the motivation, the results were impressive: fourteen million Russians watched the film in the two screenings ('Świat' 2010). Previously opinion polls had found that less than a quarter of Russians had heard of Katyn (Moshkin 2010); by mid-April this figure rose to 74 per cent. The number of people who remained unaware or unconvinced that the massacres were carried out by the NKVD, however, was still surprisingly high (Levinson 2010).[2] Wajda later said that he considered the screening of *Katyn* on Russian state television to be one of the greatest achievements of his career: 'Just as Russia is searching for a way out of [. . .] the Soviet epoch, my film is in some sense taking part in this process' (Rokossovskaia and Lisinova 2011; Rokossovskaia 2010).

Post-Smolensk Poland

The unity in grief elicited by the catastrophe was intense but short-lived. It soon broke down, exposing fault-lines that now, in a paradoxical turn of events, only seem to have been aggravated by the plane crash. In Poland, these divisions were first manifested in the protests which followed the announcement that the remains of Lech Kaczyński and his wife were to be buried in Krakow's Wawel Cathedral, a site traditionally reserved for the burial of Polish monarchs and national heroes (see Niżyńska 2010). This announcement sparked the first in a long series of battles over the meaning of the Smolensk crash.

For many Poles, the victims were killed on a pilgrimage, en route to a memorial rite of great significance. It is no exaggeration to say that many of the victims had devoted their life's work to the struggle for the memory of Katyn. Among the victims were the leading figures in that struggle, the heads of the major Katyn groups and institutions described in chapter 1, such as Andrzej Sariusz-Skąpski, the head of the Federation of Katyn Families; Andrzej Przewoźnik, head of the ROPWiM and the driving force

---

[2] Responses to the question 'Who, in your opinion, organized the executions of the Polish officers in Katyn?' were divided as follows: the Stalinist leadership of the USSR: 35%; the Hitlerite leadership of Germany: 18%; and 'don't know/ no opinion': 47%. The results for the under-25 age group were especially striking; for this group, the proportion of those responding 'don't know/no opinion' was even higher (56%). Moreover, more young people identified the perpetrators as German (23%) rather than Soviet (21%). Respondents were also asked whether they had heard that NKVD responsibility for the massacres had been established in documentary form. Forty-seven per cent said they were unaware of this fact, while another 28% said they had heard this but were unconvinced (Levinson 2010).

behind the construction of the Polish Katyn cemeteries in Russia and Ukraine; Janusz Kurtyka, head of the Institute for National Remembrance; Tomasz Merta, historian and Deputy Minister of Culture and National Heritage; the leaders of the Katyn Committee and the Polish Katyn Foundation. President Kaczyński gathered and led this group of enthusiasts of memory and clearly belonged to it. Should their deaths be remembered as a kind of martyrdom in the service of the memory of Katyn? The surviving families of some of the victims were determined that this should be the case and formed the Katyn 2010 Families' Association. The name of this association has provoked a conflict with the Federation of Katyn Families, which disputes the new group's right to use the Katyn name.

The crash rent asunder the configuration of political forces in Poland. The positing of a direct line of continuity between the two events, Katyn-1 and Katyn-2, became a political bone of contention in the months following the crash. Efforts to bury Lech Kaczyński at Wawel Castle on the banks of the Vistula River in Krakow – to install him, in effect, in a pantheon of great Polish leaders and martyrs – was the first sortie in a new memory war. Some of those who protested the burial at Wawel broke the taboo against speaking ill of the dead in spectacular fashion, rallying on the streets dressed in oversized faux crowns and bearing banners with slogans like 'Bury me in Wawel too!' Images from advertising billboards promoting 'Lech' beer with the slogan 'A Cold Lech', which appeared (apparently coincidentally) near the Presidential Palace in Warsaw around the time of the crash, went 'viral' on the Polish internet (Murawski 2011).[3] Later, the government announced that a cross erected by scout groups near the castle in April in memory of the Smolensk crash would be relocated, providing a rallying point for those who refused to accept that the crash was accidental and who instead viewed it as another act of Russian violence against Poles.

The attempt to move this makeshift cross incited a long protest, which became emblematic of the struggle over the meaning of the Smolensk catastrophe. Jarosław Kaczyński asserted that '[i]f

---

[3] The producers maintain that this advertising campaign had been planned months earlier (Odorczuk 2010).

President Komorowski removes the cross, it will be clear who he is and which side he is on in debates concerning Polish history and Polish relations' (Olszewska and Szpala 2010). For the protesters who gathered in support of the cross, the crash at Smolensk was inextricably entwined with the Katyn massacre. They bore banners reading 'Wake up Poland!', 'Katyn Isn't Over' and 'Are the Traitors and the NKVD So Powerful?'. They pledged to defend the cross 'to the death'. The resulting stand-off, which was punctuated by periodic flare-ups, dragged on through the summer of 2010. Here Poland's distinctive and highly performative memory culture was strongly in evidence. The self-styled 'defenders of the cross' tied themselves to the cross, wept and shouted, at times coming to physical blows with young participants of counter-protests, some of whom mocked and provoked the cross defenders. Other protesters saw the conflict as an opportunity to assert a secular Polish identity based on a strict separation of Church and state. The right place for a cross, they said, was a church.

These struggles were recorded in the documentary film *Solidarni 2010* (2010) and its sequel *The Cross* (*Krzyż* 2011), which aimed at demanding 'the truth about Smolensk'. The conservative media hailed Ewa Stankiewicz, who directed both films, as Poland's new Antigone (Leszczyński 2011). (For the meaning of Antigone for Wajda and his film *Katyn*, see chapter 2.) Stankiewicz's films purported to be authentic, unscripted footage of the spontaneous responses of ordinary Poles to the crash. Yet the newspaper *Gazeta Wyborcza*, a vocal opponent of the political instrumentalization of the Smolensk crash by the PiS camp, claimed that one Pole shown in the film sobbing as he alleged Putin had 'blood on his hands' was in fact a professional soap-opera actor ('Solidarni 2010' 2010). Since then, 'Solidarni 2010' rallies have featured banners proclaiming, in a surreal, metaperformative fashion, 'We are not actors!' Polish theatre scholar Dariusz Kosiński subsequently called these events 'political street theatre', enumerating the uncanny ways in which the proponents of the Smolensk myth were acting out the great works of Poland's literary canon. To an extent, his critique evoked the rhetoric that Tusk had employed over two decades earlier in his historical work:

We are concluding a pact with the dead . . . [The poet Mickiewicz asserted that] particular to the religiosity of Slavs is belief in vampires [and] werewolves [that exist] between the living and the dead and are capable of influencing the living. Those who see an element of predestination in the post-Smolensk drama [. . .] are scratching at their wounds (Kosiński 2011; see also 'Zbigniew Mikołejko' 2010, 'Stasiuk' 2011).

The hostile relations between Tusk and Lech Kaczyński, their respective relations with Russia, and the macabre character of the Smolensk catastrophe fed various conspiracy theories that proliferated on the internet and in the tabloid press (Chaciński 2010). These conspiracy theories invoked and in various ways acted out the memory of the Katyn massacre. Jarosław Kaczyński, Lech's twin brother who became the new head of the PiS party after the crash, insisted that the Katyn massacre and the crash at Smolensk be read as two consecutive chapters in the same story.[4] In fact, he used the term 'crime' (*zbrodnia*), the conventional Polish label for the Katyn massacres, to refer to the crash. Speaking at the funeral of one of the Smolensk victims, he proclaimed that 'we must bear witness – just like the generation shot in Katyn Forest and like those who perished seventy years later, wishing to pay respect to [that generation]' (Pilawski 2011a). He moderated this rhetoric as a candidate in the Polish presidential elections over the course of the summer 2010, only to resurrect it again after his loss to Bronisław Komorowski, who is a trained historian like his ally Donald Tusk. Kaczyński in fact blamed his defeat on a campaign manager who had advised him not to use the Smolensk theme (Uhlig 2010). Kaczyński's Law and Justice (PiS) party would go on to speak of the 'Smolensk assassination', advocating, with clear references to Katyn, a duty to fight for the right to remember the dead and to pursue memory in the face of those determined to falsify and obliterate it. The 'Smolensk Lie', echoing the 'Katyn Lie' of the Communist era, became a new political catchphrase.

One of the first to give a full articulation of this new 'Smolensk myth' was Polish conservative politician and publicist Ludwik

---

[4] Politicians were not the only ones giving credence to conspiracy theories. Even veteran campaigners who fought the Katyn Lie in the Communist era in both Poland and Russia lent their authority to allegations of Russian foul play or of deliberate obfuscation of the circumstances of the crash on the part of the Kremlin ('Zaniepokojeni' 2010; Trznadel 2010).

Dorn. In a series of articles and interviews in May and June 2010, Dorn made the case for viewing Smolensk as a 'blood sacrifice'. A trained sociologist, Dorn argued that, given the relatively bloodless nature of Poland's transition from Communism, the Polish Third Republic had hitherto lacked a foundation myth based on bloodshed, without which any state would ultimately remain unconvincing, in his view (Dorn 2010; Brzeziecki 2010). Previously, bitter conflicts had been fought over the creation of a foundation myth for independent Poland. While political moderates based it on the 1989 Round Table Talks that had negotiated an end to Communism, Lech Kaczyński sought to promote in its place the heroic Warsaw Uprising, viewed by many of his opponents as an emblem of the futility of the Romantic Polish tradition. According to Dorn, however, both of these events had been overshadowed by Smolensk as a foundational event.

One opponent of the mythologization of Smolensk commented bitterly, 'The Russians do not provoke us into uprisings anymore; nowadays we provoke ourselves into them. Our political scavengers fed off the Museum of the Warsaw Uprising; today they are feeding on Smolensk' (Michalski 2010). Indeed, the notion of Smolensk as a blood sacrifice inextricably connected to the memory of Katyn was a common motif in responses to the crash. In a homily, Fr Marian Putyra asked, for instance, 'Has that Katyn earth demanded still more Polish blood?! How much more of that blood needs to be spilled in order that the truth about that drama be finally made clear?' ('Ile ofiar' 2010). As Bishop of Świdnica Ignacy Dec commented on 11 April 2010, 'We hope that this sacrifice of the life of our best sons and daughters will help to show the world the truth [about Katyn]' (Szostkiewicz 2010, 22–3). Thus for some in Poland, the crash was inscribed into the Polish tradition of martyrdom and packaged as a critical 'history lesson' for the European Union. For others, however, this bloodshed could be used to transform Polish–Russian relations. In the words of Adam Michnik, 'Today, out of the blood that was spilled seventy years ago at Katyn and again last Saturday at Smolensk, an authentic community of Polish and Russian fates is being born' (Michnik 2010).

New President Bronisław Komorowski, who defeated Jarosław Kaczyński in the 2010 election, declared that his history policy would be aimed at uniting, not dividing, Polish society ('Prezydent Komorowski' 2010). His historical advisor, Tomasz Nałęcz, asserted that Komorowski opposed the use of history as a political weapon, even though he personally shared many of Lech Kaczyński's views about the past (Pilawski 2011b). Komorowski's political will was soon put to the test by events surrounding the ninetieth anniversary of the 1920 Battle of Warsaw of the Soviet–Polish War (1919–21), in which many Red Army POWs were killed. The event of these Red Army deaths during the war has been framed by some in Russia as an 'anti-Katyn'; indeed, as we noted in the introduction and chapter 6, Vladimir Putin and others have rationalized the Katyn massacre as Stalin's revenge for these Red Army losses. Komorowski's office focused the commemorative ceremonies not on the Polish victory over the Red Army, but on the unveiling of a new monument built at the site where the remains of twenty-two Red Army soldiers had been discovered two years earlier on a battlefield in Ossów, near Warsaw. A symbol of Polish–Russian reconciliation, the monument was intended to reciprocate the establishment of the memorial complexes at Katyn and Mednoe.

While they predated the Smolensk crash, the plans for the Ossów monument became prominent after the catastrophe due to a renewed public focus on Soviet war graves on Polish soil. On 9 May 2010, a large group of Polish intellectuals and civic figures – including Archbishop Józef Życiński, filmmaker Andrzej Wajda, poet and Nobel Prize laureate Wisława Szymborska, the first post-Communist Prime Minister Tadeusz Mazowiecki – issued a controversial 'Appeal' spearheaded by *Gazeta Wyborcza*. The Appeal called upon young Poles to light candles at Soviet war graves on Victory Day as a mark of respect and gratitude for the Russian response to Smolensk. Critics of this Appeal feared that it presaged a wholesale capitulation to the Russian narrative of the Red Army's liberation of Poland. Historian Adam Hlebowicz commented, for instance, 'I cannot understand at all the linkage being drawn between lighting candles on the graves of Soviet soldiers and the remembrance by Russians of the presidential plane victims . . . I have the impression that in the candle-lighting action we are dealing with ideology. But what kind, and in whose service?' (Hlebowicz 2010, 174).

The Ossów monument took the form of a large Orthodox cross and twenty-two granite bayonets sticking out of the earth. For historian Andrzej Nowak, the form of the monument represented an act of violence against the dead and served as yet another manifestation of a 'stubborn relativization of the Katyn crime' sponsored by Putin (Nowak 2011b). Following vandalism and protests, the ceremony at Ossów had to be postponed and the Russian ambassador's car turned back at the last moment (Sroczyński 2010). The monument was vandalized again, but finally unveiled on 2 November 2010, the twenty-two granite bayonets now replaced by twenty-two candle-holders.[5] The Orthodox cross, which Nowak describes as a 'giant question-mark' over the graves, remains in place (Nowak 2011c).

Post-Smolensk Russia

Meanwhile, in Russia, the post-Smolensk opening made possible new official postures towards the memory of Stalinism, a point that the Russian parliament formally acknowledged in its resolution on Katyn in November 2010. According to some, the outpouring of support and grief after the crash 'humanized' Russia in the eyes of Poland and the international community. Polish commentaries spoke, for instance, of 'Russia's new face' (Romanowski 2010a) and 'the Russia of emotions, of compassion, of the human impulse towards help and solidarity' (Sienkiewicz 2010). As Russian journalist Viktor Shenderovich (2010) remarked, 'Perhaps no one was expecting anything but vileness from us. And we succeeded in pleasantly surprising the Poles.' The warmth of the international response to the Russian handling of the Smolensk crash served as an important lesson for Moscow, highlighting the considerable political capital to be gained by technical and historical transparency. A draft of the 'de-Stalinization programme' produced by President Dmitrii Medvedev's advisers in 2011, for instance, cited the Katyn case as a model of demonstrating how Russia might profitably use memory politics in order to strengthen the country's 'international prestige'. The document notes that:

---

[5] It was defaced once more in September 2011 on the anniversary of the Soviet invasion of Poland with graffiti that read, 'You cut them down with the sickle, you finished them off with the hammer – Katyn 2010' (Sroczyński 2011).

The President's condemnation of the totalitarian regime and the Prime Minister's genuflection before the Katyn cross have already played an obvious positive role. Having recognized that the whole of Russia is a 'big Katyn', having begun to extend gestures of respect to the victims of the totalitarian regime independently, voluntarily, without coercion, the country can only arouse respect on the part of all normal people and nations ('Obshchenatsional'naia gosudarstvenno-obshchestvennaia programma' 2011).

In late June 2010, Konstantin Kosachev, chair of the Russian parliamentary committee for international affairs, argued that Russia caused damage to its reputation by defending the Soviet past in the international arena. Kosachev advocated instead the formulation of a new 'historical doctrine' that would be couched in terms comprehensible to Russia's foreign partners. He argued that such a strategy could protect Russia against future demands for compensation for the victims of Soviet crimes (Kosachev 2010). As discussed in chapter 6, Sergei Karaganov, an expert in international relations and an influential lobbyist, deployed the Katyn metonym in an article of July 2010 entitled 'The Russian Katyn'. In unusually strong words, he called upon Russia to 'find within herself the strength to admit that the whole of Russia is one big Katyn, strewn with the mostly nameless graves of millions of the victims of the [Soviet] regime'. Karaganov argued that much remained to be done in order to overcome the legacy of the twentieth century; in fact, he framed the failure to do so as 'one of the main roots of our problems'. He called for Russia to be 'strewn with monuments to the victims of Soviet Stalinism' and for crosses or other monuments to the victims of Stalinism to be erected alongside monuments to fallen soldiers. He also suggested that young people be mobilized for this task,

> a truly patriotic youth movement, which would seek out the names of these fellow citizens of ours and return them to us, so that they might be etched into these obelisks. This could also become a movement uniting the peoples [. . .] After all the regime destroyed the best individuals from all the nations [. . .] Everyone could be found amongst the butchers too (Karaganov 2010).

Responding in the pages of *Gazeta Wyborcza*, journalist Wacław Radziwinowicz noted that Karaganov's article marked a considerable departure from comments he delivered in Poznań two years earlier. 'Poles simply have a Katyn complex', he was quoted as saying. 'They must cure themselves of it on their own' (Radziwinowicz 2010). An article in the newspaper *Rzeczpospolita* gave an extended version of his remarks: 'You have a Katyn complex [. . .] you must cure yourselves of it. We are not your doctors. I will remind you that we were not [the only ones] who created the Cheka, the forerunner of the KGB: there were [also] Poles, Lithuanians and one Latvian in it' (de Lazari 2010). According to other Polish publications, Karaganov also said that '[w]e admit that Stalin murdered [the Polish prisoners], Putin even apologized for this, though I do not completely understand why. Unofficially we apologized long ago. We do not want to do so publicly, however, because you will immediately start to demand compensation' (Radziwinowicz 2010). Polish responses faulted Karaganov for his inconsistent comments, but they did not attend to a more profound issue at the heart of his use of the Katyn metonym. While admirable in its confrontation with the Stalinist past, Karaganov's claim that 'the whole of Russia is one big Katyn' threatens to deprive the Katyn massacres of their specificity. Unlike many other crimes perpetrated across the vast Soviet territory, the Katyn massacres were, after all, an act of mass murder directed against foreign nationals in an undeclared war.

Putin's return to the presidency in 2012 likely means that Medvedev's new de-Stalinization programme will not be realized. Nonetheless, the case illustrates the way in which the Smolensk crash created an opportunity to forge a template for a new narrative of the history of Soviet state terror, which could help with Russia's plans to project 'soft power' around the globe. Karaganov's formulation of Russia as 'one big Katyn', however, is far from being commonly accepted among the Russian populace. As recently as 2011, Russian tabloids and Communist newspapers circulated a competing narrative of events in which the Smolensk crash was cast as the consequence of 'stirring up' the past. The narrative aspires to the status of morality tale, positing that Lech Kaczyński, who saw himself as fulfilling a sacred mission to restore Polish memory and educate the world about Polish history, brought about the crash by showing an unseemly, unnatural level of interest in the past. Indeed, on the first anniversary of his death, *Pravda* linked the Smolensk catastrophe to Kaczyński's 'excessive attention to issues of history in current politics', asserting that '[i]n a mystical way, near Smolensk, at an historical site, the lover of history Lech Kaczyński himself became part of history'. According to *Pravda*, 'Lech Kaczyński lived in the captivity of historical myths, built his whole politics in accordance with historical myths and endlessly speculated on the problems of the past. And now his death has been transformed into a new Polish myth' ('Lekh Kachin'skii' 2011).

Smolensk One Year On

Sadly, the outpouring of shared grief after the Smolensk crash was only an abortive catharsis in Polish–Russian relations. A year after the crash, the goodwill generated by the Russian response in the days following the crash has largely dissipated and given way to mutual provocations, accusations and suspicions. This dynamic in Polish–Russian memory politics was strongly in evidence in the lead-up to the first anniversary of the crash, which was plagued by a series of scandals. The first was caused by Zuzanna Kurtyka, widow of Janusz Kurtyka, the head of the Polish Institute for National Remembrance who died in the Smolensk crash. Since her husband's death, Zuzanna Kurtyka has been a vocal and active fighter for the 'truth' about Smolensk. In the months following the crash, she was a prominent fixture in the media, functioning as an iconic personification of Poland's grief. At one point, she revealed that her husband Janusz had predicted that if he ever went to Russia, he would never return (Kurtyka 2010).

Zuzanna Kurtyka sees a direct link between Smolensk and Katyn and foregrounds it in the name of the support and lobbying group that she founded in late June 2010, the Association of Katyn 2010 Families. In November 2010, she and other widows from the Katyn 2010 group mounted a plaque to the victims of the crash during a pilgrimage to Smolensk on a memorial stone that the Governor of Smolensk had placed at the airport as a gesture of sympathy. The text of their Polish-language plaque included a phrase describing the Katyn massacre as 'genocide'. They apparently travelled to Russia carrying an electric drill and a generator for the express purpose of applying the plaque to the stone, without seeking permission or approval to do so. The Russian Foreign Ministry duly protested their actions, and the local policemen who failed to stop Kurtyka and her colleagues were reportedly dismissed over the incident (Radziwinowicz 2011). The plaque was left in place, however, until the night before President Komorowski's wife was to arrive for official commemorations of the first anniversary of the crash. At this time, the plaque was removed under cover of darkness and replaced with a bilingual Polish–Russian variant that made no mention of Katyn or genocide (Sokolov 2011).

Kurtyka's actions evoke the Antigone sequence in Wajda's *Katyn* (see chapter 2), in which Agnieszka inscribes the true facts of her brother's death at Katyn on his tombstone. The acts of mounting and dismounting the plaque were symmetrically aggressive and provocative, confirming for some the Russian stereotype of the Pole as determined at all costs to 'spoil' the prospects of harmonious relations and confirming for others the Polish stereotype of Russian officialdom as incapable of admitting its crimes.[6] While newspapers in Moscow expressed outrage that foreigners dared to enter Russia with a drill, Polish academic Włodzimierz Marciniak alleged that the Russian side had undertaken a 'professionally conducted political provocation'. Marciniak described this 'provocation' as very much in keeping with the contradictory and inconsistent history politics that Russia had been pursuing with regard to Poland for at least a year ('Prof. Włodzimierz Marciniak' 2011, 'Marciniak' 2011). Komorowski's historical advisor Nałęcz said that the Russian response had thrown relations 'back to the neolithic period' as far as the Katyn issue was concerned. He noted that this development was particularly frustrating given that the dialogue about Katyn had been 'only a few steps' from its definitive resolution ('To nas cofa do neolitu' 2011). Meanwhile, Polish Foreign Minister Radosław Sikorski, among others, soberly criticized the Katyn 2010 group for mounting the plaque unilaterally, without seeking Russian agreement. Sikorski

---

[6] Ol'ga Maiorova has traced the process whereby the Poles were labelled the Slavic family's 'vyrodok' ('black sheep') due to their Western orientation in the 1860s and the threat that their resistance posed to narratives of the Russian Empire as a peace-loving liberator (Maiorova 2001).

was in turn condemned for 'attacking widows' ('Sikorski atakuje wdowy' 2011).

The scandal prompted protests near the Russian Embassy in Warsaw, where the crowd branded Putin a 'murderer' and Tusk a 'traitor' and burned Putin in effigy (Asadchii and Chernenko 2011).[7] In Moscow, a popular newspaper described Polish society as 'on the brink of a nervous breakdown' and 'tormented by schizophrenic delirium' brought on by months of Russophobic media campaigns (Aslamova 2011). All of these events threatened to jeopardize President Komorowski's participation in the official anniversary commemoration ceremonies at Smolensk. There were reports that Komorowski refused to lay a wreath at the airport memorial stone as planned (Pashina and Lutchenkova 2011). A compromise option was devised, with the Polish and Russian presidents laying wreaths at a 'memorial birch tree' instead (Skwieciński 2011). The 'genocide' plaque that unleashed the scandal was eventually retrieved by the Katyn 2010 group and moved to the Katyn Chapel in the Warsaw Basilica of the Holy Cross and then to Poland's most important religious pilgrimage site, Jasna Góra Monastery. It featured prominently in the Family Pilgrimage ceremonies organized by the influential conservative Catholic radio station Radio Maryja in the summer of 2011, taking up a place in the ranks of Katyn's sacred relics.

This odd incident ultimately sparked a new round of debates over how to classify the Katyn massacres. The Polish Foreign Ministry adheres to the Institute of National Remembrance's 2004 definition of the massacres as genocide (Wroński 2011). This

---

[7] In May 2011, in an apparent retaliation against the 'genocide plaque' episode, unknown actors placed a plaque commemorating the deaths of Russian soldiers in Polish captivity on a memorial stone in Poland marking the ninetieth anniversary of Polish independence. The Russian-language inscription responded to the Polish assertion of 'genocide' with a reference to 'Polish death camps', setting into stone a particular memory of the past meant to provoke conflict and outrage in the present. As pointed out by Nikita Petrov, a historian from the 'Memorial' Society, the mounting of this new plaque realized a scenario that the Russian Foreign Ministry envisioned in a statement issued during the genocide plaque scandal: 'We can only imagine what the reaction of the Polish authorities would be if someone were to place any kind of emblem without permission on memorial sites in Poland' (Skwieciński and Zalesiński 2011).

official position was called into question in April, after Andrzej Wajda and presidential advisor Roman Kuźniar each stated that they did not consider Katyn to be a genocide ('Wajda o Katyniu' 2011). Responding in an open letter, a group of politicians and publicists called for Kuźniar's dismissal and demanded that President Komorowski clarify his position on this issue (Wroński 2011; 'Politycy i publicyści' 2011). Komorowski's office responded by confirming its adherence to the 'genocide' classification ('Sovetnik prezidenta' 2011).

Following the crash, references to Katyn emerged in surprising and sometimes baffling contexts. These references telescoped time and shuffled Katyn with the Smolensk crash and other central events in modern Polish history, from the Warsaw Uprising to martial law. In January 2011, upon the release of an international report on the causes of the crash, one PiS official compared the findings to a 'shot to the back of the head' ('PiS ostro o raporcie MAK' 2011). Such attempts to frame the Smolensk catastrophe according to the Katyn template and the lacrimogenetic narrative of foreign occupations and uprisings reached Brussels in 2011, when the PiS party staged a photographic exhibition in the European Parliament to mark the first anniversary of the Smolensk catastrophe. Entitled 'Truth and Memory', the exhibition featured, for instance, a photograph of an officer using a crowbar to destroy a window, apparently making a joyful gesture towards his friends. Its initial caption read: 'The Russians destroyed the wreck of the plane that crashed near Smolensk on 10 April 2010'. Other captions drew direct connections between Smolensk and Katyn: 'Many Poles call the catastrophe at Smolensk the second Katyn. The Polish elite perished in both tragic events. All of them lost their lives in Russia' ('Awantura' 2011). Before the opening of the exhibition, these captions were removed by officials of the European Parliament.

The Katyn massacre haunts the *White Book of the Smolensk Tragedy*, which was published in the summer of 2011 by the Polish parliament's Group for the Study of the Causes of the Smolensk Catastrophe, a PiS initiative dating to July 2010. The Group was led by Antoni Macierewicz, who referred to the crash as a crime (*zbrodnia*) from the outset (Potkaj 2010). The release of the *White Book* was seemingly timed to upstage a rival parliamentary investigation headed by Jerzy Miller whose report on the crash was due to be presented to Tusk shortly afterwards (Lewand-owska 2011). Macierewicz claims that the *White Book* is not a report but a collection of documents, compiled in defence of the public's right to factual information about the catastrophe. The facts gathered in the book are clearly intended to suggest that Lech Kaczyński was murdered precisely for his historical policy on Katyn. The book's appendix, for example, includes various quotations from September 2009 in which Kaczyński described Katyn as a crime of genocide (*Biała księga* 2011, 25–6), suggesting a causal connection between these statements and the events of 10 April 2010. On 10 July 2011, Jarosław Kaczyński endorsed the *White Book* in his address to participants of the monthly 'march of memory' of Smolensk, held on the tenth day of each month since August 2010 ('Kaczyński' 2011b).

The sociologist Hanna Świda-Ziemba complains that projects like the *White Book* have surrendered the memory of Katyn to Smolensk and made the massacres a mere footnote to the crash (Świda-Ziemba 2011). A singular event of unspeakable brutality in the geographical centre of Europe, Katyn has been relativized by its double, Katyn-2. This dynamic, which has also made the singular event of the crash dependent on a historical antecedent, threatens to stunt the work of mourning. In the words of Zbigniew Gluza, the head of the KARTA Centre, an authoritative NGO that collects evidence on the recent history of Poland and Eastern Europe: 'Andrzej Wajda said to me in March this year that he has the feeling that the dead victims of Katyn are still here, demanding something . . . [C]ertainly we have not yet managed to bid farewell to our dead. They still seem to be waiting' (Borowska 2010).

The dead are still waiting, while the living struggle to 'remember'. On the first anniversary of the crash, Jarosław Kaczyński held an alternative rally at the Presidential Palace in Warsaw, where he drew vague links between the Smolensk catastrophe and Polish historical struggles for survival, hinting strongly once again that the plane crash had not been accidental. The speech was framed as a defence of 'memory', which Kaczyński said had been 'trampled'. Kaczyński described the crash victims as having been 'betrayed at dawn', deploying a famous line from a poem by Zbigniew Herbert and prompting a public protest from Herbert's widow, who condemned the political exploitation of her husband's work ('Oddzielmy' 2011). At one point Kaczyński proclaimed that '[t]hose who wanted to kill memory have lost, they have failed' ('Kaczyński' 2011a). The crowd chanted in response: 'We remember! We remember!'

Bibliography

Where no author is given for a text, we provide an abbreviated title alongside the year of publication at the beginning of the reference heading. All websites were accessed on 4 January 2012.

Abraham, Nicolas and Maria Torok 1994. *The Shell and the Kernel: Renewals of Psychoanalysis*. Chicago, IL and London: University of Chicago Press.

Agamben, Giorgio 2002. *Remnants of Auschwitz: the Witness and the Archive*. New York: Zone Books.

Allenova, Ol'ga 2010. 'Katyn' kak rubezh', *Kommersant"* (14 April), http://www.kommersant.ru/doc-rss/1354628.

Andreenkova, G.A. 2009. 'K voprosu o memorializatsii ostankov sovetskikh grazhdan – zhertv repressii na territorii Memoriala "Katyn' "', *Vestnik Katynskogo Memoriala*, 9.

Andreenkova, G.A. 2010. 'K voprosu o vyiavlenii, izuchenii i publikatsii muzeinykh predmetov, sviazannykh s Katynskoi tragediei', *Vestnik Katynskogo memoriala*, 10.

Andriukhin, Vadim 2010. 'Ekho Katyni', *Novoe delo* (25 May), http://www.novdelo.ru/index.php?nav=nnews&viewart=52458.

'Andzhei Vaida' 2010. 'Andzhei Vaida atrymau navukovuiu stupen' ad Belarusi', *Radio Svaboda* (7 April), http://www.svaboda.org/content/article/2005014.html.

Aristotle 1987. 'On Memory', in J. L. Ackrill (ed.), *A New Aristotle Reader*. Princeton, NJ: Princeton University Press.

Aristotle 1997. *Aristotle's Poetics*. Montreal: McGill-Queen's University Press.

Artizov, Andrei 2010. 'Katyn. Posleslovie. Diskussiia na Kul'ture', *Youtube.com* (2 April), http://www.youtube.com/watch?v=PBcm90d W8aA.

Arumäe, Heino 2010. 'Katõn – aegumatu kuritöö inimsuse vastu', *Kultuur ja Elu*, 2, http://kultuur.elu.ee/ke500_poola.htm.

Asadchii, Aleksandr and Elena Chernenko 2011. 'Pol'sko-rossiiskie otnosheniia vyzvali k doske', *Kommersant"* (11 April), http://kommersant.ru/doc/1619189.

Aslamova, Dar'ia 2011. 'Pol'skii zhurnalist i obshchestvennyi deiatel' Adam Mikhnik: "U nas est' liudi iz zooparka s bezumnym antirossiiskim kompleksom . . ." ', *Komsomol'skaia pravda* (11 April).

Assmann, Jan 2006. *Religion and Cultural Memory*, trans. Rodney Livingstone. Stanford, CA: Stanford University Press.

Austin, J.L. 1978. *How To Do Things with Words*, second edition. Cambridge, MA: Harvard University Press.

'Awantura' 2011. 'Awantura o wystawę w PE. "Rosjanie rzucili ciała ofiar na folię" ', *Gazeta Wyborcza* (12 April), http://wyborcza.pl/1, 76842,9420395,Awantura_o_wystawe_w_PE___Rosjanie_rzucili_ciala_ofiar.html.

Bahovski, Erkki 2010. 'Katõni valus meeldetuletus', *Euroblogi* (15 April), http://blogs.ec.europa.eu/estonia/erkki-bahovski-katoni-valusmeeldetuletus/.

'Baltic Leaders' 2010. 'Baltic Leaders Attend Kaczyński's Funeral', *Baltic Reports* (19 April), http://balticreports.com/?p=15265.

Barthes, Roland 1994. *Roland Barthes*. Berkeley, CA: University of California Press.

Bartul, Snezhana 2010. 'Pavel Laptev: Srok zhizni Evropeiskogo suda mozhet byt' sokrashen', *Kommersant"* (31 May), http://www.kommersant.ru/doc/1378599.

Bell, Duncan 2003. 'Mythscapes: Memory, Mythology and National Identity', *British Journal of Sociology*, 54/1.

'Belorusy v Katyni' 2010. 'Belorusy v Katyni i poliaki v Kuropatakh', *BBC Russian Service* (30 March), http://www.bbc.co.uk/russian/russia/2010/03/100330_katyn_belorussian.shtml.

Biała księga 2011. *Biała księga Smoleńskiej tragedii*. Warsaw: Zespół Parlamentarny ds. Zbadania Przyczyn Katastrofy TU-154 M z 10 kwietnia 2010 g.

'Białoruś' 2010. 'Białoruś: władze usunęły z cmentarza Kamień Katyński', *Gazeta.pl* (18 August), http://wiadomosci.gazeta.pl/Wiadomosci/1,80 708,8267657,Bialorus__wladze_usunely_z_cmentarza_Kamien_Katynski.html.

Bogumił, Zuzanna 2010. 'Kresty i kamni: solovetskie simvoly v konstruirovanii pamiati o GULAGe', *Neprikosnovennyi zapas*, 3, http://

magazines.russ.ru/nz/2010/3/zu3.html [English-language digest of this article available at: http://www.memoryatwar.org/resources-nz].

Borowska, Katarzyna 2010. 'Tracimy zmysł historyczny', *Rzeczpospolita* (16 November), http://www.rp.pl/artykul/564434.html?print=tak.

Bragin, V. 1997. 'Kontseptsiia sozdaniia memorial'nykh kompleksov po uvekovecheniiu pamiati zhertv totalitarnykh repressii v Katyni (Smolenskaia oblast') i Mednoe (Tverskaia oblast')', *Katyn Memorial archive*, Katyn', Smolensk region.

Brier, Robert 2009. 'The Roots of the "Fourth Republic". Solidarity's Cultural Legacy to Polish Politics', *East European Politics and Societies*, 23/1 (February).

Brzeziecki, Andrzej 2010. 'Kolejka za powagą', *Tygodnik Powszechny* (4 May), http://tygodnik.onet.pl/30,0,45898,kolejka_za_powaga, artykul.html.

Bukharina, Berta 2006. 'Iskry vysekaiutsia ne zria . . .', *Moskovskaia pravda*, 31 (13 February).

Butler, Judith 2009. *Frames of War: When Is Life Grievable?* London and New York: Verso.

Chaciński, Bartek 2010. 'Prosimy nie wierzyć', *Polityka*, 18 (1 May).

Chubar'ian, Aleksandr 2010. 'Katyn. Posleslovie. Diskussiia na Kul'ture', *Youtube.com* (2 April), http://www.youtube.com/watch?v=_hX7YjV cxdw.

Cichmiński, Paweł 2007. 'Pamięc historii', *Stopklatka.pl* (12 September), http://www.stopklatka.pl/wydarzenia/wydarzenie.asp?wi=40198.

Cienciala, Anna M., Natalia S. Lebedeva and Wojciech Materski 2007. *Katyn: A Crime without Punishment.* New Haven, CT and London: Yale University Press.

Czapski, Józef 1944. *Wspomnienia starobielskie.* Rome: Oddział Kultury i Prasy 2. Korpusu.

Czapski, Józef 1949. *Na nieludzkiej ziemi.* Paris: Instytut Literacki.

Davies, Norman 1996. *Europe: A History.* Oxford: Oxford University Press.

Davis, Colin 2007. *Haunted Subjects: Deconstruction, Psychoanalysis and the Return of the Dead.* New York and Basingstoke: Palgrave Macmillan.

Day, Matthew 2009. 'Vladimir Putin Condemns Appeasement', *The Telegraph* (1 September), http://www.telegraph.co.uk/news/newstopics/ world-war-2/6122748/Vladimir-Putin-condemns-appeasement-of-Hitler-on-70th-anniversary-of-WW2-outbreak.html.

Degutienė, Irena 2011. 'Seimo Pirmininkės Irenos Degutienės kalba, pasakyta minint 70-ąsias Rainių žudynių metines', *Degutiene.lt* (23 June), http://www.degutiene.lt/?&item=953&PHPSESSID=8d89c566 45aa936c39e6a149cd4ab4a5.

' "Dėkoju jaunimui ir visiems" ' 2010. ' "Dėkoju jaunimui ir visiems, kurie tvarko šias Lietuvos skausmo vietas, kurie savo darbu ir pavyzdžiu puoselėjate ir ugdote tikrąją Toleranciją", – sakė Seimo Pirmininkė I.Degutienė', *Lietuvos Respublikos Seimas* (8 May), http:// www3.lrs.lt/pls/inter/w5_show?p_r=6125&p_k=1&p_d=98460.

de Lazari, Andrzej 2010. 'Kreml już nas nie lekceważy', *Rzeczpospolita* (10 September), http://www.rp.pl/artykul/533732.html.

Derrida, Jacques 1993. *Spectres de Marx*. Paris: Galilee.

Diukov, Aleksandr 2011. 'Kogo predlagaet reabilitirovat' prezidentskii Sovet po pravam cheloveka?' *REGNUM* (7 February), http://www. regnum.ru/news/1372424.html.

Donskis, Leonidas 2010. 'The Tragedy with Fragile Signs of Hope', *The Baltic Times* (6 May).

Dorn, Ludwik 2010. 'Na moje kopyto – Koniec grillowania', *Wprost 24*, 18, http://wprost.pl/ar/193398/Na-moje-kopyto-Koniec-grillowania/?I= 1421.

Doroga na Kuropaty 1990. Dir. Mikhail Zhdanovskii. Belarus: Belarusfilm.

Dzierzbicka, Alicja 2007. 'Lekcja historii według Wajdy', *Tygodnik Solidarność*, 28/09.

Epitafia Katyńskie 2010. Dir. Paulina Brzezińska et al. Poland: Media Kontakt.

Ermolovich, Nikolai 1994. 'Prem'ier Chernomyrdin pomog poliakam ekskavatorom', *Izvestiia*, 166 (22 September).

'Eshche raz' 1970. 'Eshche raz o Karavanskom', *Khronika tekushchikh sobytii* 13, http://www.memo.ru/history/diss/chr/.

Estam, Jüri 1996. 'Eestlaste Katõn asub Norilskis', *Kultuur ja Elu*, 2.

Etkind, Alexander 2004. 'Hard and Soft in Cultural Memory: Political Mourning in Russia and Germany', *Grey Room*, 16 (Summer).

Etkind, Alexander 2009. 'Putin's History Lessons', *Project Syndicate* (15 September), http://www.project-syndicate.org/commentary/etkind7/ English.

'Fabryka' 2007. 'Fabryka Śmierci', *Gazeta Krakowska* (24 September).

Fedoriwsky, S. 1953. 'The Pear Orchard and the Gorky Park of Culture at Vynnytsya', in S. Pidhainy (ed.), *The Black Deeds of the Kremlin: A White Book*. Toronto: Ukrainian Association of Victims of Russian-Communist Terror.

Feshchenko, P. 1969. 'Tov. Nikitchenko V. F.', №10/9736, June, 'Memorial' Society of Vasyl' Stus, http://memorial.kiev.ua/images/ stories/2009/06/05_008_andropov_znyschennia_slidiv.pdf.

Filipski, Kevin 2010. 'Yale in New York: Penderecki Conducts Penderecki', *The Flip Side*, http://flipsidereviews.blogspot.com/2010/04/ krzysztof-penderecki-interview.html.

'Filmowy' 2007. 'Filmowy Memoriał', *Kurier Szczeciński*, 14/9.

Finnin, Rory 2011. 'Forgetting Nothing, Forgetting No One: Boris Chichibabin, Viktor Nekipelov, and the Deportation of the Crimean Tatars', *The Modern Language Review*, 106/4 (30 September).

FitzGibbon, Louis 1975. *Unpitied and Unknown: Katyn – Bologoye – Dergachi*. London: Bachman and Turner.

FitzGibbon, Louis 1977. *The Katyn Memorial*. London: Gryf.

FitzGibbon, Louis 1989. 'Vynnytsya: The Forgotten Forerunner of Katyn', in I. Kamenetsky (ed.), *The Tragedy of Vinnytsia: Materials on Stalin's Policy of Extermination in Ukraine during the Great Purge 1936–38*. Toronto and New York: Ukrainian Historical Association.

Gajda-Zadworna, Jolanta 2007a. 'Płacz między ciszą', *Życie Warszawy*, 13/09.

Gajda-Zadworna, Jolanta 2007b. 'Zamiast "PostMortem" jednoznaczna kampania', *Życie Warszawy*, 12/04.

Gasztold-Seń, Przemysław 2010. 'Siła przeciw prawdzie. Represje aparatu bezpieczeństwa PRL wobec osób kwestionujących oficjalną wersję Zbrodni Katyńskiej', in Sławomir Kalbarczyk (ed.), *Zbrodnia katyńska w kręgu prawdy i kłamstwa*. Warsaw: Instytut Pamięci Narodowej.

Gawin, Dariusz and Paweł Kowal 2004. 'Polska polityka historyczna', in *Polityka historyczna. Historycy – politycy – prasa*. Warsaw: Museum of Warsaw Uprising, http://www.teologiapolityczna.pl/polska-polityka-historyczna–tekst-dariusza-gawina-i-pawla-kowala.

Gawronkiewicz, Krzysztof, Jacek Michalski, Tomasz Nowak, Jerzy Ozga and Witold Tkaczuk 2010. *1940 Katyń. Zbrodnia na nieludzkiej ziemi*. Poznań: Zin Zin Press.

Gedroits', Ie. 2008. 'Borysovi Levyts'komu, 3 July 1970', in B. Berdykhovs'ka (ed.), *Iezhy Gedroits' ta ukrains'ka emigratsiia: Lystuvannia 1952–82 rokiv*. Kyiv: Krytyka.

Golon, Mirosław 2001. 'Zbrodnia katyńska w propagandzie PRL (1944–1989). 45 lat fałszowania historii', in Andrzej Koli and Jan Sziling (eds.), *Charków-Katyń-Twer w sześćdziesiątą rocznicę zbrodni*. Toruń: Uniwersytet Mikołaja Kopernika.

Gorelik, Jevgenij 1996. *Kuropaty. Polski Ślad*. Warsaw: RYTM.

Grachev, Anatolii 1994. 'Ne trevozh'te mertvykh v Katynskom lesu', *Rossiiskaia gazeta*, 118 (25 June).

Grzybowski, Jerzy 2006. *Białorusini w polskich regularnych formacjach wojkowych w latach 1918–1945*. Warsaw: RYTM.

Gur'ianov, Aleksandr 2011. 'Reabilitatsiia zhertv Katyni: Kak vyiti iz tupika?' *Prava cheloveka v Rossii* (16 February), http://www.hro.org/node/10313.

Gurskaia, N. I. and E. S. Koneva 2010. 'Iz istorii Katynskogo lesa', *Vestnik Katynskogo memoriala*, 10.

Hałacińska, Kinga 2010. 'Irena i Ryszard', *Tygodnik Powszechny* (17 March), http://tygodnik.onet.pl/35,0,43016,2,artykul.html.

Harvey, J. (ed.) 1978. *War Diaries of Oliver Harvey*. London: Collins.

Herbert, Zbigniew 2009. 'Buttons', in *The Collected Poems 1956–1998*, trans. Alissa Valles. London: Atlantic Books.

Hirsch, Joshua 2004. *Afterimage: Film, Trauma, and the Holocaust*. Philadelphia, PA: Temple University Press.

Hirsch, Marianne 1997. *Family Frames: Photography, Narrative and Postmemory*. Cambridge, MA: Harvard University Press.

Hirsch, Marianne 2008. 'The Generation of Postmemory', *Poetics Today* 29:1 (Spring).

'Historyk Ihar Kuzniatsou' 2011. 'Historyk Ihar Kuzniatsou: Katynskaia trahedyia – heta bol' i pol'skaha , i belarus'kaha narodau, i pradstaunikou inshykh natsyianal'nasts'iau' (video material), *BelaPAN* (9 April), http://belapan.com/archive/2011/04/08/by_media_katyn/.

Hlebowicz, Adam 2010. 'Historia czy ideologia?' *Biuletyn IPN*, 5–6 (May–June), http://123abc.nowyekran.pl/post/11304,politycy-i-publicysci-apeluja-do-prez-komorowskiego-w-sprawie-katynia.

Hors'ka, A. 1996. *Chervona tin' kalyny: Lysty, spohady, statti*. Kyiv: Spalakh.

Hushchak, I. 1998. *Pleiada zaboronena, pryzabuta*. L'viv: Kobzar.

Iazhborovskaia, I.S., Iu. Iablokova and V.S. Parsadanova 2001. *Katynskii sindrom v rossiisko-pol'skikh otnosheniiakh*. Moscow: Rosspen.

Idi i smotri 1985. Dir. Elem Klimov. USSR: Belarusfilm and Mosfilm.

'Ile ofiar' 2010. 'Ile ofiar zażąda jeszcze Katyń od Polski?' *Jasielski Portal Informacyjny* (11 April).

Iliukhin, Viktor 2010a. 'Katyn'. Podlozhnoe pis'mo Berii', *Khronos* (25 May), http://www.hrono.info/statii/2010/ilyu_falsh.php.

Iliukhin, Viktor 2010b. 'Chto skazal nenazvannyi istochnik?' *KM.TV* (1 July), http://tv.km.ru/viktor_ilyuxin_kto_sfalsificziro/textversion.

Ilves, Toomas H. 2005. 'Külm rahu', *Diplomaatia*, 20 (May), http://www.diplomaatia.ee/index.php?id=242&no_cache=1&tx_ttnews[tt_news]=632&tx_ttnews[backPid]=462&cHash=6e15940332.

Ilves, Toomas H. and Lech Kaczyński 2008. 'A Call to Study and Assess Communist Crimes against Humanity and Violations of Human Rights: Joint Declaration of the Presidents of the Republic of Poland and the Republic of Estonia', *Vabariigi President* (18 March), http://www.president.ee/en/media/statements/2809-joint-declaration-of-the-presidents-of-the-republic-of-poland-and-the-republic-of-estonia/index.html.

Iser, Wolfgang 1980. *The Act of Reading: A Theory of Aesthetic Response*. Baltimore, MD: Johns Hopkins University Press.

'Istorik' 2010. 'Istorik Igor' Kuznetsov: iz pochti 22 tysiach rasstreliannykh v Katyni ne menee chetverti sostavliaiut belorusy i urozhentsy Belarusi', *News.open.by* (25 August), http://news.open.by/country/34495.

Iuzbashev, Vladimir 2004. 'Arkhitektura pokaianiia', *Novyi mir*, 4, http://magazines.russ.ru/novyi_mi/2004/4/uss21.html.

Jones, L. and B. Yasen (eds. and trans.) 1977. *The Ukrainian Herald, Issue 6: Dissent in Ukraine*. Baltimore, MD: Smoloskyp.

Juliański, Konstanty 2010. 'Tropiciele', *Tygodnik Solidarność*, 13 (26 March), http://www.tygodniksolidarnosc.com/2010/13/1_tro.htm.

Kaasik, Peeter 2006. 'Arrests of Estonian Officers and NCO-s in Värska Summer Camp', in Estonian International Commission for the Investigation of Crimes Against Humanity (ed.), *Estonia 1940–1945: Reports of the Estonian International Commission for the Investigation of Crimes Against Humanity*. Tallinn: Estonian Foundation for the Investigation of Crimes Against Humanity.

'Kaczyński' 2011a. 'Kaczyński: Ci, którzy chcieli zabić pamięć przegrali', *Gazeta Wyborcza* (10 April).

'Kaczyński' 2011b. 'Kaczyński przed Pałacem. "Jarosław, Jarosław, zwyciężymy!"' *Wiadomości* (10 July), http://wiadomosci.onet.pl/kraj/kaczynski-przed-palacem-jaroslaw-jaroslaw-zwyciezy,1,4787868,wiadomosc.html.

Kaczyński, Lech 2010. 'The Speech That Never Was . . . President Lech Kaczyński's Undelivered Speech Prepared for 70th Anniversary of the Katyn Massacre', *Lastspeech.com*, http://www.lastspeech.com.

Kaes, Anton 1989. *From Hitler to Heimat: The Return of History as Film*. Cambridge, MA and London: Harvard University Press.

Kalbarczyk, Sławomir 2007. 'Przedmioty odnalezione w Bykowni i Kuropatach świadczą o polskości ofiar', *Biuletyn Instytutu Pamięci Narodowej* 10–11 (81–82) (October–November).

Kalbarczyk, Sławomir 2008. 'Białoruska lista katyńska – brakujący element prawdy o zbrodni katyńskiej', in Marek Tarczyński (ed.), *Zbrodnia katyńska między prawdą a kłamstwem (Zeszyty katyńskie 23)*. Warsaw: Niezależny Komitet Historyczny Badania Zbrodni Katyńskiej / Polska Fundacja Katyńska.

Kamenetsky, I. 1989. 'Introduction', in I. Kamenetsky (ed.), *The Tragedy of Vinnytsia: Materials on Stalin's Policy of Extermination in Ukraine during the Great Purge 1936–38*. Toronto and New York: Ukrainian Historical Association.

Karaganov, Sergei 2010. 'Russkaia Katyn", *Rossiiskaia gazeta*, 5239 (22 July), http://www.rg.ru/2010/07/22/istoriya.html.

Karavans'kyi, S. 1966. 'From the Petition Sent to the Chairman of the Union of Journalists of Ukraine, 10 May 1966', in V. Chornovil (ed.), *The Chornovil Papers*. New York: McGraw-Hill, 1968.

Karavans'kyi, S. 1980. *Sutychka z taifunom*. Baltimore, MD: Smoloskyp.

Karavanskii, S. 1988. 'Prokuraturu SSSR, 12 August 1970', in B. Men'shagin, *Vospominaniia: Smolensk ... Katyn' ... Vladimirskaia tiur'ma*. Paris: YMCA Press.

Karawanski, S. 1988. 'Łagrowe echa Katynia', in *Katyń: Wybór publicystyki 1943–1988 i Lista Katyńska*. London: Polonia.

Karavans'kyi, S. 2010. 'Shevchenko i Bandera nerozdilymi!', *Maidan. org.ua* (16 June), http://maidanua.org/static/mai/1276636822.html.

Kärk, Lauri 2008. 'Andrzej Wajda Katõn – õigus ajaloole', *Postimees* (23 February).

Katyń 1998. *Katyń: Dokumenty Zbrodni. Tom 2: Zagłada: marzec–czerwiec 1940*. Warsaw: TRIO.

Katyń 2007. Dir. Andrzej Wajda. Poland: Akson, TVP, PFI.

'Katyn'' 2008a. 'Katyn': Bil', pam'iat', liubov', *Den'* 72 (18 April), http://www.day.kiev.ua/200170.

'Katyn'' 2008b. 'Katyn'', *Idn.npu.edu.ua*, http://www.idn.npu.edu.ua/index.php?option=com_content&task=view&id=127&Itemid=105.

Katyn'. Belorusskii spisok 2010. Belarus: Vtoroi Natsional'ny Telekanal.

Katyn Forest 1990. Dir. Marcel Łoziński. Poland/France: Wytwornia Filmow Dokumentalnych, Les Films du Losagne.

Katyń: Księga Cmentarna 2000. *Katyń: Księga Cmentarna Polskiego Cmentarza Wojennego*. Warsaw: Rada Ochrony Pamięci Wałk i Męczeństwa.

'Katyn' – Kuropaty' 2010. 'Katyn' – Kuropaty: obshchaia taina, obshchaia tragediia', *BBC Russian Service* (5 April), http://www.bbc.co.uk/russian/international/2010/04/100405_Katyn_belarus_victims.shtml.

Katyn Memorial website, http://www.katyn-memorial.ru.

Katyn'. Praz 70 hadou 2010. Belarus: BELSAT.

'Katyń Wajdy' 2007. 'Katyń Wajdy – symboliczny pogrzeb ofiar', *Gazeta Wyborcza*, 18/9.

'Katynskii rok' 2010. *New Times* (12 April).

Khachaturova, E. 2009. ' "Na kraiu vsenarodnoi, vselenskoi bedy ..." ', *Vestnik Katynskogo Memoriala*, 9.

'Kharkivs'ka Katyn'' 2010. 'Kharkivs'ka Katyn': Ukraintsi boiat'sia pro tse hovoryty', *BBC Ukrainian Service* (9 April), http://www.bbc.co.uk/ukrainian/ukraine/2010/04/100409_zinchenko_kharkiv_ie_is.shtml.

Kheifets, M. 1971. 'V ukrains'kii poezii teper bil'shoho nema ...', *Ukrains'kyi visnyk*, 2. Paris and Baltimore, MD: Smoloskyp.

Kiełpiński, Jacek 2007. 'Zostały po nich tylko gużiki', *Express Bydgoski Magazyn*, 4/10.

Kirkpatrick, Jeane J. 1988. *Legitimacy and Force: Political and Moral Dimensions*, vol. 1. New Brunswick, NJ: Transaction Publishers.

Klein, Kerwin Lee 2000. 'On the Emergence of Memory in Historical Discourse', *Representations*, 69 (Winter).

Kola, A. 2001. 'Prace archelogoiczno-ekshumacyjne na cmentarzu oficerów polskich w Charkowie', in A. Kola and J. Sziling (eds.), *Charków – Katyń – Twer: W sześćdziesiątą rocznicę zbrodni*. Toruń: Uniwersytet Mikołaja Kopernika.

Kola, A. 2005. *Archeologia Zbrodni: Oficerowie polscy na cmentarzu ofiar NKWD w Charkowie*. Toruń: Uniwersytet Mikołaja Kopernika.

Kolesnichenko, Aleksandr et al. 2010. 'Udvoenie skorbi', *Novye izvestiia* (12 April).

'Kolme Balti' 2011. 'Kolme Balti vabariigi Katõn Norilskis', *Estonian Life* (15 April).

Kolosov, N. 1988. 'Prigovor imenem Rossiiskoi Sovetskoi Federativnoi Sotsialisticheskoi Respubliki, 23 April 1970', in B. Men'shagin, *Vospominaniia: Smolensk . . . Katyn' . . . Vladimirskaia tiur'ma*. Paris: YMCA Press.

Komar, Karolina 2007. 'Widzowie po obejrzeniu filmu Katyń', *Życie Warszawy*, 21/09.

Kommel, Kutt 2009. 'Katõn teleekraanil', *Meie Maa* (9 January).

'Komorowski chce cmentarza' 2010. 'Komorowski chce cmentarza polskich oficerów w Bykowni', *Gazeta.pl* (25 September), http://wiadomosci.gazeta.pl/wiadomosci/1,114873,8425698,Komorowski_chce_cmentarza_polskich_oficerow_w_Bykowni.html.

Kornilova, O.V. 2004. 'O probleme izucheniia Katynskoi tragedii', *Vestnik Katynskogo memoriala*, 3.

Kosachev, Konstantin 2010. 'Sovetskaia li Rossiia?' *Ekho Moskvy* blog (29 June), http://www.echo.msk.ru/blog/kosachev/691501-echo/.

Kosiński, Dariusz 2011. 'Dziady Smoleńskie', *Tygodnik Powszechny* (24 May), http://tygodnik.onet.pl/30,0,63731,dziady_smolenskie,artykul.html.

Kot, Wiesław 2007. 'Krzyk Katyńia', *Wprost*, 23/9.

Kotkin, Stephen 1998. '1991 and the Russian Revolution: Sources, Conceptual Categories, Analytical Frameworks', *The Journal of Modern History* 70:2 (June).

Krasnovskii, Igor' 2001. 'Pribyl'noe zakhoronenie', *Novaia gazeta*, 77 (22 October).

Krasnovskii, Igor' 2006. 'Katyn': Yesli kaiat'sia, to pered bogom. . .', *Moskva*, 7 (15 July).

Krotov, Iakov 1995. 'Letopischik, 1995, 26 avgusta', *Krotov.info*, http://krotov.info/yakov/dnevnik/1994/hvi05_04.html.

Krzyż 2011. Dir. Ewa Stankiewicz and Jan Pospieszalski.

Krzyżanowski, Jerzy (ed.) 1995. *Katyn w literaturze*. Lublin: Norbertinum.

Kubilius, Andrius 2010. 'Putin Now Has Time for Historical Issues: Prime Minister's Interview', *The Lithuania Tribune* (6 May).

Kublik, Agnieszka 2010. 'To Katyń nr 2. Jestem zdruzgotany', *Gazeta Wyborcza* (10 April), http://wyborcza.pl/1,76842,7753298,To_Katyn_nr_2__Jestem_zdruzgotany.html.

Kulish, Nicholas and Clifford J. Levy 2010. 'Polish Crash in Russia Creates Contrarian Bond', *The New York Times* (12 April), http://www.nytimes.com/2010/04/13/world/europe/13poland.html.

Kurapaty 1993. *Kurapaty*. Minsk and New York: Belarusian Institute of Arts and Sciences.

Kurapaty 2002. *Kurapaty: Zbornik Materyialau*. Minsk: Dyiaryiush.

Kurapaty: Shliakh sumlennia 2008. Dir. Uladzimier Samoilau. Belarus: BELSAT.

Kurpiewski, Lech 2007. 'Diament ze Skazą', *Newsweek Polska*, 16/09.

Kurski, Jarosław 2010. 'Niech ta śmierć nas pojedna', *Gazeta Wyborcza* (12 April), http://wyborcza.pl/1,76842,7760643,Niech_ta_smierc_nas_pojedna.html.

Kurtyka, Zuzanna 2010. 'Dokonczyłam misję mojego Męża', *Nasz Dziennik*, 263 (10–11 November).

Kurzyńska, Ewa 2007. 'Zobaczę w kinie, jak zginął ojciec', *Gazeta Codzienna, Magazyn: Nowiny*, 21–23/09.

Kuzniatsou, Ihar 2002. 'Da likvidatsii prystupits'', in *Kurapaty: Zbornik Materyialau*. Minsk: Dyiaryiush.

Kuzniatsou, Ihar 2008. 'Predislovie', in Vatslau Areshka and Ihar Kuzniatsou (eds.), *Rastralianyia u Minsku: Indeks hramadzianau, rasstralianykh u Minsku u 1920–1950-ia hh., u 2-kh chastkakh*, vol. 1. Minsk: Dyiaryiush.

'Kwaśniewski' 2010. 'Kwaśniewski: Katyń to przeklęte miejsce', *Dziennik* (10 April), http://wiadomosci.dziennik.pl/artykuly/115477,kwasniewski-katyn-to-przeklete-miejsce.html.

Kyrylenko, S. 2007. 'Vidkrytyi lyst Kyivs'koi mis'koi orhanizatsii tovarystva "Memorial" im. V. Stusa Prezydentovi Ukrainy', *'Memorial' Society of Vasyl' Stus*, http://memorial.kiev.ua/novyny/271-bykivnja-stane-cvyntarom-orljat-u-vidnosynah-ukrajina-polshcha.html.

Laar, Mart 2009a. '22 000 mõrvatud Poola ohvitseri – miks lääs kõik need aastad vaikis?' *Postimees* (17 January).

Laar, Mart 2009b. 'Katõn – ühe vale anatoomia', *Sirp* (8 May).

Laasik, Andres 2008. 'Katõn – tapmistest, mis peideti kalevi alla', *Eesti Päevaleht* (19 December).

Landsbergis, Vytautas 2007. 'International Cooperation in Assessing the Crimes of Communist Regimes', Speech at the Conference *Communism – an International Tribunal*, Vilnius (16 June).

Landsbergis, Vytautas 2008. Address at the International Seminar *Crimes of Totalitarian Regimes in Central and Eastern Europe: Experience and Prospects of Assessment*, Vilnius (29 September).

Landsbergis, Vytautas 2009. 'New Light on Totalitarian Crimes', *European Parliament Hearings*, Brussels (18 March).

Landsbergis, Vytautas 2010. 'Lenkijos nokdaunas', *Landsbergis.lt*, http://www.landsbergis.lt/articles/view/280.

Landsbergis, Vytautas 2011. 'Tyčiotis iš žuvusiųjų, tai Rusijos tradicija', *Uważam Rze*, 10 (4 April).

Langer, Lawrence L. 2006. *Using and Abusing the Holocaust*. Bloomington, IN: Indiana University Press.

Lapikova, A. 2002. 'Katynskii les eshche ne raskryl svoi tainy', *Vestnik Katynskogo memoriala*, 1.

Latynina, Iuliia 2010. 'Katyn'-2', *Ezhednevnyi zhurnal* (13 April), http://www.ej.ru/?a=note&id=10021.

Lebedeva, Natal'ia S. 1999. 'Proces podejmowania decyzji katyńskiej', in K. Jasiewicz (ed.), *Europa nie prowincjonalna: Przemiany na ziemiach wschodnich dawnej Rzeczypospolitej (Białorus, Litwa, Łotwa, Ukraina, wschodnie pogranicze III Rzeczypospolitej Polskiej) w latach 1772–1999*. Warsaw and London: RYTM.

Lebedeva, Natal'ia S. 2001. *Katyn'. Mart 1940 – sentiabr' 2000 g. Rasstrel. Sud'by zhivykh. Ekho Katyni. Dokumenty*. Moscow: Ves' mir.

'Lekh Kachin'skii' 2011. 'Lekh Kachin'skii v kruge mistiki i spekuliatsii', *Pravda.ru* (10 April), http://www.pravda.ru/world/europe/easteurope/10-04-2011/1072678-kaczynski-0/.

Lenarciński, Michał 2007. 'Katyń – historia edukacyjna', *Dziennik Łódzki*, 22–23/09.

Leszczyński, Adam 2011. 'Ewa Stankiewicz, polska Antygona', *Gazeta Wyborcza* (15 May), http://wyborcza.pl/1,113922,9599614,Ewa_Stankiewicz__polska_Antygona.html.

Levinson, Aleksei 2010. 'Rossiiane o Katyni – posle aviakatastrofy', *Polit.ru* (29 April), http://www.polit.ru/article/2010/04/29/katyn/.

Levy, Daniel and Natan Sznaider 2006. *The Holocaust and Memory in the Global Age*. Philadelphia, PA: Temple University Press.

Lewandowska, Wiesława 2011. 'Biała Księga Smoleńskiej Tragedii', *Niedziela*, 28, http://www.niedziela.pl/warto_przeczytac.php?doc=20110707&nr=2.

Lindner, Rainer 1999. 'Besieged Past: National and Court Historians in Lukashenka's Belarus', *Nationalities Papers*, 27/4.

Lipowski, Wojciech 2005. 'Pamięć i czas', *Tygodnik Powszechny* (29 July), http://czytelnia.onet.pl/0,32694,0,4602,recenzje.html.

The Lives of Others 2006. Dir. Florian Henckel von Donnersmarck. Germany: Arte, Bayerischer Rundfunk, Creado Film, Wiedemann and Berg Filmproduktion.

Lochner, Louis P. (ed.) 1948. *The Goebbels Diaries*. London: H. Hamilton.

Łojek, Bożena 2000. 'Muzeum katyńskie, walka o miejsce pamięci', in Marek Tarczyński (ed.), *Zbrodnia katyńska po 60 latach: Polityka, Nauka, Moralność (Zeszyty katyńskie 12)*. Warsaw: Niezależny Komitet Historyczny Badania Zbrodni Katyńskiej / Polska Fundacja Katyńska.

Łojek, Jerzy 1989. *Dzieje sprawy Katynia*. Białystok: Zakłady Wydawnicze 'Versus'.

Lubelski, Tadeusz 2009. *Historia kina polskiego*. Katowice: Videograph II.

Luik, Jüri 2008. 'Meie kohustus', *Diplomaatia*, 54 (February), http://www.diplomaatia.ee/index.php?id=242&L=1&tx_ttnews[tt_news]=683&tx_ttnews[backPid]=426&cHash=24f1ca9c6e.

Macedoński, Adam 1996. 'Historia Instytutu Katyńskiego w Polsce', in Marek Tarczyński (ed.), *Zbrodnia nie ukarana: Katyń, Twer, Charków (Zeszyty katyńskie 6)*. Warsaw: Niezależny Komitet Historyczny Badania Zbrodni Katyńskiej / Polska Fundacja Katyńska.

Mach, Magdalena 2007. 'Uciekały przed bombami', *Gazeta Wyborcza*, 21/11.

Machcewicz, Paweł 2010. 'Nowa wojna pamięci', *Newsweek Polska* (4 May), http://www.newsweek.pl/artykuly/sekcje/Europa/nowa-wojna-pamieci,57726,1.

Mackiewicz, I. and M. Manowa 2007. *Cmentarz ofiar totalitaryzmu Charków – Piatichatki*. Charków: Dom Wydawniczy 'Wokrug Cwieta'.

Mackiewicz, Józef 1948. *Zbrodnia katyńska w świetle dokumentów*. London: Gryf.

Mackiewicz, Józef 1951. *The Katyn Wood Murders*. London: Hollis and Carter.

Mackiewicz, Józef 1973. 'Literatura contra faktologia', *Kultura*, 7–8.

Maimik, Peeter 2009. 'Mälu, kallis vara', *Videvik* (22 January).

Maiorova, Ol'ga 2001. 'Slavianskii s"ezd 1867 goda: Metaforika torzhestva', *Novoe literaturnoe obozrenie*, 51.

Mal'gin, Artem 2009. 'Ottalkivaias' ot proshlogo', *Nezavisimaia gazeta* (7 September), http://www.ng.ru/courier/2009-09-07/9_poland.html.

Mälksoo, Lauri 2011. 'Kononov v. Latvia', *The American Journal of International Law*, 105/1.

Mälksoo, Maria 2009. 'The Memory Politics of Becoming European: The East European Subalterns and the Collective Memory of Europe', *European Journal of International Relations*, 15/4.

'Marciniak' 2010. 'Marciniak: Teraz można stawiać żądania ws. prawdy o Katyniu', *Gazeta.pl* (13 April), http://wiadomosci.gazeta.pl/Wiado mosci/1,80708,7768700,Marciniak__Teraz_mozna_stawiac_ zadania_ws__prawdy.html.

'Marciniak' 2011. 'To klasyczna prowokacja ze strony Rosji', *Dziennik* (9 April), http://wiadomosci.dziennik.pl/opinie/galeria/330403,1,to-klasyczna-prowokacja-ze-strony-rosji-galeria-zdjec.html.

Maresch, E. 2010. *Katyn 1940: The Documentary Evidence of the West's Betrayal*. London: Spellmount.

Marples, David R. 1994. 'Kurapaty: The Investigation of a Stalinist Historical Controversy', *Slavic Review*, 53/2.

Masłoń, Krzysztof 2007. 'Po "Katyniu" można tylko milczeć', *Rzeczpospolita*, 13/09.

Meikar, Silver 2010. 'Katõni veresaun – kas genotsiid?' *Meikar.ee*, http://www.meikar.ee/blog/2010/04/katoni-veresaun-%E2%80%93-kas-genotsiid/.

Mel'nikov, Igor' 2011a. 'Katyn'. Belorusskii spisok', *Naviny.by* (12 February), http://naviny.by/rubrics/opinion/2011/02/12/ic_articles_410_172419/.

Mel'nikov, Igor' 2011b. 'Katyn'. Novye stranitsy belorusskogo spiska', *Naviny.by* (1 May), http://www.naviny.by/rubrics/opinion/2011/05/01/ic_articles_410_173463/.

Merridale, Catherine 2000. *Night of Stone: Death and Memory in Russia*. London: Granta.

Miasnikov, Viktor 2010. 'Katastroficheskii kren Katyni', *Nezavisimoe voennoe obozrenie* (16 April).

Michalski, Cezary 2010. 'Warunki do lądowania', *Krytyka Polityczna* (2 June), http://www.krytykapolityczna.pl/CezaryMichalski/Warunkidoladowania/menuid-291.html.

Michnik, Adam 2009. 'Narodowość pluszowego misia', *Gazeta Wyborcza* (14 April), http://wyborcza.pl/1,101422,6495143,Michnik__Narodowosc_pluszowego_misia.html.

Michnik, Adam 2010. 'After the Smolensk Crash: "A New Community" of Poland and Russia?' *New York Review of Books* (18 April), http://www.nybooks.com/blogs/nyrblog/2010/apr/18/after-smolensk-crash/.

Mihkelson, Marko 2008. 'Katõni tragöödia testib Venemaad', *Postimees* (23 March).

Mihkelson, Marko 2010. *Venemaa: valguses ja varjus*. Tallinn: Varrak.

Mikhalkov, Nikita 2010. 'Katyn'. Posleslovie. Diskussiia na Kul'ture', *Youtube.com* (2 April), http://www.youtube.com/watch?v=rGIIi0xb-YI.

Milosz, Czesław 1953. *The Captive Mind*. New York: Knopf.

'Minkul't otkazalsia' 2009. 'Minkul't otkazalsia nominirovat' Kuropaty na vnesenie v spisok IuNESKO', *Charter97.org* (20 January), http://charter97.org/ru/news/2009/1/20/14214/.

Mlechin, L.M. 2009. *Shelepin*. Moscow: Molodaia gvardiia.

Moshkin, Mikhail 2010. 'Parallel'nymi kursami', *Vremia novostei*, 78 (7 May).

Mularczyk, Andrzej 2007. *Katyń: Post-Mortem*. Warsaw: Muza.

Mularczyk, Andrzej 2008. *Post Mortem Katõn: filmjutustus*. Tallinn, Varrak.

Murawski, Michał 2011. 'Inappropriate Object: Warsaw's Palace of Culture after Smolensk', Presentation to the Conference *East European Memory Studies Graduate Research Triangle*, King's College, University of Cambridge, 12 March.

Nahlik, Monika 2009. 'Katyń w czasach popkultury', in Tadeusz Lubelski and Maciej Stroński (eds.), *Kino polskie jako kino narodowe*. Krakow: Korporacja Ha!art.

'Narodny khram pamiatsi' 2009. 'Narodny khram pamiatsi. (Interv'iu namesnika halounaha redaktara "Belarushkaha hystarychnaha chasopisa" Maksima Hal'piarovicha z arkhitektaram Leanidam Mendelevicham Levinym)', *Belaruski Hystarychny Chasopis* (July).

'Nasha sumlenne' 2005. 'Nasha sumlenne i bol", *Niva: Tydniovik Belarusau u Polshchy* (14 August), http://niva.iig.pl/issue/2005/33/33_2005.pdf.

Nevskaia, Tat'iana 2002. 'Nam govoriat: a mozhet, tam zhuliki lezhat?' *Gazeta.ru* (7 March), http://katyn.ru/index.php?go=Pages&in=view&id=70.

Nikitchenko. V. 1969. 'Tovarishchu Andropovu Iu. V', № 297 / H, 7 June, *'Memorial' Society of Vasyl' Stus*, http://memorial.kiev.ua/images/stories/2009/06/05_005_andropov_harkiv.pdf.

Niżyńska, Joanna 2010. 'The Politics of Mourning, and the Crisis of Poland's Symbolic Language after April 10', *East European Politics and Societies*, 24/4 (Fall).

'No Official Mourning' 2010. 'No Official Mourning in Belarus after Death of Kaczynski So Far', *Belarus Digest* (14 April), http://belarus-digest.com/2010/04/14/no-official-mourning-in-belarus-after-death-of-kaczynski.

Nora, Pierre 1989. 'Between Memory and History: Les Lieux de Mémoire [1984]', *Representations* 26 (Spring).

Nora, Pierre 1996. 'From Lieux de Mémoire to Realms of Memory', in Nora, Pierre and Lawrence D. Kritzman (eds.), *Realms of Memory: Rethinking the French Past. Vol. 1: Conflicts and Divisions*. New York and Chichester: Columbia University Press.

Novik, Ia. K. (ed.) 2009. *Historyia Belarusi, XIX – pachatak XXI st.: vucheb. dapam. dlia 11-ha kl. ahul'naadukats. ustanou.* Minsk: Vyd. Tsentr BDU.

Novikova, Liudmila 1999. 'Stali prosto zemlei i travoi, a na bol'shee – deneg ne khvatilo', *Nezavisimaia gazeta*, 25 December, http://www.muar.ru/exibitions/exibit59.htm.

Nowak, Andrzej 2011a. 'From Memory Clashes to a General Battle: The Battle for Smolensk/Katyn', *East European Memory Studies*, 6 (June).

Nowak, Andrzej 2011b. 'Jest polityka pamięci i jest polityka zapomnienia', *Nasz Dziennik* (11 April), http://wpolityce.pl/view/10134/Jest_polityka_pamieci_i_jest_polityka_zapomnienia__Wiedzieli_o_tym_ci__ktorzy_na_wieczna_rzeczy_niepamiec_zasadzili_nad_dolami_katynskimi_las.html.

Nowak, Andrzej 2011c. 'Murder in the Graveyard: Memorial Clashes over the Victims of the Soviet-Polish Wars', Presentation to the Conference *Memory and Theory in Eastern Europe*, King's College, University of Cambridge, 4 July.

Obertas, O. 2010. *Ukrains'kyi samvydav.* Kyiv: Smoloskyp.

'Obshchenatsional'naia gosudarstvenno-obshchestvennaia programma' 2011. 'Obshchenatsional'naia gosudarstvenno-obshchestvennaia programma "Ob uvekovechenii pamiati zhertv totalitarnogo rezhima i o natsional'nom primirenii" ', *Sovet pri Prezidente RF po razvitiiu grazhdanskogo obshchestva i pravam cheloveka*, http://www.president-sovet.ru/structure/group_5/materials/the_program_of_historical_memory.php.

'Oddzielmy' 2011. ' "Oddzielmy spuściznę mojego męża od polityki" ', *Gazeta.pl* (14 April), http://wiadomosci.gazeta.pl/wiadomosci/1,114873,9431913,_Oddzielmy_spuscizne_mojego_meza_od_polityki__Zona.html.

Odojewski, Włodzimierz 1984. 'Ku Dunzynańskiemu Wzgórzu idzie las', *Zabiezpieczanie śladów.* Paris: Instytut literacki.

Odojewski, Włodzimerz 1995a. 'Wstęp' in Jerzy Krzyżanowski (ed.), *Katyn w literaturze.* Lublin: Norbertinum.

Odojewski, Włodzimerz 1995b. *Zasypie wszystko, zawieje . . .* Warsaw: Państwowy Instytut Wydawniczy.

Odojewski, Włodzimierz 2003. *Milczący, niepokonani: opowieść katyńska.* Warsaw: Twój styl.

Odorczuk, Piotr 2010. ' "Zimny Lech" pod Wawelem drażni krakowian', *Gazeta Krakowska* (8 July), http://www.gazetakrakowska.pl/artykul/279586,zimny-lech-pod-wawelem-drazni-krakowian,id,t.html?cookie=1.

Olszewska, Dominika and Iwona Szpala 2010. 'Czuwają i bronią', *Gazeta Wyborcza* (3 August), http://wyborcza.pl/1,76842,8207106,Czuwaja_i_bronia.html?as=2&startsz=x.

Orłoś, Kazimierz 1995. 'Drugie wrota w lesie', in Jerzy Krzyżanowski (ed.), *Katyn w literaturze*. Lublin: Norbertinum.

Orlov, Aleksei 2000. 'Pominal'nyi zvon nad Katyn'iu', *Nasha smena* (Smolensk) (28 July), http://memonia.ru/pamyatnye-mesta/memorial/article/3-visit/84-katyn.html.

Pamiatnykh, Aleksei and Sergei Romanov [undated]. *Katynskie materialy: Dokumenty, svidetel'stva, issledovaniia, polemika*, http://katynfiles.com.

Pashina, Alena and Anna Lutchenkova 2011. 'Na pamiatnike poliakam, razbivshimsia na prezidentskom samolete v Smolenske, smenili nadpis'', *Komsomol'skaia pravda* (10 April), http://www.kp.ru/daily/25666/827843.

Pasiuta, A. 2008. 'Rezhisser Andzhei Vaida pomolilsia na mogile otsa v Khar'kove', *Komsomol'skaia pravda v Ukraine*, http://kp.ua/daily/160408/39914/.

Paul, Allen 1991. *Katyń: The Untold Story of Stalin's Polish Massacre.* New York: Scribner Book Company.

Paul, Allen 2007. 'Katyń – prawda o sowieckiej zbrodni', *Dziennik* (5 November), http://www.pomorska.pl/apps/pbcs.dll/article?AID=/20070917/ROZRYWKA01/70917028, Kultura, 17/09.

Paul, Allen 2010. *Katyń: Stalin's Massacre and the Triumph of the Truth.* DeKalb, IL: Northern Illinois University Press.

Pavlova, A.N. 2010. 'Memorial "Katyn'" za istekshii god (iiul' 2009 – iiul' 2010)', *Vestnik Katynskogo memoriala*, 10.

Pawelec, Małgorzata 2007. 'Zobacz Katyń', *Echo Dnia*, 21/09.

Peirce, Charles S. 1972. *Charles S. Peirce: The Essential Writings.* New York: Harper and Row.

Petrov, Nikita 2001. 'Desiatiletie arkhivnykh reform v Rossii', *Indeks/Dos'e na tsenzuru*, 14.

The Pianist 2002. Dir. Roman Polanski. France/Poland/Germany/UK: Studio Canal +, TVP.

Pilawski, Krzysztof 2007. 'Piętno Katynia', *Przegląd*, 23/09.

Pilawski, Krzysztof 2011a. 'Mity i Dolomity', *Przegląd*, http://www.przeglad-tygodnik.pl/pl/artykul/mity-dolomity.

Pilawski, Krzysztof 2011b. 'Polityka historyczna do kosza', *Przegląd*, http://www.przeglad-tygodnik.pl/pl/artykul/polityka-historyczna-do-kosza.

Pinkert, Anke 2008. *Film and Memory in East Germany.* Bloomington and Indianapolis: Indiana University Press.

'PiS ostro o raporcie MAK' 2011. 'PiS ostro o raporcie MAK: "Medialny strzał w tył głowy"', *Gazeta.pl* (13 January), http://wiadomosci.gazeta.pl/Wiadomosci/1,80708,8942421,PiS_ostro_o_raporcie_MAK___Medialny_strzal_w_tyl_glowy_.html.

Podgajna, Ewa 2007. 'Pójdziemy na ten film jak na egzekucje ojców', *Gazeta Wyborcza*, 17/09.

Pol'skii krest Rossii 2010. Dir. Viktor Iliukhin. Moscow.

'Polacy mogą' 2010. ' "Polacy mogą mieć kilka organizacji". Łukaszenka w pierwszej od lat rozmowie z naszymi mediami', *Gazeta.pl* (4 November), http://wiadomosci.gazeta.pl/Wiadomosci/1,80545, 8615227,_Polacy_moga_miec_kilka_organizacji___Lukaszenka_w. html.

'Politycy i publicyści' 2011. 'Politycy i publicyści apelują do prez. Komorowskiego w sprawie Katynia', *Nowy ekran* (20 April), http://123abc.nowyekran.pl/post/11304,politycy-i-publicysci-apeluja-do-prez-komorowskiego-w-sprawie-katynia.

'Posle tragedii' 2010. 'Posle tragedii: Pol'sha i my', *Grani-tv* (15 April), http://grani-tv.ru/entries/1102/.

'Posłuchaj' 2011. 'Posłuchaj odnalezionej audycji z czasów PRL-u o Katyniu', *Dwójka Polskie Radio* (13 April), http://www.polskieradio. pl/8/529/Artykul/347872,Posluchaj-odnalezionej-audycji-z-czasow-PRL-o-Katyniu.

Potichnyj, P. (ed.) 2005. *Litopys UPA – Istoriia: dokumenty i materiialy*. Toronto: Vyd-vo Litopys UPA.

Potkaj, Tomasz 2010. 'Obłędny rycerz', *Tygodnik Powszechny* (3 August), http://tygodnik.onet.pl/30,0,50269,2,artykul.html.

Pozniakov, M. 1991. 'Budu srazhat'sia za pravdu o Kuropatach', *Vo slavu rodiny* (16 August).

'President Ilves' 2008. 'President Ilves annab Varssavis režissöör Andrzej Wajdale üle Maarjamaa Risti teenetemärgi', *Vabariigi President* (31 July), http://www.president.ee/et/ametitegevus/visiidid/78-poola/4391-president-ilves-annab-varssavis-reissoeoer-andrzej-wajdale-uele-maarjamaa-risti-teenetemaergi/index.html.

'Prezydent Komorowski' 2010. 'Prezydent Komorowski o zadaniach prof. Nałęcza i polityce historycznej', *Polityka* (17 September), http:// www.polityka.pl/kraj/wywiady/1508148,1,prezydent-komorowski-o-zadaniach-prof-nalecza-i-polityce-historycznej.read.

'Prof. Włodzimierz Marciniak' 2011. 'Prof. Włodzimierz Marciniak: Rosjanie testują polskie władze', *Super Express* (11 April).

'Prosti, Bat'ka' 2009. 'Prosti, Bat'ka, chto tak dolgo iskal tvoiu mogilu', *Salidarnasts'* (24 August), http://www.gazetaby.com/index.php?sn_nid=23321.

'Protokol' 1997. 'Protokol rasshirennogo zasedaniia Koordinatsionnogo komiteta po osushchestvleniiu meropriatii, sviazannykh s uvekovecheniem pamiati zhertv totalitarnykh repressii v Katyni (Smolenskaia oblast') i Mednom (Tverskaia oblast')', *Katyn Memorial archive*, Katyn', Smolensk region.

'Protses' 1970. 'Protses Sviatoslava Karavans'koho', *Ukrains'kyi visnyk*, 1. Paris and Baltimore, MD: Smoloskyp.

Przewoźnik, Andrzej 1997. 'Polskie cmentarze wojenne w Katyniu, Miednoje i Charkowie, zamierzenia, project, perspektywy realizacyjne', in Marek Tarczynski (ed.), *Ku cmentarzom polskim w Katyniu, Miednoje, Charkowie (Zeszyty katyńskie 8)*. Warsaw: Niezależny Komitet Historyczny Badania Zbrodni Katyńskiej / Polska Fundacja Katyńska.

Przewoźnik, Andrzej 2010. 'Ból i obowiązek', *Tygodnik Powszechny* (17 March), http://tygodnik.onet.pl/35,0,43010,2,artykul.html.

Przewoźnik, Andrzej and Jolanta Adamska 2010. *Katyń: Zbrodnia Prawda Pamięć*. Warsaw: Świat Kśiążki.

Pushkar', Dmitrii 1995. 'Otdel'naia pamiat', otdel'naia skorb", *Moskovskie novosti*, 39 (7 June).

'Putin nie przywiezie' 2010. 'Putin nie przywiezie do Katynia listy białoruskiej', *Gazeta Wyborcza* (6 April), http://wyborcza.pl/1,76842,7738408,Putin_nie_przywiezie_do_Katynia_listy_bialoruskiej.html.

Radziwinowicz, Wacław 2010. 'Cała Rosja to wielki Katyń', *Gazeta Wyborcza* (23 July), http://wyborcza.pl/1,86117,8168722,Cala_Rosja_to_wielki_Katyn.html.

Radziwinowicz, Wacław 2011. 'Ta tablica musiała zniknąć', *Gazeta Wyborcza* (10 April), http://wyborcza.pl/1,75478,9405436,Krzyk_o_tablice_smolenska_niesprawiedliwy.html.

Rekulski, A. 1980. *Czy drugi Katyń?* Paris: Instytut Literacki.

Revzin, Grigorii 2001. 'Arkhitektura nad ubitymi', *Kommersant"* (20 April), http://www.kommersant.ru/doc/254589.

Ricciardi, Alessia 2003. *The Ends of Mourning: Psychoanalysis, Literature, Film*. Stanford, CA: Stanford University Press.

Ricoeur, Paul 1986. 'The Metaphorical Process as Cognition, Imagination, and Feeling', in Hazard Adams (ed.), *Critical Theory since 1969*. Tallahassee, FL: Florida State University Press.

Rogoża, Jadwiga 2010. 'Rosja', *Nowa Europa Wschodnia*, 3–4 (XI–XII) (May–August).

Rojek, Iwona 2007. 'Katyń od lat dwunastu', *Echo Dnia*, 9/10.

Rokossovskaia, Ariadna 2010. 'Chelovek iz vremeni', *Rossiiskaia gazeta* (6 December).

Rokossovskaia, Ariadna and Ol'ga Lisinova 2011. 'Ai, da Vaida!' *Rossiiskaia gazeta*, 47 (5 March).

Roliński, Adam and Andrzej Rybicki (eds.) 2000. *Kłamstwo katyńskie: katalog wystawy 8 kwietnia – 15 maja 2000*. Krakow: Fundacja Centrum Dokumentacji Czynu Niepodległosciowego/Instytut Jana

Pawła II/Instytut Katyński w Polsce/Muzeum Historii Fotografii w Krakowie/Księgarnia Akademicka.

Romanowski, Andrzej 2010a. 'Nowe oblicze Rosji', *Nowa Europa Wschodnia*, 3–4 (XI–XII) (May–August).

Romanowski, Andrzej 2010b. 'Z pamięcią katastrofa', *Gazeta Wyborcza* (26 July), http://wyborcza.pl/1,76842,8172183,Z_pamiecia_katastrofa.html.

Rosenstone, Robert A. 1995. 'The Historical Film as Real History', *Film-Historia* 5.1.

Rosenstone, Robert A. 2006. *History on Film / Film on History*. Harlow: Pearson Longman.

'Rosja' 2010. 'Rosja znów neguje Katyń', *Gazeta.pl* (24 November), http://wiadomosci.gazeta.pl/Wiadomosci/1,80708,8710346,Rosja_znow_neguje_Katyn__Rodziny_wycofuja_ze_Strasburga.html.

Rothberg, Michael 2010. *Multidirectional Memory: Remembering the Holocaust in the Age of Decolonization*. Stanford, CA: Stanford University Press.

Sadowska, Małgorzata 2007. 'W niewoli romantycznych mitów', *Przekrój*, 20/09.

Sahanovich, Henadz' 2001. 'Vaina z belaruskai historyiai' in *ARCHE* 3 (17), http://arche.bymedia.net/2001-3/sahan301.html [Re-published in English as: 'The War Against Belarusian History', *Education in Russia, the Independent States and Eastern Europe*, 20/1 (Spring 2002)].

Sahanovich, Henadz' 2009. 'Istorichaskaia politika v postsovetskoi Belarusi', *Russkii vopros*, 2, http://www.russkiivopros.com/index.php?pag=one&id=278&kat=5&csl=42.

Sanford, George 2005. *Katyn and the Soviet Massacre of 1940: Truth, Justice and Memory*. London and New York: Routledge.

Sanich, Aleksandr 1991. 'Kuropaty – zhivoi svidetel' tragedii priekh iz Maikopa', *Belorusskaia niva* (10 August).

Sawicki, Jacek Zygmunt 2007. 'Zanim powstała dolinka katyńska: Pamięć o Katyniu w pierwszych dekadach istnienia PRL-u', *Tygodnik Powszechny* (22 September), http://tygodnik2003-2007.onet.pl/3591,30122,1439914,tematy.html.

'Seimo' 2010. 'Seimo pirmininkė pagerbė lietuviškosios Katynės aukas', *Elta* (8 May), http://www.delfi.lt/news/daily/lithuania/seimo-pirmininke-pagerbe-lietuviskosios-katynes-aukas.d?id=32032523.

Seleshko, M. 1949. 'Vinnytsia – the Katyn of Ukraine', *The Ukrainian Quarterly* V/ 3.

Shakespeare, William, 1990. *The Tragedy of Macbeth*, ed. Nicholas Brooke. Oxford: Oxford University Press.

Shenderovich, Viktor 2010. 'Grani nedeli s Vladimirom Kara-Murzoi', *Ekho Moskvy* (16 April).

The Shining 1980. Dir. Stanley Kubrick. UK/USA: Warner Bros.

Shoah 1985. Dir. Claude Lanzmann. France: Historia, Les Films Aleph, Ministère de la Culture de la Republique Française.

Shved, Vladislav 2006. 'Anti-Katyn", *Nash sovremennik*, 7.

Sienkiewicz, Bartłomiej 2010. 'Wznieść się ponad własne obawy', *Nowa Europa Wschodnia*, 3–4 (XI–XII) (May–August).

'Sikorski atakuje wdowy' 2011. 'Sikorski atakuje wdowy, które zawiesiły tablicę na kamieniu w Smoleńsku', *wPolityce.pl* (15 April), http://wpolityce.pl/wydarzenia/8668-sikorski-atakuje-wdowy-ktore-zawiesily-tablice-na-kamieniu-w-smolensku-zuzanna-kurtyka-nie-spodziewam-sie-niczego-innego.

Siomkajło, Alina 2002. *Katyn w pomnikach świata / Katyn Monuments around the World*. Warsaw: Agencja Wydawnicza CB, Oficyna Wydawnicza Rytm.

Skwieciński, Piotr 2011. 'Rosyjskie media: brzoza w służbie zbliżenia Warszawy i Moskwy', *Rzeczpospolita* (12 April), http://www.rp.pl/artykul/641712_Rosyjskie-media–brzoza-w-sluzbie-zblizenia.html.

Skwieciński, Piotr and Łukasz Zalesiński 2011. 'Tablica: zamęczeni w polskich obozach', *Rzeczpospolita* (15 May), http://www.rp.pl/artykul/17,658669_Prowokacja_w_Strzalkowie___Tablica_w_Strzalkowie_.html.

Smolar, Aleksander 2008. 'Władza i geografia pamięci', in Piotr Kosiewski (ed.), *Pamięć jako przedmiot władzy*. Warsaw: Fundacja Batorego.

Snyder, Timothy 2010. *Bloodlands: Europe between Hitler and Stalin*. London: Bodley Head.

Snyder, Timothy 2011. 'Mass Killing and Commemoration: Some European Disharmonies', Lecture at the University of Cambridge, 2 June.

Sobolewski, Tadeusz 2007. 'Gest Antygony', *Gazeta Wyborcza*, 18/09.

Sokolov, Boris 2011. 'Doska dovela do skandala', *Grani.ru* (11 April), http://www.grani.ru/opinion/sokolov/m.187688.html.

Solidarni 2010 2010. Dir. Ewa Stankiewicz and Jan Pospieszalski.

'Solidarni 2010' 2010. ' "Solidarni 2010": zwykli Polacy, np. aktorzy, radny PiS', *Gazeta Wyborcza* (28 April), http://wyborcza.pl/1,98781,7823108,_Solidarni_2010___zwykli_Polacy__np__aktorzy__radny.html.

'Soojem aastaaeg' 2010. 'Soojem aastaaeg' (editorial), *Diplomaatia*, 82 (June), http://www.diplomaatia.ee/index.php?id=242&tx_ttnews[tt_news]=1142&tx_ttnews[backPid]=559&cHash=50f6b281e1.

'Sovetnik prezidenta' 2011. 'Sovetnik prezidenta Pol'shi: Bronislav Komorovski schitaet Katyn' genotsidom', *REGNUM Baltika* (20 April), http://www.newspb.ru/allnews/1396872/.

The Soviet Story 2008. Dir. Edvīns Šnore. Latvia: Documentary Film.

Spanily, A. (ed.) 2000. *Charków Katyń Miednoje: Polskie cmentarze wojenne.* Gdynia: ASP RYMSZA.

'Srebrenica' 1995. 'Srebrenica, the New "Katyn Forest"', *Executive Intelligence Review*, 22.38.

Sroczyński, Grzegorz 2010. 'Zemsta obrońców krzyża na pomniku w Ossowie', *Gazeta Wyborcza* (21 September), http://wyborcza.pl/1,75478,8403628,Zemsta_obroncow_krzyza_na_pomniku_w_Ossowie.html.

Sroczyński, Grzegorz 2011. 'Polacy, naród co pluje na cudze groby', *Gazeta Wyborcza* (17 September), http://wyborcza.pl/1,75968,10305967,Polacy__narod_co_pluje_na_cudze_groby.html.

Stanowski, Rafał 2007. 'Żałobny fresk o zbrodni', *Dziennik Polski*, 22/9.

'Stasiuk' 2011. 'Stasiuk: Kaczyński kocha występ', *Gazeta.pl* (24 April), http://wiadomosci.gazeta.pl/Wiadomosci/1,80271,9490515,_Kaczynski_kocha_wystep__On_by_te_Polske_podpalil.html.

Stolarik, M. (ed.) 2010. *The Prague Spring and the Warsaw Pact Invasion of Czechoslovakia, 1968: Forty Years Later.* Mundelein, IL: Bolchazy-Carducci Publishers.

Strzembosz, Tomasz and Krzysztof Jasiewicz 1992. 'Posłowie', in Ewa Wosik (ed.) and W. Materski (trans.), *Katyń. Dokumenty Ludobójstwa. Dokumenty i materiały archiwalne przekazane Polsce 14 października 1992 r.* Warsaw: Instytut Studiów Politycznych Polskiej Akademii Nauk.

Swianiewicz, Stanisław 1976. *W cieniu Katynia.* Paris: Instytut Literacki.

'Świat' 2010. 'Świat ogląda "Katyń"', *Gazeta Wyborcza* (14 April), http://wyborcza.pl/1,75475,7768575,Swiat_oglada__Katyn_.html.

Świda-Ziemba, Hanna 2011. 'Z niewolą Polakowi do twarzy', *Gazeta Wyborcza* (9 May), http://wyborcza.pl/1,97863,9553927,Z_niewola_Polakowi_do_twarzy.html.

Szczepkowska, Ewa 2002. *Cykl podolski Włodzimierza Odojewskiego: Postacie. Krajobrazy. Obszary Pamięci.* Warsaw: Instytut Badań Literackich.

Szerszunowicz, Jerzy 2007. 'Smutny film o zabijaniu', *Kurier Poranny*, 26/09.

Szostkiewicz, Adam 2010. 'Królestwo wawelskie', *Polityka*, 18 (1 May).

Tarczyński, Marek 1996. 'Obchody Roku Katyńskiego. Instytucje, programy, efekty', in Marek Tarczyński (ed.), *Zbrodnia nie ukarana: Katyń, Twer, Charków (Zeszyty katyńskie 6).*

Tarnashyns'ka, L. 2010. *Ukrains'ke shistdesiatnytstvo: profili na tli pokolinnia.* Kyiv: Smoloskyp.

Tarnavskii, Georgii, Valentin Sobolev and Evgenii Gorelik 1990. *Kuropaty: sledstvie prodolzhaetsia.* Moscow: Iuridicheskaia literatura.

Terlikowski, Tomasz P. 2007. 'Walka o dusze: nieoczywista apoteoza fałszu', *Gazeta Polska*, 26/09.

'To nas cofa do neolitu' 2011. ' "To nas cofa do neolitu ws. Katynia. Ale prezydent spotka się z Miedwiediewem" ', *Gazeta.pl* (10 April), http://www.tokfm.pl/Tokfm/1,103087,9407408,_To_nas_cofa_do_neolitu_ws__Katynia__Ale_prezydent.html.

Toeplitz, Krzysztof Teodor 2007. 'Polityka ucalenia', *Przegląd*, 30/9.

Tokarz, Tomasz 2011. 'Koncepcja "polityki historycznej" w myśli konserwatystów polskich', *Kultura i Historia*, 1, http://www.kulturaihistoria.umcs.lublin.pl/archives/2468.

Toom, Marju 2010. 'Katõn seob NKVD ja Gestapo', Presentation at *The General Assembly of the Memorial Society MEMENTO*, Tallinn, 20 April.

Tragediia v Katynskom lesu 1944. Dir. I.M. Posel'skii. Dokumental'nyi Fil'm.

Trznadel, Jacek 1994. *Powrót rozstrzelanej armii: Katyń – fakty, rewizje, poglądy*. Warsaw: Wydawnictwo Antyk.

Trznadel, Jacek 1995a. 'Józef Mackewicz i inni pisarze świadkowie Katynia', in Marek Tarczynski (ed.), *II półwiecze zbrodnia: Katyń Twer Charków (Zeszyty katyńskie 5)*. Warsaw: Niezależny Komitet Historyczny Badania Zbrodni Katyńskiej / Polska Fundacja Katyńska.

Trznadel, Jacek 1995b. 'Polski Hamlet', in Jerzy Krzyżanowski (ed.), *Katyń w literaturze*. Lublin: Norbertinum.

Trznadel, Jacek 2007. 'Film Andrzeja Wajdy "Katyń": między fikcją a kiczem', *Jacektrznadel.pl*, http://www.jacektrznadel.pl/index.php?option=com_content&task=view&id=69&Itemid=31.

Trznadel, Jacek 2010. 'List otwarty. Do Prezes Rady Ministrów RP Donalda Tuska', *Jacektrznadel.pl*, http://www.jacektrznadel.pl/index.php?option=com_content&task=view&id=73.

Tusk, Donald 2010. 'Przemówienie premiera Donalda Tuska podczas uroczystości upamiętniających ofiary Zbrodni Katyńskiej, wygłoszone w Katyniu', *Kancelaria Prezesa Rady Ministrów*, http://dev.premier.gov.pl/premier/przemowienia/przemowienie_premiera_donalda_,4427/.

Tvardovskii, Aleksandr 1991. 'Po pravu pamiati', *Dom u dorogi: poemy i proza*. Voronezh: Tsentral'no-Chernozemnoe knizhnoe izdatel'stvo.

'U Mensku pomniats' ' 2010. 'U Mensku pomniats' pra Katyn'-1940', *Radio Svaboda* (24 June), http://www.svaboda.org/content/article/2081842.html.

Uhlig, Dominik 2010. 'Kluzik-Rostkowska i Jakubiak wyrzucone z PiS', *Gazeta Wyborcza* (5 November), http://wyborcza.pl/1,75478,8619068,Kluzik_Rostkowska_i_Jakubiak_wyrzucone_z_PiS.html.

Ujazdowski, Kazimierz M. 2007. 'Wajda i jego lekcja historii', *Dziennik*, 14–15/04.

'Ukaz' 1995. 'Ukaz Prezydenta Ukrainy No. 766/1995: Pro zasnuvannia vidznaky Prezydenta Ukrainy "Orden kniazia Iaroslava Mudroho"', *Verkhovna Rada of Ukraine*, http://zakon1.rada.gov.ua/cgi-bin/laws/main.cgi?nreg=1549-14.

Uluots, Ülo 1999. *Nad täitsid käsku: Eesti ohvitseride saatus*. Tallinn: Eesti Sõjahaudade Hoolde Liit.

'Usio zhe adzin dzen' 2010. ' "Usio zhe adzin dzen' khatsia b varta bylo abvestsits' zhalobu"', *Radio Svaboda* (16 April), http://www.svaboda.org/content/article/2015828.html.

'Valerii Innokent'evich Kharazov' [undated], *Pseudology.org*, http://www.pseudology.org/Bolsheviki_lenintsy/XarazovVI.htm.

Voronov, Vladimir 2010. 'Palach v kozhanom fartuke', *Sovershenno sekretno*, 3/250, http://www.sovsekretno.ru/magazines/article/2429.

'Vpervye v Kuropatakh' 2008. 'Vpervye v Kuropatakh zaderzhany vandaly', *Charter97.org* (1 November), http://charter97.org/ru/news/2008/11/1/11672/.

'W Rosji' 2010. 'W Rosji musi gdzieś być białoruska lista katyńska' [Interview with Natal'ia Lebedeva by Wacław Radziwinowicz], *Gazeta Wyborcza* (7 April), http://wyborcza.pl/1,76842,7739094,W_Rosji_musi_gdzies_byc_bialoruska_lista_katynska.html.

Wajda, Andrzej 2008. *Katyń*. Warsaw: Proszynski i S-ka.

'Wajda o Katyniu' 2011. 'Wajda o Katyniu: Ludobójstwo . . . Myślę, że to nie jest to określenie', *Gazeta.pl* (13 April).

Wakar, Jacek 2007. 'Wajda Has Paid Off His Debt to History', *Dziennik*, 21/09, http://movie.douban.com/subject/2286418/discussion/25414661/.

Wasilewski, Witold 2009. 'Pamięć Katynia: działania opozycji', *Biuletyn Instytutu Pamięci Narodowej*, 5–6.

Wasilewski, Witold 2010. 'Klamstwo katyńskie – narodziny i trwanie', in Sławomir Kalbarczyk (ed.), *Zbrodnia katyńska w kręgu prawdy i kłamstwa*. Warsaw: Instytut Pamięci Narodowej.

Whalley, G. 1974. 'Metaphor', in A. Preminger et al. (eds.), *Princeton Encyclopedia of Poetry and Poetics*. Princeton, NJ: Princeton University Press.

Winter, Jay 1995. *Sites of Memory, Sites of Mourning: The Great War in European Cultural History*. Cambridge: Cambridge University Press.

Winter, Jay 2010a. 'The Performance of the Past: Memory, History, Identity', in Karin Tilmans, Frank van Vree and Jay Winter (eds.), *Performing the Past: Memory, History, and Identity in Modern Europe*. Amsterdam: Amsterdam University Press.

Winter, Jay 2010b. 'Thinking about Silence', in Efrat Ben Ze'ev, Ruth Ginio and Jay Winter (eds.), *Shadows of War: A Social History of*

Silence in the Twentieth Century. Cambridge: Cambridge University Press.

Wojciechowski, Marcin 2010. 'Katyń rosyjski jak Katyń polski', *Gazeta Wyborcza* (29 July), http://wyborcza.pl/1,76842,8188165,Katyn_rosyjski_jak_Katyn_polski.html.

Wolsza, Tadeusz 2008. *'Katyń to juz na zawsze katy i katowani'. W 'polskim Londynie' o sowieckiej zbrodni w Katyniu (1940–1956)*. Warsaw: Instytut Historii PAN.

Wood, Nancy 1999. *Vectors of Memory: Legacies of Trauma in Postwar Europe*. New York and Oxford: Berg.

Wosik, Ewa (ed.) and W. Materski (trans.) 1992. *Katyń. Dokumenty Ludobójstwa. Dokumenty i materiały archiwalne przekazane Polsce 14 pa dziernika 1992 r*. Warsaw: Instytut Studiów Politycznych Polskiej Akademii Nauk.

Wroński, Paweł 2011. 'Kłótnia o Katyń i ludobójstwo', *Gazeta Wyborcza* (19 April), http://wyborcza.pl/1,75248,9459204,Klotnia_o_Katyn_i_ludobojstwo.html.

Yakubovich, Pavel 2009. 'Kuropaty: mir pod sosnami', *Sovetskaia Belorussiia* (29 October), http://www.pda.sb.by/post/93010.

'Zaiavlenie' 2010. 'Zaiavlenie Gosudarstvennoi Dumy o Katynskoi tragedii i ee zhertvakh', *Kommersant"* (26 November), http://www.kommersant.ru/doc/1547722.

'Zakończyła' 2007. 'Zakończyła się uroczysta premiera "Katynia" A. Wajdy', *Wirtualna Polska* (18 September), http://wiadomosci.wp.pl/kat,1342,title,Zakonczyla-sie-uroczysta-premiera-Katynia-A-Wajdy,wid,9217492,wiadomosc.html?ticaid=1d1b5.

Żakowski, Jacek 2007. 'Przesłuchanie: Andrzej Wajda zaklinacz duchów', *Onet.film* (17 September), http://film.onet.pl/wiadomosci/publikacje/wywiady/przesluchanie-andrzej-wajda-zaklinacz-duchow,1,3811465,wiadomosc.html.

'Zaniepokojeni' 2010. 'Zaniepokojeni przebiegiem śledztwa', *Rzeczpospolita* (24 May), http://www.rp.pl/artykul/2,484507.html.

Zaorska, Aldona 2009. 'Jeżeli ja zapomnę o nich, Ty Boże na niebie zapomnij o mnie', *Gazeta Finansowa* (18 December), http://www.gazetafinansowa.pl/index.php/component/content/article/3134-qjeeli-ja-zapomn-o-nich-ty-boe-na-niebie-zapomnij-o-mnieq-.html.

Zavorotnov, S. 2003. *Khar'kovskaia Katyn'*. Khar'kov: Konsum.

Zawodny, J.K. 1962. *Death in the Forest: The Story of the Katyn Forest Massacre*. South Bend, IN: University of Notre Dame Press.

'Zbigniew Mikołejko' 2010. 'Zbigniew Mikołejko: 10 kwietnia 2010 – czas apokalipsy', in Jan Osiecki, *Polaków rozmowy o polityce*. Warszawa: Prószyński i S-ka, http://smolensk-2010.pl/2010-10-

06-zbigniew-mikolejko-10-kwietnia-2010-%E2%80%93-czas-apokalipsy.html.

Zerubavel, Eviatar 2010. 'The Social Sound of Silence: Toward a Sociology of Denial', in Efrat Ben Ze'ev, Ruth Ginio and Jay Winter (eds.), *Shadows of War: A Social History of Silence in the Twentieth Century*. Cambridge: Cambridge University Press.

' "Zhaloba" u Belarusi' 2010. ' "Zhaloba" u Belarusi: ad 12 da 18 gadziny', *Radio Svaboda* (16 April), http://www.svaboda.org/content/article/2016008.html.

Zhavoronkov, G. 2006. *O chem molchal Katynskii les, kogda govoril akademik Andrei Sakharov*. Moscow: Dipak.

Zieliński, Ryszard [Jan Abramski and Ryszard Zywiecki] 1977. *Katyń*. Warsaw: Społeczny instytut pamięci narodowej im. Józefa Piłsudskiego.

Zinchenko, O. 2011. *Hodyna papuhy: Ukrains'ki storinky Katyni*. Kyiv: Dukh i litera.

Zubrzycki, Genevieve 2006. *The Crosses of Auschwitz: Nationalism and Religion in Post-Communist Poland*. Chicago, IL: University of Chicago Press.

Index